D0429230

Nightly Business Report Presents

Lasting Leadership

What You Can Learn from the Top 25 Business People of Our Times

Ideas. Action. Impact.
**Wharton School
Publishing**

In the face of accelerating turbulence and change, business leaders and policy makers need new ways of thinking to sustain performance and growth.

Wharton School Publishing offers a trusted source for stimulating ideas from thought leaders who provide new mental models to address changes in strategy, management, and finance. We seek out authors from diverse disciplines with a profound understanding of change and its implications. We offer books and tools that help executives respond to the challenge of change.

Every book and management tool we publish meets quality standards set by The Wharton School of the University of Pennsylvania. Each title is reviewed by the Wharton School Publishing Editorial Board before being given Wharton's seal of approval. This ensures that Wharton publications are timely, relevant, important, conceptually sound or empirically based, and implementable.

To fit our readers' learning preferences, Wharton publications are available in multiple formats, including books, audio, and electronic.

To find out more about our books and management tools, visit us at whartonsp.com and Wharton's executive education site, exceed.wharton.upenn.edu.

Nightly Business Report Presents

Lasting Leadership

What You Can Learn from the Top 25 Business People of Our Times

Mukul Pandya and Robbie Shell

Written by Knowledge@Wharton Editor Mukul Pandya and Managing Editor Robbie Shell, with help in reporting and writing from Susan Warner, Sandeep Junnarkar, and Jeff Brown.

Ideas. Action. Impact.
Wharton School Publishing

Library of Congress Publication in Data: 0131531182

Publisher: Tim Moore
Editorial Assistant: Richard Winkler
Development Editor: Russ Hall
Marketing Manager: Martin Litkowski
International Marketing Manager: Tim Galligan
Cover Designer: Sandra Schroeder
Managing Editor: Gina Kanouse
Project Editor: Lori Lyons
Copy Editor: Sarah Cisco
Senior Indexer: Cheryl Lenser
Interior Designer: Gloria Schurick
Senior Compositor: Gloria Schurick
Manufacturing Buyer: Dan Uhrig

Ideas. Action. Impact.
Wharton School Publishing

© 2005 by Pearson Education, Inc.
Publishing as Wharton School Publishing
Upper Saddle River, New Jersey 07458

Wharton School Publishing offers excellent discounts on this book when ordered in quantity for bulk purchases or special sales. For more information, please contact U.S. Corporate and Government Sales, 1-800-382-3419, corpsales@pearsontechgroup.com. For sales outside the U.S., please contact International Sales at international@pearsoned.com.

Company and product names mentioned herein are the trademarks or registered trademarks of their respective owners.

Printed in the United States of America

Second Printing November 2004

ISBN 0-13-153118-2

Pearson Education LTD.
Pearson Education Australia PTY, Limited.
Pearson Education Singapore, Pte. Ltd.
Pearson Education North Asia, Ltd.
Pearson Education Canada, Ltd.
Pearson Educación de Mexico, S.A. de C.V.
Pearson Education—Japan
Pearson Education Malaysia, Pte. Ltd.

Ideas. Action. Impact.
Wharton School Publishing

C. K. Prahalad
THE FORTUNE AT THE BOTTOM OF THE PYRAMID
Eradicating Poverty Through Profits

Yoram (Jerry)Wind, Colin Crook, with Robert Gunther
THE POWER OF IMPOSSIBLE THINKING
Transform the Business of Your Life and the Life of Your Business

Scott A. Shane
FINDING FERTILE GROUND
Identifying Extraordinary Opportunities for New Ventures

Contents

Introduction   xiii

Chapter 1:   Best of the Best: Inside Andy Grove's
Leadership at Intel   1

Chapter 2:   Leadership and Corporate Culture   21

Chapter 3:   Truth Tellers   47

Chapter 4:   Identifying an Underserved Market   73

Chapter 5:   Seeing the Invisible   103

Chapter 6:   Using Price to Gain Competitive Advantage   131

Chapter 7:   Managing the Brand   159

Chapter 8:   Fast Learners   183

Chapter 9:   Managing Risk   209

Chapter 10:   Conclusion   237

References   243

Index   261

Acknowledgments

We are grateful to several people without whom the book you hold in your hands would not exist.

Our thanks go, first, to three journalists who helped us report and write the book and deserve a substantial part of the credit for any merits it may possess. Susan Warner, a former business reporter for *The Philadelphia Inquirer,* who is now a freelance writer, was responsible for seven of the leaders (Herb Kelleher, Jack Welch, Sam Walton, Lee Iacocca, Michael Dell, Frederick Smith, and Richard Branson); Sandeep Junnarkar, former New York bureau chief for CNET News.com, who now teaches business and online journalism at Indiana University in Bloomington, was responsible for six of the 25 (Jeff Bezos, Peter Drucker, Ted Turner, Lou Gerstner, Charles Schwab, and William George); and Jeff Brown, who has written the syndicated personal finance column for *The Philadelphia Inquirer* since 1995, was responsible for five of the 25 (John Bogle, Warren Buffett, Alan Greenspan, Oprah Winfrey, and Peter Lynch). Without their reporting and writing, this book would never have been completed—especially not on a tight deadline. They were always responsive, cheerful, and above all, professional in their work. *Lasting Leadership* was the result of a tremendous team effort. We are lucky that Susan, Sandeep, and Jeff were part of that team.

We would also like to acknowledge Ed Voves, a former researcher at *The Philadelphia Inquirer*, who gathered data on the Top 25 leaders and helped us obtain the necessary permissions for our usage of secondary sources. He carried out these sometimes thankless jobs with incredible persistence and good grace.

Before the book could be researched or written, however, it had to be conceived. For that, we thank our collaborators at *Nightly Business Report*, who first came up with the idea of identifying the Top 25 leaders of the past 25 years. Linda O'Brien, Stuart Zuckerman, Rodney Ward, Wendie Feinberg, Susie Gharib, and Jack Kahn were enthusiastic about taking a television program planned to mark NBR's 25th anniversary to the next stage by turning it into a book. During the months that the manuscript was being prepared, NBR worked with us as a true partner in matters large and small—from helping open doors at certain companies to carefully reviewing the manuscript and improving it with thoughtful suggestions.

We are grateful to Pearson, Wharton's partner in Wharton School Publishing, for publishing the book. Tim Moore, editor-in-chief of Pearson Education, was enthusiastic about the book from the time it was just an idea, and he played a patient and encouraging role all the way through its completion. We also thank Russ Hall for helping edit the manuscript; Lori Lyons for invaluable assistance in its production; and John Pierce and Martin Litkowski for their help with marketing and publicity.

At Wharton, several people played a key role in helping this book see the light of day. Deputy dean David S. Schmittlein, who oversees *Knowledge@Wharton*, defined the vision and set the standard for what this book could potentially be. He not only helped us avoid possible missteps, but also deserves credit for shaping the themes reflected in the book. We are grateful to Jerry Wind, editor of Wharton School Publishing, for his guidance and enthusiastic assistance. Robert E. Mittelstaedt, Jr., former vice dean of executive education at the school, played a key role in developing the concepts for some chapters, as did Michael Useem, director of the Wharton School's Center for Leadership and Change Management. Other Wharton faculty members who contributed to shaping the ideas in this book include Peter Cappelli, Barbara Kahn, and Raffi Amit. Barbara Gyde and Teresa Regan of Wharton School Publishing also contributed greatly to the project.

We would like to thank our colleagues Jamie Hammond, Bruce Brownstein, David Siedell, and Sanjay Modi for their encouragement, support, and good-humored accommodation of our crazy schedules as we juggled the writing of this book with publishing *Knowledge@Wharton* every two weeks. Everyone should be so lucky to have such co-workers. In addition, Michael Baltes, Peter Winicov, Tracy Liebman, Meghan Laska, Phyllis Stevenson, and Joanne Spigonardo in Wharton's Communications Department deserve thanks for their support throughout.

Last, but not least, we are deeply grateful to our families. A book is a demanding taskmaster, and during the months when we worked on this project, our families, too, paid the price. Ultimately it is their love, patience, and understanding that make such labors worthwhile.

Mukul Pandya and Robbie Shell
Philadelphia
August 2004

About the Authors

Mukul Pandya is editor and director of *Knowledge@Wharton*, a web-based journal of research and business analysis published by The Wharton School of the University of Pennsylvania.

A winner of four awards for investigative journalism, Mr. Pandya has more than twenty years of experience as a writer and editor. His articles have appeared in *The Wall Street Journal*, *The New York Times*, *The Economist*, *Time Magazine*, *The Philadelphia Inquirer*, and many other publications. He coauthored *Knowledge@Wharton on Building Corporate Value*.

Mr. Pandya, who has an M.A. in economics from the University of Bombay, lives in Ewing, NJ, with his wife and daughter.

Robbie Shell, the managing editor of *Knowledge@Wharton*, has worked as a business reporter and editor for national news services, newspapers, and magazines throughout her career. She has covered both the White House and U.S. Supreme Court and taught journalism at the University of Virginia. Her freelance work most recently appeared in *The Wall Street Journal*. A graduate of Princeton University, she lives in Wynnewood, PA, with her husband and two sons.

Introduction

In June 2000, John Bogle, founder and former CEO of the Vanguard Group, spoke about leadership at the Wharton School of the University of Pennsylvania. As an avid group of executives listened to the man who popularized the principle of index-based investing—and in the process built the Vanguard Group into a firm managing more than $550 billion in assets—Bogle ended his speech quoting James Norris, a Vanguard manager, who wrote: "While it is revealing to consider...what constitutes a leader, your search for understanding, for some kind of leadership formula, is apt to end in frustration. It is like studying Michelangelo or Shakespeare: You can imitate, emulate, and simulate, but there is simply no connect-the-dots formula to Michelangelo's David or

Shakespeare's Hamlet. I suppose, when all is said and done, it really comes down to this: People are leaders because they choose to lead."

The heart of leadership is as simple as that: It is a matter of choice and determination. It is equally true, however, that no two leaders are exactly alike. Gandhi and Churchill rallied millions behind them, but not quite in the same way or for the same reasons. In the business world, John Bogle's leadership of Vanguard might have something in common with the way Warren Buffett runs Berkshire Hathaway, but the two also have big differences— although both are involved, broadly, in the "investment" business. Andrew Grove and Bill Gates are chairmen of high-tech companies with commanding positions in their respective markets—but while Gates grew up as the privileged son of a wealthy attorney, Grove spent his early years enduring the rigors of Stalinist Hungary. These vastly different backgrounds are reflected in their approaches to leadership.

If this is true, then people who choose and are determined to become influential business leaders can benefit from observing other leaders and using their observations to discover and nurture their own leadership style. The purpose of studying other business leaders is not so much to imitate their qualities as to discover which attributes resonate with one's own and, thus, can be cultivated to further enhance one's leadership skills and capabilities. Leaders are made, not born. Discovering the attributes of lasting leadership can help people increase their impact in their own spheres. Someone who does this might not become another Jack Welch or Mary Kay Ash, but he or she might become a better leader than would otherwise be possible in the absence of this knowledge.

Our book, *Lasting Leadership: What You Can Learn from the Top 25 Business People of Our Times,* is based on that premise. It is the result of collaboration between *Nightly Business Report* (NBR), the most-watched daily business program on U.S. television, and *Knowledge@Wharton* (http://knowledge.wharton.upenn.edu), the online research and business analysis journal of the Wharton School of the University of Pennsylvania. To celebrate NBR's 25th anniversary in January 2004, Wharton and NBR worked together

to identify the 25 most influential business leaders of the past 25
years. NBR's viewers nominated more than 700 business people
from around the world, and a panel of six Wharton judges selected the Top 25.

The winners are, in alphabetical order, Mary Kay Ash, founder
of Mary Kay Inc.; Jeff Bezos, CEO of Amazon.com; John Bogle,
founder of The Vanguard Group; Richard Branson, CEO of Virgin
Group; Warren Buffett, CEO of Berkshire Hathaway; James
Burke, former CEO of Johnson & Johnson; Michael Dell, CEO of
Dell Inc.; Peter Drucker, the educator and author; William Gates,
chairman of Microsoft; William George, former CEO of
Medtronic; Louis Gerstner, former CEO of IBM; Alan Greenspan,
chairman, U.S. Federal Reserve; Andrew Grove, chairman of Intel;
Lee Iacocca, former CEO of Chrysler; Steven Jobs, CEO of Apple
Computer; Herbert Kelleher, chairman of Southwest Airlines;
Peter Lynch, former manager of Fidelity's Magellan Fund; Charles
Schwab, founder, CEO and chairman of The Charles Schwab Corp.;
Frederick Smith, CEO of Federal Express; George Soros, founder
and chairman of The Open Society Institute; Ted Turner, founder
of CNN; Sam Walton, founder of Wal-Mart; Jack Welch, former
CEO of General Electric; Oprah Winfrey, chairman of the Harpo
group of companies; and Muhammad Yunus, founder of Grameen
Bank.

To arrive at this list from among hundreds of nominees, the
Wharton panel searched for business leaders who created new and
profitable ideas. They looked for people who had affected political,
civic, or social change in the business/economic world; created new
business opportunities or more fully exploited existing ones;
caused or influenced dramatic change in a company or industry; or
inspired and transformed others. The judges included Michael
Useem, director of the Center for Leadership and Change
Management; Peter Cappelli, director of the Center for Human
Resources; Raffi Amit, director of the Goergen Entrepreneurial
Research Program; Barbara Kahn, vice dean of the Wharton
undergraduate division; Robert E. Mittelstaedt, Jr., former vice
dean and director of the Aresty Institute of Executive Education
(now dean of the W.P. Carey School of Business at Arizona
State University); and Mukul Pandya, editor and director of
Knowledge@Wharton.

Andy Grove: Best of the Best

NBR asked the Wharton judges to pick the most influential leader among these 25. That honor went to Intel's Andy Grove. To understand why, consider this: When Grove got his Ph.D. from the University of California, Berkeley in 1963, he was a corporate recruiter's dream candidate. He had a number of job options, perhaps the best of which was with Bell Labs, at the time the Mecca of research in solid-state physics. But Grove made a different choice. Rather than head for Bell Labs, he joined Fairchild Semiconductor, a West Coast upstart, where he worked under the legendary Gordon Moore, who led the company's research operation. That was an early example of out-of-the-box thinking from Grove, who five years later left Fairchild with Moore and others to co-found Intel.

After he succeeded Moore as Intel's CEO in 1987, Grove took other steps that shunned conventional logic—perhaps most visibly during the "Intel Inside" campaign of the 1990s. Back then, the most recognized brands in the computer industry were hardware makers, such as IBM or software firms like Microsoft. Intel, though it supplied more than 80% of the microprocessors to the world's computers, was hardly known outside a small band of industry insiders. Determined to change that narrow perception, Grove led Intel into an aggressive branding campaign that made the company a household name by the end of the decade. Today, as its products play an increasingly critical role in stitching together a globally networked economy, Intel has emerged as one of the world's top technology companies, with 2003 revenues of more than $30 billion.

Grove's leadership of Intel—marked as it has been by unconventional thinking, imagination, and integrity—was instrumental in his being named the most influential business leader of the past 25 years. "My life has been intertwined with Intel," Grove told NBR co-anchor Susie Gharib. "My proudest accomplishment has been to contribute to the creation of a company that has helped put a billion PCs into people's hands."

Learning from Leaders

In addition to identifying these individuals as influential leaders, the Wharton judges discussed aspects of their character that contributed to their success. In Grove's case, for example, his openness to unconventional ideas was a critical factor. In his or her way, however, each of these leaders has traits from which others could learn.

Consider Warren Buffett, whom Michael Useem describes as "a man for all seasons." According to Useem, not only is Buffett "an investor extraordinaire" who has delivered enormous returns to investors in Berkshire Hathaway, but he was also highly successful as the hands-on CEO of Salomon Brothers, helping restore confidence in the Wall Street firm when it faced a severe management crisis. These days, "Buffett has become the conscience of the Street, offering great wisdom on contentious topics like expensing stock options," Useem says. In other words, in addition to his genius at spotting good investment opportunities, Buffett's influence derives from his moral stature and integrity. In the aftermath of accounting and governance scandals that have rocked U.S. companies in the past few years, it is difficult to overemphasize the importance of ethics as a factor in leadership.

Bogle, like Buffett, owes his influence to having delivered great value to investors—though his approach was strikingly different. The former CEO of the Vanguard Group has long argued that "owning the entire stock market at very low cost is the ultimate investment strategy." This belief led him to launch the Vanguard Group in 1975. Bogle was a pioneer in introducing and helping popularize index funds—which kept fees extremely low for investors. Says Peter Cappelli: "One of the reasons why Bogle is on this list is because of the enormous impact he had on the average person."

Sam Walton's approach to Wal-Mart's customers was similar, according to Robert E. Mittelstaedt, Jr. The goal of making a wide range of products available to average people at the lowest possible price enabled him to take the retail company from a single store to a megacorp that is now ranked No. 1 on the Fortune 500. "Walton's legacy is that a single person can make a huge difference in an industry," says Mittelstaedt. "It doesn't happen overnight, especially in an industry like retail, but it can happen over a period of years. Walton believed in delivering great value at low prices to his customers."

Jack Welch's leadership delivered great value to GE's shareholders. One measure, according to Useem, is that GE's stock price saw a 40-fold increase during Welch's tenure, consistently outpacing the S&P 500. But his greatest strength, says Useem, was spotting and nurturing other leaders. "Welch has written the textbook on leadership. He has often said that he doesn't know how to make jet engines or produce Tuesday night television shows at NBC, the GE subsidiary. But he does know how to pick people with leadership potential, give them the resources to meet their goals, and get rid of them if they cannot. As a result, Welch built one of the best leadership teams anywhere."

Mittelstaedt notes that team-building also counts among Bill Gates's strengths as a leader. Gates saw the potential of the PC to transform the world, and he built Microsoft into a software powerhouse. In addition, he is among those rare entrepreneurs whose abilities have expanded to keep pace with the growth of his enterprise. "Very few successful people who have started as entrepreneurs have led their companies until they grew to a very big size," says Mittelstaedt. In Gates's case, he has had the vision to bring in people and then let them serve the company "in a way that most entrepreneurs are not capable of doing."

Each leader on the list offers similar leadership lessons. While most of them are recognizable names, a few are less well known or are simply no longer in the public eye. James Burke, for example, was J&J's CEO when the company faced its well-known Tylenol crisis in 1982. Seven people died after taking the pain killer, and it turned out that someone had introduced cyanide in the pills as an act of sabotage. Burke's handling of that has become a textbook case for companies facing crises. Bill George, the former CEO of Medtronic, has recently written a book about *Authentic Leadership* that draws upon his experiences. Yunus, the founder of Grameen Bank in Bangladesh, has been a pioneer in the field of microfinance, providing loans as small as $10 to impoverished people. His great innovation was recognizing that lending could be separated from collateral and still be the basis for operating a sound financing business. Micro-lending programs modeled after Grameen's have now spread to more than 100 countries.

Themes and Structure

Of the 25 leaders profiled in this book, two have died—Sam Walton in 1992 and Mary Kay Ash in 2001. We were able to get interviews with 15 of the other 23, including Jeff Bezos, John Bogle, James Burke, Michael Dell, William George, Louis Gerstner, Lee Iacocca, Herb Kelleher, Andrew Grove, Peter Lynch, Charles Schwab, Fred Smith, Ted Turner, Jack Welch, and Muhammad Yunus, in addition to Mary Kay Ash's son, Richard Rogers. We would like to thank all of them for their willingness to talk to us openly about their companies and themselves. We were not able to interview Richard Branson, Warren Buffett, Peter Drucker, Bill Gates, Alan Greenspan, Steve Jobs, George Soros, and Oprah Winfrey. For information on these leaders, we relied on books about or by them, speeches and interviews, and newspaper and magazine articles.

Our book explores the theme of lasting leadership in ten chapters. The first takes a close look at Grove's approach to leadership and discusses the attributes that helped him and Intel succeed. It includes a timeline of Grove's life and discusses the biggest challenge he faced in his career—the Pentium flaw crisis of 1994—and how he dealt with it. The eight chapters that follow provide brief introductions to all the leaders through short chronologies that cover the major tipping points or milestones in their lives. These are accompanied by articles that describe a major challenge in their business careers and how they tackled it.

What is fascinating about these challenges is their enormous variety. For example, Kelleher's challenge was getting Southwest Airlines off the ground—literally. Gates's challenge was dealing with regulators on both sides of the Atlantic so Microsoft could continue to grow. Ash had to motivate a sales force of thousands. Walton wielded pricing strategy like a fencer wields a saber to keep Kmart, his main rival, at bay. Jobs had to contend with a large rival—IBM—which threatened to put a fledgling Apple Computer out of business.

Eight Attributes of Lasting Leadership

In *Lasting Leadership*, we identify eight attributes or qualities that have enabled the 25 individuals to overcome major challenges as well as to nurture their own leadership styles. These attributes—each of which has its own chapter in the book—include

- Building a strong corporate culture
- Truth telling
- Finding and catering to under-served markets
- "Seeing the invisible"—that is, spotting potential winners or faint trends before their rivals or customers do
- Using price to build competitive advantage
- Managing and building their organization's brand (which, in some cases, may be their own name)
- Being fast learners
- Managing risk

None of the leaders in this book has all these attributes. If that were a requirement of lasting leadership, the world would have no leaders at all. At the same time, one attribute alone is not enough to ensure long-lived leadership. A leader with a single attribute may succeed briefly, but the success will not be sustained unless other qualities exist to keep the momentum going.

Which combinations of attributes are most effective? That question has no easy answer: The combinations are as varied as the leaders, which is why all 25 individuals in this book are so unlike one another. What makes Michael Dell or Jeff Bezos prosper in their industries is different from what makes Peter Lynch or Oprah Winfrey thrive in theirs. In that reality lies great cause for optimism: If countless combinations of leadership attributes are possible, each person reading this book should find at least a few qualities in himself or herself that, properly nurtured, can be cultivated into a deeper and more effective leadership style. In short, there is hope for the rest of us.

Yet if there is one trait that each of these leaders shares, it is tenacity. Unlike so-called serial entrepreneurs who cash out of their companies after a few years and move on to their next venture, these leaders have had a long-term vision. They have been willing to ride out the lows with the highs. This willingness to slog it out and stay in the game for the long haul has been reflected in the success of their enterprises and in the endurance of their own influence as leaders.

Asked why he never left Intel to start another company, Grove replied: "Intel is like a river. It changes every day and behind every bend there is a new start, a new challenge. I cannot think of any place where I would rather have worked."

Best of the Best: Inside Andy Grove's Leadership at Intel

When Andrew S. Grove was a student of engineering at New York's City College in the mid-1950s, he faced a problem. The one-year scholarship he received as a Hungarian refugee was about to run out, and to speed up his graduation, he needed to take courses in the chemical engineering department. The chairman, Professor Al Xavier Schmidt, taught a crucial course—Chem E 128. Unable to schedule an appointment with Schmidt, Grove, then a young man of 20, waited outside the classroom one day and seized his chance to present his case to the formidable professor.

As Grove spoke, Schmidt, a short man with a fierce moustache, fixed his eyes on the nervous student and subjected him to an interrogation. "He cross-examined me on the spot," Grove recalls.

"He asked me about my courses, who I took them from, and my grades." Schmidt apparently liked Grove's replies—he had failed one exam in physics but got an A in the subject the next time—and admitted him to his course. "He was testing me, testing my background," says Grove.

That incident was an early example of a pattern that appears frequently in Grove's life—converting a negative situation into a positive one through resourcefulness. As chairman and former CEO of Intel, a company he co-founded in 1968, Grove has repeatedly faced setbacks during the past 35 years but found ways to turn them into stepping stones. In the process, with Grove at its helm, Intel has grown into the world's largest chipmaker, with 78,000 employees and more than $30 billion in annual revenues in 2003.

That, in itself, is not unusual. Many companies and leaders profiled in this book have seen remarkable success during the past 25 years. Still, Intel occupies a special place among them. As the company that introduced the world's first microprocessor in 1971, Intel has played a seminal role in the evolution of modern computing. It is impossible to conceive of today's global, networked economy without Intel, or to imagine Intel without Andy Grove. As this chapter shows, Grove's life and career consistently reveal his imagination, resolution, and integrity. That is why his leadership has lasted as long as it has.

This book argues that lasting leadership results from individuals possessing—and cultivating—certain qualities and combinations of attributes. While all the leaders featured here have some of these attributes, Grove stands out because he has personified so many of them in specific ways over a span of nearly 50 years.

Inspired by Schmidt, Grove developed a leadership style based on truth-telling. At a time when Intel was facing a crisis of mammoth proportions—triggered by Japanese inroads into the company's core market of memory chips in the mid 1980s—he discovered an underserved market and rejuvenated the business. A decade later, confronted by another severe disaster involving a flaw in its Pentium microprocessors, Grove was forced to recognize how market conditions had changed. He was able to build the Intel brand (through the famous "Intel Inside" campaign) and used his savvy in managing risk to steer the company clear of antitrust regulators.

Above all, Grove espoused and upheld values that have given Intel its unique corporate culture, or what he calls its "very strong immune system."

A business leader who combines all these attributes and deploys them consistently over his or her life is not just rare; he or she is unique. That is why Wharton and *Nightly Business Report* named Andy Grove "most influential" among the Top 25 leaders profiled in this book. The attributes that make him special, however, are not unique; they are available to everyone. Learning how to nurture these qualities in yourself will not turn you into Andy Grove. It may, however, make you a better leader.

1936: Born in Budapest, Hungary, on September 2 and named Andris Grof. The secular Jewish family is modestly prosperous; his father, George, is a dairyman; his mother, Maria, a book-keeping clerk.

1938: The Grof family moves to the commercially vibrant Pest section of Budapest where George Grof expands the dairy business.

1940: An acute attack of scarlet fever nearly kills four-year-old Andris. The illness leaves him almost completely deaf for years, until surgery finally corrects the problem.

1942: George Grof is drafted into a work brigade in the Hungarian army, and he disappears for three years. During World War II, as Jews in Hungary are being rounded up, young Andris and his mother go into hiding, changing their name to Malesevics and moving in with Christian acquaintances.

ANDREW S. GROVE

The Challenge:

Dealing with the Pentium Flaw Debacle

Ask Andy Grove, chairman of Intel, about his toughest business challenge, and a pensive look appears in his piercing blue eyes. Two situations vie for the position. One is the time when Intel almost went under during the mid-1980s as a result of fierce competition from Japanese chipmakers. The second crisis—which is highlighted in this section—came a decade later, when the company was slammed by its customers and the media for a flaw in its Pentium microprocessors. The flaw eventually led to large-scale product replacements and ended with Intel taking a $475 million write-off. "The net present value of the pain involved is hard to compare," Grove says in his precise voice. "They both tore me up. It seems that the more recent one tore me up more, but that may be because it is more recent."

It happened in the fall of 1994. At that time Intel, which had $10 billion in annual revenues, was already the world's largest chipmaker. The company was busy preparing for the launch of the Pentium, its latest generation microprocessor—an operation that involved a heavy-duty manufacturing effort and a massive advertising campaign. As optimism about Intel's prospects increased, the company's stock soared. In the last week of November, it traded in the high 60s after a Merrill Lynch analyst predicted a big increase in fourth-quarter sales.

Under the radar screen, however, trouble was brewing. Several weeks earlier, discussions had begun in various Internet newsgroups about a flaw in the Pentium's floating point unit, the part of the chip that handles advanced number-crunching. Intel executives, including Grove, didn't pay much attention. They were aware of the flaw and, after a thorough examination, concluded that it was insignificant. According to Grove, the design error "caused a rounding error in division once every nine billion times." This meant "that an average spreadsheet user would run into the problem only once every 27,000 years of spreadsheet use."

Soon, however, the online discussion caught the attention of trade publications, which started writing about it. Matters came to a boil on November 22, 1994, the Tuesday before Thanksgiving. A CNN crew showed up at Intel's headquarters in Santa Clara, California, and the next day, the cable news channel aired a nasty piece about the Pentium flaw. Soon the story began to appear in *other* publications in the U.S., and then in other parts of the world. For example, *The New York Times* ran an article titled, "Flaw Undermines Accuracy of Pentium Chips." Customers, too, were up in arms, because news reports said Intel had already shipped two million computers with Pentium chips. Says Grove, "We had a daily monitor of incoming nasty calls, of customer complaints."

Grove's reaction, as usual, was to set the record straight. On Thanksgiving Day, he wrote a memo and posted it on the Internet, identifying himself as the CEO of Intel, and pointing out that while the floating-point unit did have an error, it would only affect "users of the Pentium processor who are engaged in heavy-duty scientific/floating-point calculations." Much to his amazement, not only did people pooh-pooh his arguments about the Pentium flaw, but they also didn't believe that he had written the memo.

1950: At age 14, he aspires to become a journalist and is a reporter for the youth newspaper, which is under the influence of the government. After a relative is imprisoned without trial, the newspaper stops publishing Andris's articles. The experience turns him off journalism. "I was crushed as only a slighted adolescent can be," he later writes. "I did not want a profession in which a totally subjective evaluation, easily colored by political considerations, could decide the merits of my work." He turns from journalism to science.

1956: In December, as Soviet tanks crush Hungary's October rebellion, Andris and a friend escape from Hungary, initially crossing the border into Austria and then sailing to the U.S. The International Rescue Committee, a relief organization, helps bring him from Vienna to New York City. Later he Americanizes his name to Andrew Grove.

1956: Enters City College of New York to study engineering. Meets Professor Al Xavier Schmidt, chairman of the Chemical Engineering department, who gives Grove a job and becomes his mentor.

1958: Marries Eva Kaston in New York; he had met her the previous year while working as a busboy at a holiday resort in New Hampshire where she worked as a waitress.

1960: Graduates from the City College of New York with a bachelor's degree in chemical engineering. Knowing that Grove loves America but hates New York, a professor suggests Grove might prefer California.

1963: Completes his Ph.D. at the University of California at Berkeley.

1963: Joins the research and development laboratory of Fairchild Semiconductor. Founded in 1957, the company initially started out making transistors for IBM and other customers, but the company became well known after researcher Robert Noyce co-invented the integrated chip in 1959.

1967: Becomes assistant director of R&D at Fairchild Semiconductor, working under Gordon Moore, one of the top chemists of the century.

1967: Publishes his first book, *Physics and Technology of Semiconductor Devices.* It is widely used in schools and colleges.

1968: Co-founds Intel—short for Integrated Electronics—with Moore and Noyce. The company initially focuses on making integrated chips.

"There was a *huge* amount of discourse on the web claiming that it wasn't I who had written it," Grove says. "I typed the f***ing thing with my own two fingers [but] nobody believed what it said, and nobody believed that I wrote it. Everything I said in it was true, and I wrote it. I was shocked."

Outraged customers began demanding replacement chips for their computers. Sticking to Grove's policy of insisting that the error was minor, Intel initially resisted replacing the chips unless the customers could establish that the chips would be used for advanced math calculations. As *Information Week* wrote in an article titled, "Intel to Users: 'Humbug!',", "Users, upon reaching Intel's 800 number, apparently go through a lengthy interview process to see if Intel deems them worthy of receiving a corrected chip. If you can't convince Intel that you may encounter the bug in daily life, you just don't make the cut." Soon, jokes ridiculing Intel were making the rounds on the Internet, including a top-ten list of reasons to buy a Pentium machine. "Reason number 10.0000001: Your current computer is too accurate."

By December, the volume of complaints declined a little, and Grove began to feel optimistic that the worst might be over. Unexpectedly, another blow fell. Grove arrived at his office one Monday to find a message with a news flash on his desk. It said, simply, that IBM had stopped shipments of all Pentium-based machines. According to Grove, "All hell broke loose again... The phones started ringing furiously from all quarters. The call volume to our hotline skyrocketed. Our other customers wanted to know what was going on. And their tone, which had been quite constructive the week before, became confused and anxious. We were back on the defensive again in a major way."

Why did Intel respond to the Pentium flaw crisis the way it did, in a manner that one observer called "a textbook example of how not to handle a delicate situation"? In part, it followed from Grove's approach, modeled as it was after his former chemistry professor's tough, no-nonsense style of stating the facts and refusing to bow before pressure. In retrospect, says Grove, he thinks he "mishandled the floating-point debacle about as badly as possible. By the way, Schmidt probably cheered me on as I mishandled that situation. I stuck with the facts and told our customers to get with it." It was apparent, however, that Grove's "Schmidt approach," while it may have worked in previous situations, was not only ineffective during the Pentium flaw crisis but was making matters worse. Eventually, "after a number of days of struggling against the tide of public opinion, of dealing with the phone calls and the abusive editorials, it became clear that we had to make a major change," according to Grove. When this realization sank in, Intel reversed its policy. The company announced it would replace anyone's chip who wanted it replaced. It set up a huge operation to answer customer phone calls—staffing it initially with volunteers who wanted to help cope with the disaster. Ultimately, as Intel replaced hundreds of thousands of chips, the crisis passed. When it ended, Intel had to take a $475 million bath. "It was the equivalent of half a year's R&D budget, or five years' worth of the Pentium processor's advertising spending," says Grove.

While Grove's "Schmidt-style" response may have aggravated the Pentium flaw crisis, it alone was not responsible for the way he dealt with it. As he explained two years later in his book *Only the Paranoid*

1971: Researchers at Intel invent a new kind of integrated chip, the microprocessor, which can be programmed to do calculations. This allows microprocessors to become the "brains" of a computer. The 4004, a four-bit silicon chip, packs as much computing power as the ENIAC, the world's first electronic computer—which filled a room—in a chip smaller than a thumbnail.

1972: Intel develops an eight-bit microprocessor, the 8008, with twice the power of the 4004.

1976: Intel researchers create the Multibus, a mechanism that makes it possible to interconnect large numbers of microprocessors. This innovation is used to develop products such as automatic teller machines.

1979: Grove becomes president of Intel.

1983: His book, *High Output Management*, is published. The book is translated into 11 languages.

1987: Becomes CEO of Intel; G.P. Putnam's Sons publishes *One-on-One with Andy Grove*. Grove is a "Dear Abby of the Workplace," offering business advice as a columnist for Knight Ridder.

1994: Controversy explodes around Intel as it releases flawed Pentium chips; after initially saying the problem is minor, Intel changes direction and agrees to spend $475 million to replace the flawed chips.
1994: In December, Grove's doctors diagnose cancer of the prostate. He reads all the research he can find on the subject and decides upon his own treatment.
1996: *Only the Paranoid Survive: How to Survive the Crisis Points That Threaten Every Company* is published by Currency/Doubleday. In this book, Grove explains his concept of strategic inflection points—make-or-break situations that bring about a sea change in an industry—with examples from Intel's experience. *Forbes* magazine calls it "probably the best book on business written by a business person since Alfred Sloan's *My Years with General Motors.*"
1997: Becomes chairman and CEO of Intel.
1997: *Time* magazine names Grove "Man of the Year."
1998: Steps down as CEO but remains chairman; named "Distinguished Executive of the Year" by the Academy of Management.

Survive, Intel at that time was going through a "strategic inflection point," or a key turning point, when the rules by which the company did business changed.

The rules changed, ironically, because of the success of another initiative, the "Intel Inside" marketing campaign. During its relatively brief history, Intel had pioneered the development of innovative memory chips and microprocessors. It had set the standards for its products and marketed them to computer makers (rather than computer users). "Whatever problems we had in the past, we used to handle with the computer manufacturers, engineer to engineer, in conference rooms with blackboards, based on data analyses." A few years before the Pentium crisis hit, however, Intel had embarked on an aggressive marketing campaign to build the Intel brand. Its "Intel Inside" slogan was plastered on billboards, appeared in TV commercials, and, in China, even on bicycle reflectors. By the time the campaign ended, Intel had become a world-famous brand with international name recognition.

As a result, when the Pentium crisis hit, the customers who were concerned were not just engineers (who might have understood why a minor design flaw was not a big deal) but millions of non-technical folks who didn't give a hoot about intricate mathematical arguments. They just knew they wanted an accurate chip to replace a flawed one. Grove was still trying to communicate about product standards according to the old rules, without realizing that as a result of its marketing campaign, Intel's customer base had fundamentally changed. Intel was no longer an industrial products company; it had evolved into a mass consumer products company.

Another factor, Grove realized in retrospect, was also at work. He still thought of Intel as an innovative start-up, but the external view of the company was that it had grown into a global IT giant. As such, when thousands of customers thought Intel was not responding to their complaints about the Pentium's flaw, they lambasted it as they might any insensitive big-business megacorporation. Here, too, Grove's perception of Intel was at odds with that of its customers.

That disconnect was brought home strongly to Grove after Christmas 1994. One Sunday, Grove was speaking to Dennis Carter, Intel's head of marketing, about having survived the crisis. Carter said, "I'm glad you called, because I have drawn completely the opposite conclusion. We may have survived, but it was shocking how little public goodwill there was for us to tap into. It was as if the public was just waiting for us to stumble." Carter argued that "Intel would have to change its approach to business dramatically: It would have to court its public, be sensitive to the needs of vast numbers of customers, and build equity of goodwill."

Grove was livid. "I told him to go f*** himself," he says. "I didn't have the patience to listen to bullshit like this. Again, Schmidt probably cheered me on. We talked for hours. I was standing in front of the kitchen phone. And as usually was the case when Dennis and I fought, Dennis won." Intel had learned its lesson: It implemented several actions to win back the public's trust and confidence. Eventually it won a spot on *Fortune* magazine's list of most admired companies.

Grove's experience shows that when faced with a challenge of such enormous magnitude, just being a truth teller may not be enough; it is equally important to be a fast learner, recognizing how the rules of the game have changed and adapting to the new realities. Grove, with some help from his colleagues, was able to do just that. "So, did I learn? Yeah," he says. "But did I learn from the incident? Hell, no."

2001: In November, *Swimming Across: A Memoir,* is published. The book is an account of the first 20 years of Grove's life, beginning with his childhood in Hungary up until his move to California. Grove tells media host Charlie Rose that he did it mainly for his grandchildren.

2004: Grove is named the "most influential" business leader of the past 25 years by Wharton and *Nightly Business Report.*

Style of communication needs To adjust To the needs of The audience, and To their receptivity.

Be aware of how you are perceived.

i.e. JSU students Treating me like Heather Leackler

Leadership Lessons

About Schmidt: Telling the Truth

Schmidt captivated Grove as a teacher from the very first lecture. As Grove remembers, Schmidt came to the class and wrote a problem on the board. "It seemed very complicated, though in retrospect it was very simple," he says. "He tortured us with it. After making it more and more complicated, he showed us how to solve it with one long line of conversions. At the end of that class, Professor Schmidt said, 'Our statistics show that 60% of you will be unable to finish this course, and that is alright with me. The rest of you will approach problems in the fashion I just showed you.' I was just blown away."

Schmidt soon was to help Grove in another way. When he learned the young man's scholarship was about to run out, Schmidt called Grove to his office. He asked how much money Grove would need, pulled out a long slide rule, did some calculations, and offered Grove a job at $1.79 an hour—estimating that by working 20 hours a week he could make as much money as the scholarship paid. Almost speechless with surprise, Grove agreed. As he later said, "So I ended up working for crusty Professor Schmidt, running his copies and his errands, typing with two fingers, filing, whatever—and supported myself through my remaining years of college that way."

The years that Grove worked for Schmidt helped shape his style as a leader. Schmidt was "down to earth, had no airs, said what he had on his mind, took no nonsense from anyone, did what he said he would do." Almost everyone who encountered Schmidt was terrified of him (except for his secretary, who terrorized the formidable professor). Grove, too, was a resolute truth-teller. Years later, in a book that offered management advice, he was to write: "Be straight with everyone. I hate it when people are not honest with me, and I would hate myself if I weren't straight with them. This isn't an easy principle to stick to. There are always many reasons (better to call them excuses) to compromise a little here or there. We may reason that people are not ready to hear the truth or the bad news, that the time isn't right, or whatever. Giving in to those tempting rationalizations usually leads to conduct that can be ethically wrong and will backfire every time."

Grove and Moore: Teamwork at the Top

After finishing his Ph.D. at the University of Berkeley, Grove joined Fairchild Semiconductor, where he encountered the second person who helped him mold his leadership style. Gordon Moore, the legendary chemist who headed research operations at Fairchild, is now widely known for "Moore's Law," which predicted that the number of transistors placed on a computer chip would double every two years—the phenomenon that has made it possible for the computer industry to produce increasingly powerful computers at declining prices. Moore took Grove under his wing. "He guided me from a freshly minted Ph.D. to a reasonably knowledgeable technologist in the semiconductor industry," says Grove.

Soon Grove left Fairchild with Moore and Robert Noyce, the highly respected scientist who had invented the integrated circuit in 1959, to co-found Intel. Grove's leadership qualities, already evident as Moore's deputy at Fairchild, now gained freer rein. Moore, who became Intel's chairman and CEO, was very different from Schmidt. Despite Moore's brilliance, "if I had relied on his leadership style, I would have been in deep trouble because Gordon is not an activist," says Grove. "My role was to be exactly the opposite of Gordon."

One example sharply reveals the difference between Moore and Grove. One time, Grove went to Moore to discuss an issue related to plastic packaging. Moore delivered a lecture on the history of plastic packaging, the various problems that had been encountered in its evolution, and the solutions that were implemented. Grove took notes. By the time Moore had finished, it was as if Grove had taken a course on plastic packaging. "Moore has encyclopedic knowledge of the technologies that are relevant to our business," says Grove. "But he was not an activist. That was not his thing to do." As a consequence, acting on knowledge he gained from Moore to achieve objectives became Grove's "thing to do." He did what it took to get results.

Moore was once asked what Intel would have been like without Grove. Moore's response, says Grove, was, "It would have been a much more pleasant place and a whole lot smaller." The corollary question might be what Intel would have been like without Moore. Says Grove, "The answer is: It would have been an Intel without Andy Grove. Gordon came to the conclusion in the first half-hour that I interviewed with him at Fairchild that I would be the person to succeed him there. In a minor detail, that turned out to be wrong, but I did become the person to succeed him at Intel." Grove says Moore first told him in 1971 (when Grove was just 33) that he had him in mind to run Intel. "It was a compliment that I didn't take literally at all," says Grove. "But he acted on what he said. He brought me along and tutored me. If he hadn't been there, I would have been a happy, productive engineer and I might have done pretty well, but I don't think I would have ended up running the company."

Over time, the bond between Grove and Moore grew uncannily deep. Grove recalls a meeting when some 20 Intel executives were sitting around a table, discussing an issue. From the corner of his eye, he saw Moore and noticed a subtle change of expression on his face. Grove knew that Moore would never interrupt or enter a discussion if something bothered him. Grove stopped the discussion at once, and asked, "Gordon, what's the matter?" and then Moore went on to explain what was on his mind. "Gordon produced ideas that he never would have voiced—thoughts that would never have received the hearing they deserved—until he expressed them and I amplified them," says Grove. "I didn't read his mind; I read his body, his face." Later, Moore told Grove, "You're getting to be scary. You know me as well as my wife."

In contrast, Grove and Noyce were essentially friends; Grove didn't regard Noyce either as a guide or role model. Asked how he, Moore, and Noyce worked together at Intel, Grove points to Peter Drucker's 1954 book, *The Practice of Management*, in which Drucker argues that the activities that make up a chief executive's job are too varied to be performed by a single person but should be divided between three: a "thought man," a "man of action," and a "front man." Grove says that during the 1970s, that description applied to Intel's three co-founders. Moore, with his encyclopedic mind, was the "thought man;" Noyce, a charming man who had enormous standing in the semiconductor industry, was Intel's public persona or the "front man"; and Grove, with his Schmidt-inspired, no-nonsense style, was the "man of action" who got things done.

By the 1990s, Grove increasingly took on the public role that Noyce had played in the 1970s, while Craig Barrett, now Intel's

CEO, became the "man of action." In other words, these roles aren't static; they change over time.

From Chips to Microprocessors: Targeting an Underserved Market

Intel's core business, which initially focused on memory chips, also changed over time. The way in which that change came about is now a well-documented part of Intel's history. As Grove tells the story in *Only the Paranoid Survive*, Intel went through a "crisis of mammoth proportions" as it "got out of the business it was founded on and built a new identity in a totally different business." Grove says that although this experience was unique to Intel, the lessons it teaches are universal.

The episode also offers an excellent instance in which Grove, as Intel's leader, rescued the company from potential extinction by discovering an underserved market and turning the company around by catering to it.

When Moore, Grove, and Noyce first started Intel, their goal was to produce memory chips. Its first product was a chip with a 64-bit memory. Over time, the company developed chips with increasing numbers of transistors packed in closer proximity. Initially, Intel owned 100% of the market because it had invented these products. In the early 1970s, some U.S. competitors, such as Unisem and Mostek, made their appearance. "If you don't recognize the names, it's because these companies are long gone," notes Grove. By the end of the decade, the U.S. had about a dozen memory chip companies that competed with one another, but Intel still was a dominant player in the memory game.

By the time the 1980s came, the nature of the business changed. Japanese chip makers entered the market in a big way—Grove describes it as "overwhelming force"—offering better quality and beating the U.S. chip makers on price. In an effort to beat back this competition, Intel tried to ramp up its manufacturing efforts. "During the 1970s, we were parallel to our competition," says Grove. "In the 1980s, the competition became better than us, but we didn't respond until Craig [Barrett] took charge of it." As Intel kept improving its manufacturing and laboratory operations to keep pace with the competition, Grove adds, it went from being an "okay manufacturer" to a "superb manufacturer, though it didn't happen overnight."

Despite Intel's efforts, the Japanese producers kept gaining ground. "Their principal weapon was the availability of high-quality product priced astonishingly low," Grove wrote. By the mid-1980s, Intel's memory chip business continued to head south, with steadily declining sales and rising inventories. Grove felt that he and his colleagues at Intel had lost their bearings and were floundering for direction.

In the middle of 1985 came a watershed moment. As Grove explains in a frequently quoted passage from *Only the Paranoid Survive*, he was sitting in his office with Moore, then Intel's chairman and CEO, discussing their situation. "Our mood was downbeat. I looked out the window at the Ferris wheel of the Great America amusement park revolving in the distance, then I turned back to Gordon and I asked, 'If we got kicked out and the board brought in a new CEO, what do you think he would do?' Gordon answered without hesitation, 'He would get us out of memories.' I stared at him, numb, then said, 'Why shouldn't you and I walk out the door, come back, and do it ourselves?'"

As Grove discovered, getting Intel out of memory chips was easier said than done. The more difficult question was, when Moore and Grove walked back through the door again, on what market should they focus? Most of Intel's organization—including its manufacturing and R&D facilities—was geared toward producing memory chips. More importantly, the mindset of every Intel employee had long been focused on trying to beat the company's rivals. Turning that around and getting Intel to focus instead on a different line of business was hardly easy. And yet, such an opportunity did exist. It was an underserved market: microprocessors.

Since 1981, Intel had been supplying microprocessors for IBM PCs. As demand for personal computers exploded, demand for Intel microprocessors grew as well. In addition, its next generation microprocessor, the 386, was about to go into production. Grove made the case—resisted at first by employees and then gradually accepted—that Intel should leave the declining memory business and concentrate R&D and manufacturing efforts on producing better microprocessors. As a result, Intel's fortunes gradually swung up again.

Grove's leadership in turning Intel away from memory chips and toward microprocessors helped Intel retain its lead. It might otherwise have gone the way of Mostek, Unisem, and other chipmakers whose names no one now remembers.

Intel Inside: Building a Brand

While Intel continued on its growth path, it faced a unique problem on the branding front. Most of its customers were computer makers, who used Intel's increasingly powerful microprocessors—286, 386, and so on—but the average computer user was no more aware of Intel than an average car driver is of the company that made the engine for his or her automobile. Consumers knew that Compaq or IBM had made their computers, but few were aware of Intel's role in producing the chip inside them.

Intel also faced a related problem: Its products were identified by numbers rather than names. When other chip makers offered products identified by similar numbers, Intel had a difficult time differentiating its products from those of its rivals. For example, other microprocessor manufacturers wanted to produce their own "386" product, and Intel was powerless to stop them because the numbers could not be trademarked. Again, Intel was vulnerable because its brand was not as strong as it could be.

Determined to change this situation, Intel embarked at the end of the 1980s on its Intel Inside campaign. As Grove observes, it "was the biggest campaign the industry had ever seen—in fact, it ranks up there with big-time consumer merchandising campaigns. Its aim was to suggest to the computer user that the microprocessor that's inside his or her computer is the computer."

Intel spent massive amounts of advertising dollars on its campaign, consciously targeting a new customer base. Rather than selling to computer companies, as it had in the past, the messages targeted the emerging mass market of computer users. (As previously noted, this shift in Intel's customer base came back to haunt the company a few years later when it faced the Pentium floating-point unit crisis.) In addition, Intel partnered with computer manufacturers to display Intel's logo in their advertising campaigns. This met with some resistance among manufacturers who thought Intel's emerging brand identity might reduce their ability to distinguish their own brands from that of their competitors.

All in all, the campaign was a huge success. Grove believes that by 1994, "our research showed that our logo had become one of the most recognized logos in consumer merchandising, up there with names like Coca-Cola or Nike."

Push, but Mitigate: Managing Risk

As Intel's brand recognition spread, the combination of its higher profile with its growing clout prompted some to wonder whether it might face pressure from antitrust regulators. In many ways, its market dominance resembled that of another IT giant that had prospered with the proliferation of personal computers—Microsoft. To be sure, from time to time Intel did face antitrust inquiries, but these never assumed the enormous proportions faced by Microsoft.

Grove was acutely aware of this potential danger. When the company was getting ready to introduce the 386 microprocessor, executives in Intel's legal department turned to him to say that Intel might potentially be heading into a monopoly situation. As Grove remembers, they asked, "We need to decide how we are going to play this. Do you want to play this aggressively, or would you rather stay on the safe side of the line?"

Grove and his colleagues had two examples before them of the consequences of antitrust actions. "The first example was AT&T—and this was two or three years after the modified final judgment [that mandated the breakup of the company]," says Grove. "The second was IBM, which had been in litigation forever." Grove decided the way Intel would approach the issue was "not pushing it to the line. That meant that even though we may be in trouble, we could avoid going down the AT&T path."

So, where did Grove draw the line? "There are certain rules that you can make combinations of products more attractive," he says. "You can be aggressive about the conditions under which you do that." For example, one reason why Microsoft in 2004 faced antitrust problems in Europe was because of its decision to bundle software for audio and video formats with its Windows operating system. Intel, however, under Grove's direction, resisted going down that path. "We left a lot of money on the table," Grove says. "Generally, we are very conservative in our business philosophy. We never push it to that last ounce. That philosophy continues."

Grove's guarded approach to the antitrust issue explains in part why Intel, while it was blasted in the media during the Pentium crisis, still has generally not faced the kind of hostility that has hounded Microsoft. It also says a lot about Grove's attitude toward managing risk. "I am a very cautious risk taker," Grove says. "And I mitigate. I push, but I mitigate the risk by over-preparation. Push, but mitigate. It's like trust, but verify. I am comfortable with risks that I am prepared for."

Beyond the Signing Sheet: Building Intel's Corporate Culture

As Grove emphasized his values through repeated actions and decisions, these became part of Intel's DNA. The company developed a unique corporate culture. Nowhere is this clearer than in Grove's answer to a question about mistakes he has made during his career. His response: "Every attempt I ever made to hire a senior person for the company failed. No exceptions."

Grove doesn't know if the mistake lay in trying to hire outsiders "because there was a systemic problem: Intel has a very strong immune system, and only autologous transplants work. Or I didn't understand the criteria by which we could identify people who fooled the immune system." A related error, Grove believes, was that he did not fire people sometimes a year or two years after he realized he should get rid of them. "About people I had hired, I was a ridiculous wimp," he says. "I would rationalize and say, 'I haven't tried X.' That is not my general image—but my general image is wrong in this regard. Every single time it caused pain and suffering to the organization. It led to a lot of wasted time on my part. But the same kind of attitude also allowed a lot of people to become successful. It gave them time to find their footing and succeed. So, on balance, it was probably good—but I wish I knew where to cut my losses earlier."

Hard as he found it to fire people he hired, Grove long believed in setting fair standards of discipline at Intel. One of his most unpopular actions was instituting a so-called signing sheet that people had to sign if they were more than five minutes late for work. "It was one of my more controversial management moves," he recalls. "Absolutely nothing was done with those sheets," but the engineers were furious. "It was as if we had seduced their sisters. What really got me going was watching people drift in and out. This was during the 1970s, with hippies and flower children. That was the kind of environment in which we were trying to build an organization. We had Hispanic women who were paid a dollar above minimum wage to work in our factories. If they were five minutes late, they got a tardy mark. If they had three 'tardies' in a month, they faced disciplinary action. These people who made products that paid our salaries had to be at their workstations on time, no matter what the traffic or the situation with their children. But these highly paid engineers could do what they wanted. It seemed the height of unfairness."

Intel's corporate culture also played a role when it came time for Grove to choose his successor as Intel's CEO. Barrett got the job, says Grove, because of his "knowledge, integrity, and leadership." Grove's tongue-in-cheek definition of leadership is someone whom people follow. "I tried teaching leadership," he says. "It is such a hokey bunch of psychobabble. I tried to substitute the psychobabble with something useful—such as the definition of a leader as someone whom people follow. People followed Craig. He always had his act together. Every job he had, he exceeded everyone's expectations."

An important attribute Grove saw in Barrett is that he has the "right kind of ambition." That, Grove explains, is crucial. "An individual's productivity depends on ambition. If you plot productivity on a vertical axis and the degree of ambition on a horizontal axis, the curve goes through a peak. If you have too little ambition, you don't push or work hard. If you have too much ambition, you put yourself ahead of others, elbow them out of your way, people stop trusting you, and your output drops. You need just the right amount of ambition. Craig was always ambitious, but in a healthy fashion. He had ambition for his team to win. He wouldn't put himself ahead of anyone else. He has his head screwed on right; he was never political, never competed with his peers. He's just a very competent, well-put-together guy."

Fifty years from now, how would Grove like people at Intel to remember him? "People will probably remember me for the signing sheet," he says with a laugh. "Inasmuch as I'm remembered, it will be for all the mythical good things—the turkey was big, the popcorn was fresh, the trains ran on time...except for the signing sheet, he was a good guy. That is probably how I will be remembered by people who think they know me."

Then the twinkle in Grove's eyes gives way to a quiet thoughtfulness. "What I would like to be remembered for is helping build an organization that sustains itself long afterward," he says slowly. "A bit like Sloan. He did pretty damn well."

Have Ambition, but in the right amount . . . and in a healthy fashion.

Have Ambition for your team to win. ✗✗✗

2

Leadership and Corporate Culture

A strong corporate culture, like charisma, is hard to define. But we know one when we see one, and nowhere is that more apparent than at Southwest Airlines. Chairman and former CEO Herb Kelleher, who founded the Dallas, Texas-based airline more than 30 years ago, injected two core values into the firm right from the beginning: a light-hearted irreverence for bureaucracy and an emphasis on teamwork. He came to company events dressed as Elvis Presley and rode into headquarters on his Harley. He encouraged employees to learn one another's jobs and make common-sense decisions without concern for channels, and he also expected them to dress up for Halloween. "One of the things that promotes our approach is a disinterest in titles, hierarchy, and bureaucracy. You say the heck with all that stuff. It just slows you down," says Kelleher.

Kelleher suggests that Southwest's culture is its best defense against other low-fare carriers that continually pop up with an eye toward duplicating his success. "It's the intangibles that are the hardest for your competitor to imitate," he notes. "You can buy an airplane and a terminal, but you can't buy the spirit of the people."

That "spirit of the people" is a big part of what management experts mean when they talk about corporate culture. The beliefs and values that guide employee behavior can improve performance by motivating workers toward a common goal and instilling in them a sense of purpose. They become loyal not to the CEO or their immediate boss, but to the company's vision.

Many of the Top 25 business leaders in this book successfully defined a culture for their organizations, either by creating one from the ground up—as did Kelleher and Mary Kay Ash—or by transforming one they inherited, as was the case with Johnson & Johnson's Burke. In some instances, the culture reflected both their own personalities and the needs of their organization. For example, Burke, a self-professed gambler by nature, inspired Johnson & Johnson employees to be risk-takers when it came to identifying and championing new products. Ash, a victim of workplace discrimination against women, opened the doors of her company to anyone willing to work hard and help others. Kelleher built a culture at Southwest Airlines by constantly reminding employees that they were the company's most valued asset.

"Most companies achieve a culture by accident," says Wharton management professor Peter Cappelli. "I think at Southwest it was more purposeful. Kelleher has been quite masterful in the role of manager of the corporate culture, creating a competency driven in part by the motivation and attitudes of employees. He's played this role of chief morale officer extraordinarily well." Doing that requires "not only skill," Cappelli adds, "but a certain amount of self-effacement to make the culture go. And that's something you rarely see CEOs able to do."

HERB KELLEHER

The Challenge:

Giving Southwest Airlines Its Wings

Getting Southwest Airlines off the ground at all was Herb Kelleher's greatest feat.

The upstart Texas airline, catering to low-fare, no-frills flyers, was blocked at the gate for more than three years as established carriers filed lawsuits to protect their turf. Kelleher, who was Southwest's lawyer in those early days, fought all the way to the U.S. Supreme Court, clearing the way for Southwest's first flights in 1971. Later, Kelleher was back in court fighting to keep the airline at Love Field in Dallas. "It was a long and difficult battle. It even continued after Southwest began operations," says Kelleher. "The other carriers exerted a massive effort to get us out of business."

Ultimately, executives at two competing airlines were indicted on antitrust charges. Southwest grew to become one of the nation's largest carriers, with planes painted like killer whales, flight attendants popping out of overhead bins, and in-flight meals consisting of a simple bag of peanuts. Those initial battles gave Southwest its wings, but they also helped shape Southwest's celebrated culture, one marked by humor, loyalty, and a fierce resistance to corporate bureaucracy.

During the early courtroom struggles, before the airline was flying, Southwest was just Kelleher, a small group of investors, and a plan sketched out on a cocktail napkin. "It was only a couple of us

1931: Born March 12 in Haddon Heights, New Jersey, son of a Campbell Soup executive and a mother who was a homemaker.

1953: Completes English degree at Wesleyan; considers becoming a journalist.

1956: Graduates from NYU Law School and clerks for a New Jersey Supreme Court Justice.

1960: After working for a Newark law firm, moves to San Antonio, Texas, his wife's hometown, with an eye out for entrepreneurial opportunities.

1966: Hired as outside counsel by Texas businessman Rollin King, who plans to launch an intrastate airline. Business plan is drawn up between the two men on a cocktail napkin in a local bar.

1967: Files application with the Texas Aeronautics Commission to fly Air Southwest Co., later renamed Southwest Airlines, between Dallas, Houston, and San Antonio.

1968: Commission approves Southwest's application, but the following day Braniff, Trans Texas, and Continental seek a restraining order arguing that Dallas, Houston, and San Antonio are adequately served.

1969: After losing the trial and an appeal, Kelleher asks the Southwest board to "go one more round." Postpones legal fees and takes the case to the Texas Supreme Court, which overturns the lower court rulings.

1970: U.S. Supreme Court refuses to hear appeal by competing airlines to overturn Texas Supreme Court decision.

1971: After yet another last-minute trip to the Texas Supreme Court to block another restraining order, Southwest begins flights.

1972: Southwest refuses to vacate Love Field in Dallas and move to a new airport farther from town. Competing airlines and airport officials file suit, arguing Southwest must comply with an agreement signed by other airlines as part of a bond issue to finance construction of the airport. Southwest argues it was not at Love Field when the agreement was made, so it should not have to comply.

1973: Southwest fends off Braniff in a fare war by offering customers a fifth of scotch, whiskey, or vodka, making it the largest distributor of liquor in Texas for two months. Southwest turns a profit and has not lost money since.

1974: Southwest expands beyond its original three cities—Houston, Dallas, and San Antonio—to the Rio Grande Valley, proving to itself that markets in smaller cities exist and opening the way to expansion to other cities, such as El Paso, Austin, Lubbock, Corpus Christi, and Midland-Odessa.

fighting the legal battles, day in and day out, against a whole cadre of lawyers from the other carriers," Kelleher recalls. "Persistence was very important. The other thing that was important was not accepting the conventional wisdom that it wouldn't work. I think probably only one in four people in Texas thought Southwest had a chance of flying, much less of being successful. I say, 'If it's conventional, it ain't wisdom, and if it's wisdom, it's not conventional.'"

In 1973, when competitors again took legal action against Southwest, this time to make it leave Dallas's Love Field, flight attendants, baggage handlers, and reservations clerks rallied around the company. "Our people were stimulated and challenged and responded with warrior-like spirit," says Kelleher. "I think that inculcated in them the idea that survival in the airline industry is a game of inches, and by golly, we've got to pitch in. The company became a crusade that they enlisted in. It's been pretty much the same ever since."

Kelleher rejected the conventional notion of putting the customer first. At Southwest, employees come first, in the belief that a company with happy and productive workers will have happy, paying customers. He loves to tell the story of an executive who complained it was easier for a baggage handler to get in to see the chief executive than it was for him. Kelleher told the executive that was because the baggage handler was more important.

As it was attempting to get off the ground, Southwest's management team was made up of refugees from other airlines who had lost jobs in the recession of the early 1970s. Some were free spirits who did not fit in at other carriers. Many had a lot of experience and became known inside Southwest as the Over-the-Hill-Gang. "The original employees were not young, but they were looking for new opportunities. They were looking for ways to do things differently," says Kelleher. "When they came to Southwest, they were unleashed. They could begin to say what they really thought. That group was seminal to turning the corner at Southwest Airlines, making it profitable and creating the blueprint for how we operated."

From the start, Southwest resisted traditional hierarchies and built flexibility into its operations. Kelleher says his days playing high school football and basketball taught him how a team should work. "If you play football, you don't say to the tackle, 'That's your territory, I'm not going to make that tackle.' Teams don't function effectively under those circumstances...Team play is a fundamental concept, and playing team sports brings that home to you very strongly. If you want to succeed, if you want to win, you have to play as a team."

As the young airline developed its operations, Southwest focused on substance, not process, says Kelleher. Southwest made use of every second to keep its planes in the air. Pilots, flight attendants, and ticket agents helped clean planes to turn them around within 10 minutes for the next flight. To fill every seat, the company pioneered low, off-peak fares.

With little capital for advertising—the company spent half its first year's marketing budget of $700,000 in the first month—Kelleher relied on word-of-mouth to generate interest. Southwest flight attendants dressed in orange hot pants and white go-go boots for the 8 a.m. flight from Dallas

1975: Braniff and Texas International officials indicted on U.S. antitrust charges for conspiring against Southwest. They plead "no contest" and are fined $100,000. The Fifth Circuit Court of Appeals allows Southwest to remain at Love Field. The U.S. Supreme Court refuses to hear the case.

1978: After having backed the airline as an investor, Kelleher joins Southwest as chairman and hires Howard Putnam from United as CEO.

1979: Following airline deregulation, Southwest begins first interstate flights to New Orleans.

1981: Putnam resigns to become President and chief operating officer at Braniff International.

1982: Appointed CEO of Southwest, Kelleher is confronted by a recession and an air-traffic controllers' strike.

1985: Southwest buys airline started by first Southwest CEO, Lamar Muse, triggering fare war with Frank Lorenzo, CEO of Texas Air. Southwest eventually sells the airline to Lorenzo.

1992: Loses arm-wrestling contest to the chairman of a South Carolina-based aviation sales and maintenance firm over rights to the advertising slogan, "Plane Smart." The contest raises $15,000 for charity.

1993: Southwest expands to East coast with service to Baltimore/Washington International Airport.

1994: Employees take out an ad in *USA Today* honoring Kelleher on Boss's Day, thanking him for running the only profitable major airline, for singing at the holiday party, and for singing only once a year.

1995: Southwest offers ticketless travel system-wide.

1996: Florida added to Southwest's routes.

2001: Relinquishes CEO title in June and turns duties over to James Parker and Colleen Barrett. Parker jokes the two will divide the work, with Parker in charge of drinking and Barrett overseeing smoking.

2004: Southwest enters market in Philadelphia, faces competition nationally from new generation of low-cost airlines including JetBlue, AirTran, and Delta's Song subsidiary—all modeled on Southwest. Gary Kelly, formerly Southwest's CFO, is named CEO. He replaces Parker, who announces his retirement.

to Houston, dubbed the "Love Bird" flight by the company.

Despite all the fun and games at Southwest, the company has maintained a disciplined business strategy, says Kelleher. When airline deregulation took place in 1978, Southwest had the opportunity to become a larger interstate airline competing for more lucrative, longer routes. "We said, 'We have a particular niche in the airline industry, and we're basically going to continue as an intrastate airline within Texas.' That took a great deal of discipline when the other alternatives were available," says Kelleher. Gradually, carefully, Southwest did expand, but only with enough cushion to ride out an emergency without having to cut people or profits.

Kelleher figures the airline industry is good for two major crises every 10 years, such as an oil-price hike, a war, an air-controllers' strike—even another 9/11. Each crisis leads to massive layoffs and bitterness. But Southwest has never furloughed an employee. "It's very important if you are going to be successful that people's jobs are secure, so they don't have all the haunts and worries about whether they are going to [be jobless] next week. That's how people at airlines have always felt."

Leadership Lesson

Flying High, Coming In Low

Kelleher talked openly of leading an organization based on soul rather than systems. (Southwest's ticker symbol is LUV, a reference that harks back to Love Field in Dallas but one that also sums up the company's cultural mindset.) "Things happen naturally, not programmatically. It's as much a matter of spirit and soul as the mind. The way you deal with people has to emanate from the heart. That's what gives it meaning and sincerity and provides motivation. We didn't sit down and say, 'We're going to be funny because it's good for business.'" Yet, if a CEO instills the right kind of culture, employees will work hard at keeping costs low, says Kelleher, who once held a 2 a.m. barbeque—with himself and the pilots as chefs—after hearing that mechanics on the graveyard shift had trouble attending company picnics.

While the company pays salaries that are lower than competitors' salaries, it also offers stock options to everyone, not just executives. In addition, Southwest's compensation system states that its officers receive pay increases that are no larger, proportionally, than what other employees receive. "And in bad times, we take reductions," Kelleher says. But no matter how bad the times get, the company refuses to lay off employees—a policy that has promoted financial discipline by discouraging managers from hiring too many people when the industry is thriving. Good employee relations also has, for the most part, prevented labor strife at Southwest and encourages sometimes extraordinary customer service. On a Southwest flight to Oklahoma City for a court hearing, a passenger who had forgotten to bring along a tie looked up to see a flight attendant presenting him with one she had borrowed from another traveler, along with the traveler's address so that the tie could be returned.

In a culture that encourages informality, pilots crack jokes over the loudspeaker system during flights, Kelleher once arm-wrestled with a manager at another airline during a trademark dispute, and prospective pilots are asked to trade their suits for Bermuda shorts during job interviews.

Kelleher's efforts to build Southwest's culture complemented his overall strategy for the airline, which focused on travelers for whom air travel was financially just out of reach; he gave them an alternative, no-frills option. While Southwest was engaged in bitter fare wars and legal battles with other airlines, its true competition was the automobile—one reason why Kelleher always resisted suggestions to raise ticket prices. Once, when Braniff was charging $62 to fly between Dallas and San Antonio and Southwest's fare was only $15, a shareholder asked Kelleher if the company couldn't charge an additional $2 or $3. Kelleher said no. "You don't understand," Kelleher told him, "We're not competing with other airlines. We're competing with ground transportation."

According to Kelleher, when Southwest started out in 1971, only 15% of U.S. residents had flown in an airplane. It's now 85%. To keep that 85% coming back, Southwest has had to run fast and lean. While the best symbol of this is the standard Southwest in-flight meal—a bag of peanuts—real cost savings came from Kelleher's approach of taking the simplest, most direct route. For example, he avoided the vogue of establishing hubs and stuck to Southwest's original point-to-point system. Southwest also bypassed travel agents, instead selling directly to consumers (and along the way pioneering the concept of ticketless travel). Kelleher balked at participating in computer reservation systems that charged airlines a fee. In addition, he kept his fleet simple. By training pilots and mechanics only on Boeing 737s—and having access to interchangeable parts—Southwest was able to cut training and maintenance costs.

An eye for thrift is an essential part of Southwest's culture and a key ingredient of its success. The company keeps its planes in the air more than its competitors, driving down the cost of carrying the equipment and other overhead expenses. In 1972, Southwest had four planes and 70 employees. When it could not meet payroll, Kelleher contemplated selling a plane, which would have resulted in layoffs and a breach of the company's commitment to its workforce. Instead, employees cut turnaround time at the gate to squeeze more revenue out of the planes it already had. The company also "hedges" its fuel costs by buying most of it in advance, and it saves on fuel usage by flying light, "flying at higher altitudes…and coasting into landings at a slower descent speed."

In 2004, Southwest announced it would begin flights out of Philadelphia where US Airways has dominated the market with 68% of daily flights. Southwest offered fares as low as $29 one way, with a ceiling price of $299 each way. US Airways had been charging last-minute fares of up to $1,000, but began adding flights and cutting prices to cities targeted by Southwest. The two airlines had already gone head-on at Baltimore-Washington International Airport where Southwest has now displaced US Airways as the lead carrier.

"They beat us on the West Coast, they beat us in Baltimore, and if they beat us in Philadelphia, they're going to kill us," former US Airways Chief Executive David Siegel told workers in Philadelphia in early 2004. "It's going to be a battle for our lives." Siegel directed workers' attention to a screen showing Kelleher dressed as Uncle Sam, pointing his finger at the viewer, next to the words, "I want your job!" It was Siegel's attempt to get employees to agree to more labor concessions. Within a few months, Siegel himself was dismissed by the US Airways board, in part for alienating the airline's labor force.

Maintaining a strong balance sheet and expanding cautiously is the best way to avoid layoffs during times of turbulence, says Kelleher. "On September 11, when the airline industry as a whole experienced the greatest crisis in its history, Southwest did not cancel a flight or lay off any people. Why? Were we lucky or was it because we had the lowest costs for available seat-mile and had the greatest liquidity and access to capital?" asks Kelleher.

A vigilant approach to costs, in good times and in bad, is part of his "corporate wellness plan" for Southwest. "If you're fit," he says, "you're ready to encounter anything. You're ready to take on any competition."

May 12, 1918: Born Mary Kathlyn Wagner in Hot Wells, Texas, outside of Houston. At age 7, starts taking care of her father, a tuberculosis victim, while her mother works full-time managing a restaurant.

1935: Marries Ben Rogers with whom she has three children. Marriage dissolves upon his return from World War II.

Early 1940s: Joins Stanley Home Products selling household goods at parties in women's homes. Attends annual sales meeting in Dallas where top salesperson is crowned Queen of Sales and given an alligator handbag. The next year, inspired by previous year's sales meeting, Ash herself wins Queen of Sales award. Instead of the coveted handbag, she receives a "flounder light," a device pinned onto hip boots for night fishers.

1953: Joins another direct-sales company, World Gifts.

1957: Receives promotion to National Training Director.

1963: Resigns from World Gifts when a male employee she trained is promoted over her at twice her salary.

1963: A month before the opening of Mary Kay Cosmetics, second husband George Hallenback dies after suffering a heart attack at the kitchen table.

MARY KAY ASH

The Challenge:

Motivating a Sales Force of Thousands

"Most companies create a sales force to enhance their products," says Richard Rogers, Chairman and CEO of Mary Kay Inc., and the son of Mary Kay Ash. "But Mary Kay created a product to enhance the work of her sales force."

And what a sales force it has turned out to be. Mary Kay Inc., the direct seller of beauty products founded in 1963 by Mary Kay Ash, currently has 1.1 million independent sales reps in more than 30 markets worldwide. Every summer, thousands of these reps convene in Dallas for a three-day, action-packed "seminar" that includes loving tributes to Ash (who died in 2001), testimonials, and presentations on new sales techniques. But the highlight is awards night, when top performers are crowned, seated on thrones, and given prizes ranging from furs and vacations to diamonds and the famous pink Cadillacs. These lucky women have earned the ultimate reward—the approval of the company and the admiration of their peers.

How was Ash, who started Mary Kay Inc. at age 45 with $5,000 in savings, able to motivate a sales force of mostly unskilled, unemployed or underemployed women over a span of nearly three decades?

She didn't rely on bonuses, stock options, or other financial incentives, as many companies do. Instead, she treated her beauty consultants like celebrities, and along with small and large gifts, she gave them constant support and encouragement. "Mary Kay Cosmetics is known for 'praising people to success,'" she wrote in her autobiography, *Mary Kay: You Can Have It All*. "We think this is so important, we base our entire marketing plan on it." According to Ash, the last time many women are acknowledged for achievement is when they graduate from high school or college. "Women need praise," she states. "It's been my experience that a woman will often work for recognition when she won't work for money."

Ash realized this early on. At her first annual awards night in 1964, she treated 200 sales reps to Jell-O salad and home-cooked chicken in the company's small Dallas warehouse. Two years later she set up the Golden Goblet Club, which handed out gold-plated goblets to every sales consultant who sold $1,000 worth of wholesale merchandise in a month. She initiated the "ladder of success," a gold brooch "on which each rung and each jewel represented a different personal plateau." And in 1968, Ash started awarding diamond pins in the shape of bumblebees—a symbol for women who have "flown to the top." The pins were "badges of merit," instantly recognizable by any other salesperson at a Mary Kay function.

But ultimately, it didn't matter what the prizes were. They could be ribbons, gold-colored stars, a special red jacket, a designer suit, praise in the company's monthly magazine, or a Go-Give Award for an act of kindness. They could be an invitation to Mary Kay Ash's 30-room Dallas mansion for tea and cookies or a personally signed letter of congratulations for meeting a sales or recruitment

1963: Launches Mary Kay Cosmetics—later called Mary Kay Inc.—on Friday, Sept. 13, with $5,000 of savings, the help of her youngest child, 20-year-old Richard Rogers, and a skin cream formula she purchased from the family of J.W. Heath, an Arkansas leather tanner. Mary Kay Cosmetics, which has nine independent beauty consultants and revenues of $200,000 its first year, is located in a 500-square-foot Dallas storefront.

1964: Holds first annual staff meeting for 200 sales people.

1966: Marries third husband, Mel Ash, who dies in 1980.

1968: Company goes public.

1969: Settles lawsuit with former employees who claim they own the rights to the Arkansas tanner's original formula for beauty cream. Employees use that formula to start their own rival company, BeautiControl, which is later sold to a New Jersey direct-sales firm.

1969: Company awards first pink Cadillacs to its five top sellers.

1971: First international subsidiary opens in Australia.

1976: Company is listed on the New York Stock Exchange.

1979: Mary Kay Inc. surpasses $100 million in sales and first beauty consultant makes more than $1 million in commissions. Ash is profiled on CBS's *60 Minutes*, during which Morley Safer asks her whether she is "using God" to promote her company. She replies, "I like to think God is using me."

1981: Writes first of three books: an autobiography called *Mary Kay*, a second book called *Mary Kay on People Management* in 1984, and a third book called *Mary Kay: You Can Have It All* in 1995. All make best-seller lists.

1982: Long-running fight begins with BeautiControl, which has been bought from the New Jersey company by former employee Richard Heath. With his wife Jinger, Heath relaunches the company to compete with Mary Kay.

1984: First edition of the "100 Best Companies to Work For" features Mary Kay Inc.

1985: An investment group led by Ash and son Richard Rogers takes the company private in leveraged buyout.

1987: Mary Kay Ash becomes chairman emeritus of the company; her son Richard becomes chairman.

1992: Mary Kay Inc. makes the list of Fortune 500 companies.

1993: Subsidiary opens in Russia.

1993: Mary Kay Ash sets up museum to archive the stories of its sales force leaders and the company history.

goal. "Anything can be a symbol for recognition," Ash said. "We applaud each little success one after another, and the first thing you know, [these salespeople] actually become successful."

By the 1980s, according to Rogers, Ash was head of a "massive sales force grounded in the philosophy of…leaders creating leaders." Supporting that philosophy was a carefully defined career path based on promotions to different levels within the sales force, ranging from director to independent sales director to the most coveted spot of all, independent national sales director—a status earned by only 300 people in the company's history.

Mixed in with Ash's praise was always an emphasis on raising the bar—recruiting more sales reps, selling more products, getting the next promotion. She didn't just tell women to support each other's efforts; she also made sure they saw how well the other sales reps were doing. One national sales director remembers being on stage at the Dallas Seminar, thinking she had done a great job and then looking over at Ash, whose comment was "Yes, but next year, we'll see you as the queen."

In 1985, 17 years after Mary Kay Inc. had gone public, the company bought back all outstanding shares and once again operated as a privately held family company. That year also marked a decision by corporate headquarters to update its image and refocus on its closest "customers"—its sales force. One of Ash's favorite sayings was: "When I meet someone, I imagine her wearing an invisible sign that says, 'Make me feel important.'" Ash did. In *Mary Kay: You Can Have It All*, she wrote: "The media have described our seminars held at the Dallas Convention Center as the 'ultimate form of praise,' and they're right. Because that's exactly our purpose in holding them...When our top beauty consultants and directors are recognized for their accomplishments in front of an appreciative audience of their peers, the applause ranks among the most meaningful praise anyone can receive."

1994: Operations expand into 22 markets, including Japan, Argentina, Canada, and Germany.

1996: Mary Kay Ash Charitable Foundation is established to fund research on cancers affecting women; expands four years later to help victims of domestic violence.

1996: Mary Kay Ash suffers debilitating stroke.

1997: Operations open in Ukraine, Czech Republic, and the Dominican Republic.

2000: Establishes subsidiaries in Kazakhstan, Slovakia, and the Philippines.

2000-2002: Company overhauls its cosmetics business with new packaging, formulations, and product forms.

2001: Richard Rogers resumes role as CEO of Mary Kay Inc. Rogers had been on sabbatical from day-to-day operations since the early 1990s, while retaining position of chairman of the board of directors of Mary Kay Holding Corp.

2001: Mary Kay Ash dies on Thanksgiving Day at age 83.

2002: CBS premieres movie entitled "The Battle of Mary Kay," depicting the well-publicized rivalry between Mary Kay Ash and Jinger Heath, co-founder of BeautiControl Cosmetics.

2004: Mary Kay Inc. is one of the largest direct sellers of skin care and color cosmetics in the world, with 200 products and 1.1 million independent consultants worldwide in more than 30 markets. Sales for 2003 totaled a record $1.8 billion at wholesale level.

Leadership Lesson

Members of a Very Large Family

A focus on employees is at the heart of every successful company, but creating a distinctive culture for those who work there is highly individualized. For example, shortly after Mary Kay Ash started up her cosmetics and skin care company, she solved a critical incentive problem for her employees by emphasizing the joys of adopting. She was referring, in this case, to her sales force.

Mary Kay beauty consultants, as they are called, operate under an elaborate system in which consultants receive commissions on the sales of people they recruit into the company. This encourages an incentive-based mentoring program, but it leaves a gap when a consultant moves away from the home base—and her original mentor—into a new area. That is where Ash's "adoptee program" comes in. The program requires an established director to "take [the newcomer] under her wing and treat [her] as one of her own," although commissions still go to the person who initially recruited her. The metaphor explicitly appeals to Mary Kay's largely female workforce.

Anticipating the criticism that some established reps might not help a newly arrived transplant since they won't receive any commissions on her sales, Ash responded: "If you adopted a child, you would not say to her, 'No, you can't have steak tonight. Only my own children can have steak.' No decent mother would treat her adopted child like this, and neither would our directors with their adoptees."

The family analogy was quintessential Mary Kay Ash, who set up a corporate culture that emphasized, among other things, the importance of relationships and a sense of inclusion. Unlike most companies in the beauty industry, which traditionally sell their heavily advertised product lines in department stores and drug stores, direct sales companies sell their products wholesale to women who work as independent contractors. These women then resell the products directly to consumers at marked-up prices. Mary Kay's rewards for those who do well under this system include the famous pink Cadillacs, which even today remain synonymous with a highly motivated, top-performing sales force whose devotion to Ash was legendary. (The pink color eventually softened into a pearlized white.)

According to Richard Rogers, CEO of Mary Kay Inc. and Ash's son, "relationship-building is engrained in our sales force as a business model." At the company's annual seminar in 2003, Rogers told the 50,000 sales reps in attendance that "forging bonds and establishing high levels of trust are essential. The ability to get along with people is the Mary Kay connection..." Although the company currently has sales of $1.8 billion at the wholesale level, Rogers said they operate "the same way we did with mother and a handful of consultants and directors...We are still an extended family. We are just worldly now. A relationship-based culture is at the core of all that we do."

In *Mary Kay: You Can Have It All*, Ash stressed over and over the importance of forging relationships with customers and other sales reps. Her chapters include subheads like "P&L Means People and Love," "Respect for Others," and "Do the Right Thing." When a director is promoted to national sales director, she wrote at one point, "she takes an oath before a packed audience of Mary Kay people at the Dallas convention center" in which she "vows to abide by the Golden Rule. These vows are not idle words. At Mary Kay, they are how we live."

The same system exists today. As Rogers says, "Somebody is always coaching, encouraging, and advising someone else in order to get to the next level." Mary Kay Inc. just opened an operation in Poland, Rogers adds. "We send in sales directors to teach [the reps] about motivating, caring, and helping one another...They feel like they are part of a structure that will help them succeed."

This sense of inclusion is constantly reinforced as part of the Mary Kay Inc. corporate culture. In 1993, the company set up a museum to archive the success stories of its top sales leaders as well as the history of Mary Kay Ash and the company. In 2000, it published a book called *Paychecks of the Heart*, a compilation of personal stories by 113 Mary Kay independent national sales directors who grew up in the company under Ash's tutelage. The stories were recorded by Yvonne Pendleton, the company's director of corporate heritage. Every year since 1978, the company has bestowed a Go-Give Award recognizing those "who unselfishly inspire and motivate others with no thought of personal gain." And in 2002, the company opened its Keeper of the Dream Gallery to honor top salespeople. The 300 women who have achieved independent national sales director status have their portraits hanging in the gallery alongside Ash's. There is space for more.

As Rogers told the sales reps at the Dallas Seminar in 2002: "Let me assure you, there will always be room at the top of this company for you."

No Ceilings, No Boss

The genius of Mary Kay was not that she created a particularly unique product, but that she so brilliantly created a culture that nurtured two very important markets: the women she recruited to sell Mary Kay products, and the millions of consumers who bought them.

When Ash started her company in 1963, she knew from experience that few jobs existed for under-skilled women who were brought up to believe that family, not career, was their first priority. What Ash offered was a job they could do part-time, before the kids came home from school or after dinner, and a clearly defined career path. By selling more cosmetics and recruiting more sales reps, these women could earn commissions that rivaled the salaries of some chief executives. Just as importantly, they gained status within the Mary Kay organization as top producers.

Mary Kay Inc., one newspaper said, offered women "the ultimate opportunity with no ceilings, no boss."

The offer has had enduring appeal. Tom Whatley, president, Global Sales and Marketing, at Mary Kay Inc., suggests that "what made working for a direct seller interesting to women years ago—enabling them to get out of the house—offers the opposite attraction today. Now, it allows women to stay home." A recent newspaper article put it this way: "Through bra burning and, decades later, the dominance of black clothing and grunge chic, Mary Kay remains. It's not hard to figure out why. This is not about the people of high fashion so much as it's about everyone else. Mary Kay is about the suburbs and, beyond that, the small towns." Ash, the article said, "liberated hundreds of thousands of women...who had not yet seen themselves in an entrepreneurial light. She taught them certain truths about beauty, equality, success, and the color pink..."

When Ash died in 2001, tributes to her company and her leadership came from all over the world. Angela Stoker, a Mary Kay beauty consultant for 21 years, made $2.5 million in commissions and earned the use of 13 Cadillacs. Ash, she said, "understood women. She created a company so women could really have a career, a home life, a family, and be involved in [their] community." Ash herself told countless stories of how women like Stoker were inspired by her company, and how she herself was inspired by their life stories. One of her books, *Mary Kay*, is "dedicated to the thousands of women who DARED to step out of their 'comfort zones' and use their God-given talents and abilities...." Many of Ash's beauty consultants could have written a similar dedication to her.

His mother, says Rogers, didn't care as much about the business side of running the company as she did the human side. "Every month I would get an envelope from her with her checkbook in it, and I would balance it and send it back. If she had given a lot of money away to charities and so forth during that month, then I would make a wire transfer to her account. All she cared about was motivating and encouraging people. She always understood that it was easier to be successful when you could look around you and see people just like you succeeding."

The aspirations of the company's beauty consultants and the needs of its customer base coincided with Ash's remarkable ability to identify and serve both: She gave a career to one group and cosmetics to the other. For Ash, it was all part of her life's plan. As she wrote in *Mary Kay: You Can Have It All*, "My prime motivation for going into business was to help women. I wanted to provide opportunities for them to create better lives...and to realize their dreams."

1925: Born February 28 in Rutland, Vermont. Father was a marble company salesman and then a life insurance salesman; mother was a homemaker. As a young boy, Burke sold daffodils from a field near his home outside Albany, New York because, he says, "they were beautiful and they were going to waste." He offered to split the profits with the owner of the field, but she never accepted any money. He also sold Christmas trees and strawberries door to door. "I was a marketing person beginning in fourth grade," he says.

1942: Enters Holy Cross College; during that time Holy Cross participates in the Navy's V-112 program, which requires students to enlist in the service. Burke is commissioned as an ensign and spends one year as a skipper on a landing craft tank (LCT) in the South Pacific. Returns to college when the war is over.

1947: Graduates from Holy Cross College with B.S. in Economics.

1949: Earns MBA from Harvard Business School; joins Procter & Gamble.

1953: Joins J&J as a product director; chafes under company's lack of emphasis on new product development; makes plans to leave but is persuaded to stay with assurances of more tolerance for risk-taking.

JAMES BURKE

The Challenge:

The Tylenol Crisis

On the wall of an executive's office at Johnson & Johnson's headquarters in New Brunswick, New Jersey, hangs a quote from the year 1982. It reads: "A flat prediction I'll make is that you will not see the name Tylenol in any form within a year. I don't think they can ever sell another product under that name. There may be an advertising person who thinks he can solve this, and if they find him, I want to hire him, because then I want him to turn our water cooler into a wine cooler." The quote is from Jerry Della Femina, chairman of the ad agency Della Femina Travisano Partners, and it refers to one of the most notorious product tampering cases ever recorded. Seven people in the Chicago area died that fall after taking cyanide-laced, extra-strength Tylenol capsules, a pain reliever sold by J&J subsidiary McNeil Consumer Products Co.

Anyone given a list of defective product incidents occurring over the past 25 years would see that there is clearly a wrong way to handle such crises. Consider Coca-Cola's mismanagement of the "contaminated can" incident in Europe in 1999, Intel's initial failure to respond quickly to the calculation errors imbedded in its Pentium chip in 1994, and Firestone's initial failure to accept responsibility for SUV roll-overs caused by poorly manufactured tires in 2000.

The most prominent—and by now legendary—example of good crisis management remains Johnson & Johnson's handling of the Tylenol disaster. That incident was clearly the biggest challenge of his career, says James Burke, chairman and CEO of Johnson & Johnson from 1976 until his retirement from J&J in 1989. His actions in the weeks after the first death, which was reported on September 30, 1982, have been the subject of case studies in numerous business schools and management texts, not to mention the impetus for a new sub-specialty in public relations.

Burke not only preserved the reputation of his highly respected consumer goods company, but he saved the Tylenol brand. At no point did he try to back off from the company's responsibility in the incident, even though it was later proven that the tampering had occurred at the retail level. "When those seven people died," Burke says, "I realized there were some things we hadn't done right. Responsibility for that incident had to be, in part, ours. It wasn't easy to take that responsibility…but it was clear to us, to me especially, that whether we could be blamed for the deaths or not, we certainly could have helped to prevent them. How? Through packaging. The fact is that the package was easily invaded. You could take the capsule out, open it up, put the poison in and then put the capsule back together. It was easy to do. I felt, and still feel, that it was our responsibility to fix it."

Burke's conviction, and his total commitment to the safety of the customer, led the company to spend $100 million on a recall of 31 million bottles of Tylenol, which before the tampering, had been the country's best-selling over-the-counter pain reliever.

1954: Launches several over-the-counter medicines for children, all of which fail.

1955: Moves up to director of new products.

1962: Becomes general manager of Baby & Proprietary Products.

1964: Appointed executive vice president of marketing for Consumer Products Division.

1965: Promoted to general manager of J&J Domestic Operating Company; becomes president in 1966.

1971: Promoted to vice chairman of the J&J Executive Committee.

1973: Named president of the corporation and chairman of the Executive Committee.

1976: Elected chairman of the board and CEO of J&J.

1979: Meets with top management team to reconfirm commitment to J&J credo.

1982: Seven people die in September and early October after taking cyanide-laced extra-strength Tylenol capsules in five Chicago stores. Tylenol, sold by McNeil Consumer Products, a division of J&J, had 35% of the $1.2 billion analgesic market before the deaths. Market share suddenly falls to 7%. J&J spends $100 million to recall 31 million bottles of Tylenol and then re-launches the product two months later in tamper-proof packaging.

1983: By mid-year Tylenol's share of the analgesic market climbs up to 30%, reaching its pre-tampering level of 35% by year-end.

1984: Tylenol comes out in caplet form.

1986: Woman in New York dies in second product tampering case. J&J halts production and offers consumers option of swapping their capsules for tablets. Company makes decision to stop marketing Tylenol in capsule form.

1988: J&J introduces gel caps, which look like capsules but cannot be taken apart.

1989: Burke retires from J&J, after staying on four years longer than he expected due to Tylenol crisis.

1989: Becomes chairman of the Partnership for a Drug-Free America (PDFA), a non-profit organization founded in 1985 by the American Association of Advertising Agencies and best known for its national anti-drug media campaign.

1989: Agrees to chair the Business Enterprise Trust, a group founded by Norman Lear and committed to fostering corporate ethics and social responsibility. Lear will disband the Trust in 2000 due to lack of funding.

The recall decision, Burke says, "was a highly controversial one because it was so expensive. There were plenty of people within the company who felt there was no possible way to save the brand, that it was the end of Tylenol. Many of the press reports said the same thing, that we would never survive this incident. But the fact is, I had confidence in J&J and its reputation, and also confidence in the public to respond to what was right. It helped turn Tylenol into a billion dollar business." Indeed, within eight months of the recall, Tylenol had regained 85% of its original market share and a year later, 100%.

But during the days immediately following the deaths, Burke's clearest and most pressing challenge was dealing with the public hysteria. According to media reports, the Tylenol crisis led the news every night on every station for six weeks. In an action that proved to be typical of Burke's willingness to meet the crisis directly, he contacted the head of each network's news division in order to keep lines of information open and assure them of his accessibility. "We were straight with them," Burke says. "There were times I wasn't too pleased with what some members of the media were doing, but by and large they were very sensible."

Burke also met with the heads of the FBI and the FDA and, against their advice, decided on the recall. Johnson & Johnson immediately asked the country to stop taking any type of Tylenol, and offered customers free replacements and coupons. In addition, J&J stopped all advertisements, examined its production and distribution facilities for possible contamination, and cooperated with law-enforcement agencies to identify possible suspects. Within two months, the company reintroduced the product in a triple-sealed tamper-resistant package. Surveys done at the time showed that J&J's quick response to the tragedy helped to reestablish consumer confidence in both the brand and the company.

The person who tampered with the Tylenol was never found. Nor was anyone caught when a similar incident involving cyanide-laced Tylenol caused the death of a New York woman in 1986. In 1984, J&J replaced capsules with caplets, and in 1988, the company introduced gel caps, which look like capsules but can't be taken apart.

Burke had one other tool at his disposal that was and is unique to J&J: the company credo, which goes back to the founding of J&J in 1887. The credo clearly states that the company is responsible first to its customers, then to its employees, the community and the stockholders, in that order. "The credo is all about the consumer," Burke says.

Burke had first addressed the credo in the late 1970s by initiating discussion in J&J offices around the world as to whether it should be kept, modified, or scrapped altogether. "The credo came alive because of those debates," says Burke. "Some people asked why we needed it. Others said it wasn't necessary to have a credo to confirm what we already knew." Still others suggested that of course when issues arose, the consumer would come first, not the shareholders. "So that all sounded pretty simple, but in a business environment it wasn't that simple at all," Burke says.

For Burke, though, it was. When those seven deaths occurred, "the credo made it very clear at that point exactly what we were all about. It gave me the ammunition I needed to persuade shareholders and others to spend the $100 million on the recall. The credo helped sell it."

1990-92: Under Burke, PDFA achieves media goal of $1 million per day in donated time and space—reaching over 90% of American households with an anti-drug message every other day. Research studies confirm significant declines in use of illegal drugs.

1992-1997: Is a founding member, and serves as director of, the National Center on Addiction and Substance Abuse at Columbia University, whose mission is to study and combat substance abuse.

1993-94: PDFA launches Inner City Program, specifically targeting anti-drug attitudes of New York City's low-income young people.

1994-96: Drug use increases among young people, remains stable among adults.

1997-98: Burke works with director of Office of National Drug Control Policy to develop concept of "public-private partnership" to use federal money to buy media time and space for PDFA.

1999-2000: Early results of National Youth Anti-Drug Media Campaign are encouraging. Media donations for match of paid time and space exceed expectations. Independent research supports effectiveness of PDFA media messages.

2000: Burke is awarded the Presidential Medal of Freedom by President Bill Clinton for his outstanding achievements and contributions to society as chairman of PDFA and J&J.

2002: Becomes chairman emeritus of the Partnership.

2003: Named the sixth greatest CEO of all time by *Forbes* magazine.

2004: In a study on corporate reputations conducted by Harris Interactive and the Reputation Institute, Johnson & Johnson ranks number one (out of 60) for the fifth consecutive year. Report also shows that the average reputation score for all companies falls, indicating a deeper distrust of corporate America than in the recent past.

2004: McNeil Consumer and Specialty Pharmaceuticals, the unit of J&J that makes Tylenol, announces a new $100 million ad campaign for Tylenol in an effort to reposition the brand. The ad campaign's theme is "Stop. Think. Tylenol."

Leadership Lesson

A Credo Culture

In the lobby of Johnson & Johnson's headquarters in New Brunswick, New Jersey, corporate culture is literally chiseled in limestone. As noted earlier, the company's credo states that J&J's responsibility is first to its customers, then to its employees, then to the community and finally, to its shareholders. Of course, many companies have codes and mission statements. But the best corporate leaders have a gift for giving those words meaning, especially in a time of crisis.

James Burke displayed that gift during his handling of the Tylenol crisis in 1982. Brian Perkins, worldwide chairman of J&J's consumer pharmaceuticals and nutritionals group, was then a 28-year-old product director with J&J subsidiary McNeil Consumer Products, the maker of Tylenol. He remembers Burke as a man "who had a clear vision and could galvanize an organization around what seemed like doing the impossible. Right after the first death was reported, he came to a McNeil meeting, got up in front of our sales and marketing people and said, 'Look, I have a challenge for you. I will give you an extra week's pay if you can do this. I don't know that you can, but I want you to know that the challenge is there.'"

What Burke wanted, and got, was an immediate plan of action that included recalling 31 million bottles of Tylenol worth $100 million, setting up a toll-free hotline for consumers, and working closely with the media, health-care community,

FBI, and FDA to share information and keep the public informed. "He was so much in command of the situation, connecting the dots of what was important every single hour during those days,"says Perkins. Four years later, on February 10, 1986, when another person died from taking a cyanide-laced Tylenol, the company knew exactly what to do: Within two weeks, the entire sales force had created and set in motion a series of actions to control the damage.

Burke's adherence to the credo defined the culture at J&J throughout his tenure as CEO from 1976 to 1989. As Perkins says, "whenever we were faced with a really hard decision, he would always point to the credo for guidance. He had a way of making a very difficult and complex situation pretty simple when you think about doing what is right for your customer. It was a powerful message."

Burke also read the credo to include something that had fallen by the wayside—an emphasis on risk taking. After graduating from Harvard Business School in 1949 and spending three years at Procter & Gamble, Burke joined J&J, "because that was the place everyone who was interested in marketing wanted to go." Within the first few months, he let it be known that he was looking for a new job because, he said, the company wasn't willing to take risks in the consumer products field.

"I felt they had a huge opportunity in consumer products, but I couldn't sell it to anybody so I decided to look around," Burke remembers. "Then I got a call from General Robert Wood Johnson's office. I assumed I was going to be fired, because I had introduced four new products and all but one had been failures (including a children's aspirin and chest rub). I was stumbling and I knew it. I thought they had every right to fire me. But I felt cocky enough that I decided I would explain why it was a bad idea to do that."

General Johnson, Burke says, "listed my failures—he had all the details in front of him—then he stood up and shook my hand and said he wanted to congratulate me. He understood that business involved risk taking and that consumer products was a high-risk business. So at the end of the meeting, he said I would now report to his son, and we would be responsible for new products worldwide. Then he sat down and got back to work."

Burke continually emphasized a customer-focused culture where risk taking was rewarded. "It was always about the consumer," he says. "The closer you were to the consumer, the more power you had to decide what should be done, and to take risks doing it. I believed strongly in decentralization. The name of the game was bottom up and not top down, as it was in most other companies. The consumer business more than any other had to be that way because you had to have people close to the consumer. That meant decentralizing decision-making downward."

Annual reports from J&J during the years that Burke was chairman and CEO list the "most important products and introductions" of each year. During Burke's tenure, those lists included approximately 175 new products; in addition, about 15 acquisitions were completed or new units set up. Just before his retirement, Burke was described in a (1988) *BusinessWeek* article as a man with "a passion for urging people to take risks. A demanding boss who can shout his way through a rowdy staff meeting, he has spent years encouraging his managers to be daring...he continually energize[d] the system."

Working with Addiction

After retiring from J&J, Burke extended his ideas about risk-taking to the world of non-profits—specifically, the Partnership for a Drug-Free America. Burke, who started smoking on his 12th birthday and gave it up when he turned 42, says he was up to two packs a day and had clearly become addicted. "It was an addiction I struggled with over and over again. Finally I decided I had one last chance to stop, and I did. As a result of quitting, I came to the conclusion that I should be able to help others with addictions. I realized that with the right attitude, you can do almost anything. That's how I got interested in the idea of the Partnership for a Drug-Free America."

Burke became chairman of the PDFA in 1989 when he retired from J&J, and held the position for 13 years. The Partnership was founded in 1985 by the American Association of Advertising Agencies, a group that had a strong belief in the power of advertising to change behavior. Under Burke, the partnership grew to become the single largest public-service media campaign in advertising history. From the beginning, he was able to gather together other people from the media and advertising industries to make PDFA into "a big deal. The more we talked, the more excited we got and the more people we were able to involve. I was totally convinced this was the right thing to do," he remembers.

As PDFA chairman, Burke took marketing risks once again, just as he had done with Tylenol. In the late 1990s, the group ran an edgy TV ad showing a teenage girl smashing up dishes, windows and other appliances in her kitchen to illustrate how heroin smashes up relationships. Another ad zeroed in on a person holding an egg and telling the audience that the egg is their brain. He points to a hot frying pan and says the pan represents drugs. Then he cracks the egg into the frying pan, where it immediately sizzles and burns. The message: This is your brain on drugs. A third ad shows a young man revving up a car so high that the engine explodes. This is how it feels to your heart to be on meth, he tells the audience, referring to methamphetamine. "The difference is you can't rebuild a heart."

What's interesting, says Burke, is that "drug use, cigarette use, and alcohol use are all joined at the hip and all are going down at the same time. We believed this was going to happen. We all fundamentally believed that attitudes can in fact change behavior, and that you can change attitudes with advertising. My whole life was spent in marketing. I believe in it intensely. I believe you can apply the lessons that you learn in business to social issues."

Burke is still speaking out on lessons he learned during a long career in both public and private service. For example, before it became fashionable to talk about truth and trust as core values, he did. In a 1996 interview with the American Management Association during which he was asked what advice he would give to others, he responded, "I have found that by trusting people until they prove themselves unworthy of that trust, a lot more happens." In an interview with the Harvard Business School alumni magazine, he noted that the business community has "corrupted the system by hiring boards of directors that feel beholden to the CEO." Not only should an independent board and lead director govern companies, but business executives also need to "recreate a trust agenda. Nothing good happens without trust. With it you can overcome all sorts of obstacles. You can build companies that everyone can be proud of."

In his interview for this book, he also spoke about trust. "Trust has been an operative word in my life. The word trust embodies almost everything you can strive for that will help you to succeed. You tell me any human relationship that works without trust, whether it is a marriage or a friendship or a social interaction; in the long run, the same thing is true about business, especially businesses that deal with the public." The accounting scandal at Enron, he adds, has brought that truth home.

As for the current scandals in the brokerage houses and investment banks, "there is a big difference in how some people look at the word trust. There are still a lot of people who are abusing their privileges and their right to make money properly. But a lot of them are paying the price for that…Everyone who influenced me beat into me the importance of being trustworthy. And I think those influences are still out there. Trust is gaining. I can't prove it and most people would call me an optimist, but I honestly think it's happening."

3

Truth Tellers

Truth lies at the heart of all true leadership. To understand how the two relate to one another, consider Mohandas ("Mahatma") Gandhi, whom more than a billion Indians call the father of their nation. Confronted by unjust laws imposed by the British Empire in the last century, he developed a doctrine of peaceful non-cooperation that he called *Satyagraha*, or insistence on truth, whose aim was to "wean opponents from error by patience and sympathy" rather than by subjecting them to violence. After early successes in South Africa, Gandhi's principles spread like wildfire in India, where they helped unite millions in the subcontinent against British rule. "*Satyagraha* is a relentless search for truth and a determination to reach truth," Gandhi wrote. "It is a force that works silently and apparently slowly. In reality, there is no force in the world that is so direct or so swift in working."

If this principle applies to political leadership, it applies even more to the world of business. In these times of corporate scandals at Enron, WorldCom, and Parmalat, truth-telling is as critical as vision when it comes to lasting leadership. Just as leaders need sensitive antennae to spot opportunities that aren't obvious to others, they also need the ability to communicate their vision in a way that wins the trust of their constituents. Integrity builds trust; dishonesty—while it may succeed temporarily—ultimately undermines it. It is only when constituents—whether they are members of a board of directors, employees, or Wall Street analysts—are convinced the leader is a straight-shooter who is expressing a complete and credible view of reality that they will accept it. Once that happens, constituents often become followers, which is the litmus test of leadership.

In their own ways, all Top 25 leaders in this book are truth tellers. Warren Buffett famously helped re-establish the credibility of Salomon Inc. after John Gutfreund, its chairman and CEO, led the Wall Street investment bank into a bond-trading scandal in the early 1990s. Wharton's Michael Useem, who wrote about the issue in his book *The Leadership Moment*, says this helped Buffett become known as "the conscience of the Street." Jack Welch, former CEO of General Electric, made a clear statement about truth telling when he titled his recent autobiography, *Jack: Straight from the Gut*. Welch's penchant for plain speaking played a key role in his rise to the top at GE and in his ability to elevate the company to new heights as its CEO.

Peter Drucker, the perennial outsider who studied companies but never joined them, also built his reputation by writing about management issues without fear or favor. In articles and books produced over a lifetime, Drucker, Marie Rank Clarke Professor of Social Science and Management at Claremont Graduate University in California, brought a sharp, skeptical eye and a trenchant pen. In an article about leadership, for example, he noted that the most effective leaders he had encountered subjected themselves to a "mirror test"—by making sure that the person they saw in the mirror in the morning was the kind of person he or she wanted to be, respected, and believed in, thus protecting themselves from the temptation of taking popular but wrong actions.

William George, the former CEO of Medtronic, has made truth-telling the cornerstone of his philosophy of authentic leadership. Asked what he would tell a young and ambitious manager about becoming a successful leader, George responds: "Be yourself, follow your own style, be what you really are, and think about why it is that you want to be a leader. Don't just try to get a title or power or money because in the end, these are not fulfilling."

Truth-telling as an attribute of lasting leadership works at two levels. First, the leader must be able to perceive and express an accurate understanding of reality, which goes hand in hand with an intolerance of humbug.

Second, leaders must be able to communicate the truth as they see it without being afraid it might alienate their constituents. The ability to speak the unalloyed truth calls for courage. Temptations to hide or distort facts are often rooted in fear of the consequences if the truth were to be revealed. Why do companies cook their books or sales managers pad their sales figures? Fear of the consequences. Why do executives praise their CEOs' half-baked ideas instead of speaking up about the emperor's palpable nakedness? Fear of the consequences. In the business world, so many factors militate against truth-telling that those who tell the truth consistently and fearlessly (though not tactlessly) earn credibility. People who are ruthlessly honest may not be wildly popular, but they are usually respected and believed. And inspiring belief, as the experiences of Welch, Drucker, and George show, is indispensable to lasting leadership.

1935: John Frances
Welch Jr. born in Salem,
Massachusetts, the only
child of a railway con-
ductor and a mother
who pushes him to
excel and fostered self-
confidence. She famous-
ly explains Welch's stut-
ter as the simple inabili-
ty of her son's tongue
to keep up with his
quick mind.

1957: Graduates from
University of
Massachusetts with a
B.S. in chemical engi-
neering, enters
University of Illinois and
earns M.S. and Ph.D.
degrees in chemical
engineering.

1960: Joins GE as a
junior engineer in
Pittsfield, Mass., at a
salary of $10,500 and
begins to question the
company's bureaucracy.

1961: Feeling slighted
by a standard $1,000
raise, announces he's
quitting. Boss talks him
into staying.

1963: Explosion in a
tank at a pilot plastics
factory under his super-
vision tears a hole in
the roof. No one is
hurt.

1965: Helps develop
Noryl, a plastic product
that grew to become a
$1 billion business.

1968: Appointed general manager of GE's plas-
tics business.

1970: Plastics division
sales doubled in three
years.

JACK WELCH

The Challenge:
Eliminating the Weak Links

Jack Welch, former chairman and chief executive officer of General Electric, had to look no further than Syracuse, New York, where General Electric was manufacturing television sets, to see the global future. It cost GE more to make a television in Syracuse than it cost to buy a Japanese-made set. "You didn't need to be a genius to see it," says Welch. "We were in businesses that had no technological advantage—housewares, hairdryers, irons. The barriers to entry were low and foreign competitors could quickly come at it."

In 1981, when Welch became the youngest CEO in GE history, he began a crusade to eliminate the company's weak links before they could drag down the entire organization. His goal was a radical restructuring that would get rid of problem products and focus on profitable businesses immune to foreign competition, particularly in the financial, high-tech, and service sectors. The strategy would earn Welch the nickname "Neutron Jack" because it eliminated tens of thousands of workers but left plants and office buildings intact.

"My biggest challenge, without question, was changing a company—which the outside world and the inside world thought was perfect—to face the realities of global competition in the 1980s and 1990s," says Welch. Everything, he said, appeared to be "running well. There was no burning bridge. It was not a turnaround. I had to create a sense of urgency and desire for radical change in the face of what appeared to be smooth sailing."

Welch himself was a product of GE, a company founded in 1892 with a long reputation for progressive and effective management. Independent, scrappy, and opinionated, Welch often went against the GE grain. Still, after an elaborate selection process, he was named CEO in 1981 and took control of the company's mixed bag of businesses as well as its entrenched interests, traditions, and bureaucracy.

Almost immediately he launched his controversial restructuring. GE managers were ordered to fix, sell, or close down businesses that were not first or second in their markets. In all, GE made 1,700 acquisitions and divested 408 businesses while Welch was CEO.

Among the first units to go was central air-conditioning in 1982, followed by Utah International, a $2 billion natural resources business. Those sales proceeded smoothly, but GE employees and the public were roiled when Welch sold the $300 million housewares business. These low-tech products, like the television sets in Syracuse, were sitting ducks for low-cost foreign competitors, Welch argued.

Another deal driven by concern about foreign competition was GE's 1985 acquisition of RCA, including its NBC television network. Welch says he went after NBC because he felt foreign ownership rules governing television networks would give him some cover from rival companies abroad. "We had to convince people of the

1971: Promoted to head of chemical and metallurgical division managing a wide portfolio of materials beyond plastics, such as industrial diamonds and insulation. Restructures management.

1973: Writes in a performance review that his long-range career objective is to become CEO of the company.

1974: After another promotion that adds medical systems and appliance and electronics components to his responsibilities, gets special permission to remain in Pittsfield, Mass., and run the businesses from there instead of moving to corporate headquarters in Fairfield, Conn.

1977: Promoted to sector executive for GE's consumer product business and finally moves to Fairfield.

1979: GE chairman Reginald Jones begins search for a successor, asking Welch who should be the next chairman of the company if both Welch and Jones are killed while traveling on the company jet.

1981: Becomes GE's youngest and eighth chairman and CEO.

1982: Nicknamed Neutron Jack by *Newsweek* magazine because of his restructuring strategies.

ing strategies.

1983: Sells GE's housewares business to Black & Decker, a move that causes an uproar among his critics because the products were so familiar to GE's traditional customers.

1985: Acquires RCA and the NBC television network.

1987: Eight months after acquiring Kidder Peabody, federal officials raid the Wall Street firm and find ties to Ivan Boesky, who pleaded guilty to insider trading charges. GE pays $26 million in fines.

1993: Attempts to increase financial holdings by buying Primerica from Sandy Weill, but negotiations stall.

1994: Joseph Jett, a trader at Kidder Peabody, fabricates $350 million in trades. Later in the year, Kidder Peabody is sold to PaineWebber.

1996: Launches Six Sigma initiative to improve quality by reducing defects to 99.99966% of perfection.

1998: After a lifetime playing golf, which fed his love of competition and drive for perfection, Welch has his ultimate game, shoots a 69 off the back tees at the Floridian in a match with pro golfer Greg Norman who shot 70 from the

foreign competitive threat," he says. "IBM and others did turnarounds, but they did that after they were almost gone. We changed before we had to."

Even though Welch was a tough CEO, these changes were painful. "You have to know who you are and what you're doing and be comfortable in your own shoes. It's an awful thing to be labeled something [Neutron Jack] because you are making an organization more competitive...The only thing that counts is a winning company. Broke dot-com companies can't do much for society. Companies that go bankrupt don't do much for society."

As Welch sold off industrial businesses, he began to focus on developing the company's financial arm, GE Capital, figuring that it would be more profitable than "grinding metal. So I put a lot of resources and time and effort into [that]. After 20 years in manufacturing businesses, I couldn't believe how easy it was to make money, relatively speaking."

For Welch, GE became a giant management laboratory where he could experiment with ideas and strategies. When something worked in one division, he would transfer it to another. "One of the nice things about a big company is you can try a lot of that stuff. It's a great hothouse," he says. "A small company can make a big mistake. Shame on a big company that doesn't take a lot of small risks."

Welch acknowledges that there is an element of luck and timing in business and that even the greatest corporate leaders cannot control external circumstances. "Being a CEO in the 1990s, with the wind at your back in the markets and giving out options, sure helped make the case for a winning company. I took over in a very rough period. Unemployment was high. The prime rate was at 21%. President Carter said we were in a malaise. It wasn't hard to go up from there."

Welch says that despite his long tenure as CEO he was always able to keep himself energized by launching new company initiatives, such as his Six Sigma push, designed to bring GE quality to near-perfection. Each year Welch unveiled his latest strategic bent to managers at their annual meeting in Florida after New Year's, until he retired at the company-mandated age of 65. "I had one job title for all those years, but I was many people," he says of his ongoing personal restructuring. "You reinvent yourself all the time."

It was a process that Welch seemed to enjoy. "You get hooked on these different new things. There was India. Find out all you can about India. Then find out all you can about China. There's always a new [opportunity]. You're the same core person, but your eyes are constantly being opened to new worlds."

pro tees.

1999: Admits to being late in recognizing the importance of the Internet and launches a company-wide e-business initiative.

2000: Offers to buy Honeywell, but European antitrust regulators thwart the merger.

2001: Retires after 20 years as CEO during which GE's market value rose. Writes best-selling business book, *Jack: Straight from the Gut,* published in September 2001.

2003: Surrenders lavish GE retirement perks, including a Manhattan apartment, golf course memberships, and a helicopter after the package is made public in divorce papers. Maintains $9 million annual pension.

2004: Signs reported $4 million book deal to write *Winning,* a business how-to book due out in 2005.

Leadership Lesson

Bitter Truths

In 1998, Jim McCann, CEO of 1-800-Flowers.com, wrote a short piece for *Fast Company* magazine about having to fire a senior executive at his company. McCann knew, as did his colleagues, that the person was not right for the job, but he could not bring himself to let him go. McCann was friends with the person in question, and firing him, McCann felt, was not only difficult, it was almost brutal.

As he was agonizing over this dilemma, McCann happened to meet Jack Welch at a dinner party and told him about the problem. Welch asked McCann, "When was the last time anyone said, 'I wish I had waited six months longer to fire that guy?' Always err on the side of speed." Encouraged by Welch's advice, McCann dealt with the situation. It initially hurt, then it brought relief, and eventually McCann made up with his friend. The lesson McCann learned from Welch was clear: The truth can be more bitter than a sweet illusion, and making the right decision can involve unpleasant confrontations. Firing someone is never easy, especially for managers who cherish loyalty and are as loyal to their colleagues as they expect their colleagues to be to them. Still, doing the right thing—which usually involves truth-telling—tends to work out well for everyone in the end.

Welch himself learned this lesson the hard way. When he came to GE in 1981 as newly appointed chairman and CEO, he undertook a massive restructuring, a process that involved not only recasting General Electric's product portfolio, but also significant staff layoffs as he attempted to stamp out bureaucracy. Although the layoffs didn't go down well, Welch's gut instinct about the merits of streamlining the company eventually paid off. As he told a group of Wharton students in a speech in 1999, GE took five years to break through its lumbering bureaucracy. "An organization is like a building," Welch said. "Every floor is a layer, and every layer is a nuisance. Every wall is a functional wall. Think about detonating that building."

Traditionally, GE had been organized by industry, with managers reporting up through sectors to the chief executive's office. The restructuring that Welch engineered led to the idea of a "boundaryless" company in which the values and culture of GE were more binding than a particular business or geographic market. "The boundaryless company I saw would remove all the barriers among the functions: engineering, manufacturing, marketing, and the rest. It would recognize no distinctions between domestic and foreign operations. It meant we'd be as comfortable doing business in Budapest and Seoul as we were in Louisville and Schenectady," Welch writes in his autobiography.

Welch's straightforward truth-telling was also in evidence at the company's training facility in Crotonville, New York, where Welch regularly lectured from "The Pit" in the center's main classroom. In June 1983, when the manager of Crotonville was preparing a presentation for the GE board requesting $46 million for renovations, Welch looked at the payback analysis on his last chart, and then drew an "X" over the executive's transparency and scribbled "infinite" across the page. It was a telling gesture: Welch was totally committed to overhauling the company, investing millions in some divisions even as he was laying off thousands of workers in others.

At Crotonville, Welch was upfront with rising executives about his own management problems; in the late 1980s, he extended the give-and-take throughout the company in a program called "workout." During these sessions, patterned after a New England town meeting, management and workers in a GE business held two- to three-day meetings to brainstorm ways to increase efficiency. At a 1990 work-out session in GE's appliance business, as a union worker was making a presentation on improving refrigerator door production, the chief steward of the plant jumped out of his seat to interrupt. "You don't know what the hell you're talking about. You've never been up there," the steward shouted, then snatched the magic marker from the presenter and quickly sketched out a solution that was endorsed by all those in the meeting. "It was absolutely mind-blowing to see two union guys arguing over a manufacturing process improvement," writes Welch in his autobiography. "Here were the guys with experience, helping us fix things."

In a letter to shareholders in 1992, Welch quantified four types of leaders at GE. Type One, the star, delivers on commitments and shares in the values of the company's management. Type Two neither delivers results nor shares values and should be working elsewhere. Type Three misses commitments, but shares the company's values and should get a second chance. Welch was most concerned about Type Four, the leader who delivers on commitments but does not share the company's values. He described Type Fours as tyrants, overly concerned with short-term performance, and having the potential to destroy morale. "In an environment where we must have every good idea from every man and woman in the organization, we cannot afford management styles that suppress and intimidate," wrote Welch.

Welch's analysis shows the important relationship between truth-telling and corporate culture. When a leader insists on truth-telling to a fault, integrity becomes integrated into corporate practice. Wharton's Peter Cappelli says that unlike many other executives who preach simplicity, Welch, whose own personal style was direct and simple, was able to actually change the company's culture. "He understood management at a fundamental level and he had the enormous willingness to persevere and change an organization to take simple principles seriously."

Welch blames himself for not picking up on problems that led to what he considers GE's greatest failure during his watch, the Kidder Peabody scandal that centered on rogue trader Joseph Jett. Welch said he allowed Kidder to operate outside the integrity-based culture he had fostered at GE and behave like its counterparts on Wall Street, with their emphasis on superstars and huge bonuses. After the fraud was uncovered, GE managers from other divisions offered to kick in funds from their businesses to keep the company from missing its quarterly numbers. Not the Kidder managers. "Instead of pitching in, they complained about how this disaster was going to affect their incomes," Welch writes in his autobiography. "The two cultures and their differences never stood out so clearly in my mind."

When Welch retired, he was asked to name the single achievement at GE of which he was most proud. His response was: Building a company where everyone feels important, where new ideas are welcome and where every person benefits from the organization's successes.

PETER DRUCKER

The Challenge:

Inventing the Discipline of Management Studies

Peter Drucker, Marie Rank Clarke Professor of Social Science and Management at Claremont Graduate University in California, single-handedly kicked off an expedition to map, as he put it, the "dark continent of management." Up through the 1940s, the prevalent practice at most U.S. corporations was to drive employee productivity higher through intimidation and fear. During those years, Drucker came across just two companies—Sears Roebuck and the British retailer Marks & Spencer—that saw any value in developing managers, according to biographer Jack Beatty. And in stark contrast to the present, only three universities listed continuing education programs aimed at managers. The union-busting, hard-nosed manager was held as the ideal.

Drucker was eager to understand how the world of business was changing, but not as an insider. Despite his study of human nature and his uncanny ability to draw lessons from business trends, he was never tempted to enter the corporate world. Some companies tried to lure him in, but Drucker quietly declined each offer, choosing to retain the objectivity—and credibility—of the perceptive outsider. In the process, he unintentionally became the world's preeminent and earliest management guru. "An observer, not a

1909: Born in Vienna, Austria, to Adolph and Caroline Drucker. His father is an economist and lawyer who becomes a senior civil servant in the Austro-Hungarian Ministry of Economics; his mother is one of the earliest women medical doctors of the era. During his formative years, Drucker is surrounded by rich cultural and intellectual discussions that take place during his parents' weekly soirees.

1929: Writes article that appears on October 15 in a prestigious European economic journal published by the *Frankfurter Zeitung*. Argues that stocks on the New York Stock Exchange could only climb higher. U.S. stock market collapses a few weeks later. Forswears making predictions about the stock market, although he builds a reputation for being prescient in spotting business trends.

1929: Becomes a senior editor for finance at the *Frankfurter General-Anzeiger* newspaper. Duties include writing six to eight editorials per week and managing all foreign and economic news. Realizing that a journalist has to cover diverse subjects, disciplines himself to read about as many topics as possible at the end of his work hours.

1931: Earns his doctorate in international and public law at Frankfurt University while working full-time as a journalist at the *General-Anzeiger* from 6 a.m. to 2 p.m. Credits his editor, Erich Dombrowski, with instilling in him an intense sense of discipline.

1933: Moves to London after declining to enroll in the Nazi Party and also turning down a job with the Nazi Intelligence office. In London, analyzes distressed securities but is thoroughly bored with finance. Realizes his interests increasingly lie in studying and writing about human nature.

1937: Marries Doris Schmitz, a former student at the London School of Economics, where Drucker substitutes occasionally for a professor.

1937: Leaves London for the United States where he begins to write for the American press.

1939: Publishes his first book, *The End of Economic Man: The Origins of Totalitarianism*, which explores the intense irrationality and nihilism of fascism and draws a parallel between fascism and communism. Book is read by Henry Luce, the founder of Time Inc., who asks Drucker to join his staff as the foreign news editor. Drucker turns down the job, a life-long pattern of never working for a single employer.

participant—making him, for his refusal to participate, all the keener as an observer," *Forbes* magazine said of him.

Drucker has filled shelves with books on every aspect of management from leadership and corporate governance to decision-making and non-profit management. He has published more than 30 books since 1939. The challenge that launched his nearly 80-year career as a management theorist (he sees himself as a "social ecologist") came after he published his second work, *The Future of Industrial Man,* in 1942. At the time, Drucker was a professor of politics and philosophy at Bennington College in Vermont, but academics soundly criticized his book for mixing economics with social science. Still, it caught the attention of legendary General Motors chief Alfred P. Sloan, who invited Drucker to study the automaker.

The president of Bennington College, Lewis Jones, urged Drucker to forego the GM project, warning him that it would derail his academic career in both economics and political science. Even trying to fit the project into an academic area wouldn't work because there was *no* established discipline that studied corporations and how they functioned. "I am ashamed to admit how little I knew about management," said Drucker. "It was amazing, not because I was so ignorant, but because *nobody* knew anything." And it seemed, also, that nobody cared. Drucker's publisher questioned the value of such a book, asking, "Who the hell wants to know how a big company is organized?"

It was a daunting challenge to venture into a field where little work had been done before— and in the face of discouragement from his peers.

Still, Drucker followed his own beliefs, and ultimately, his decision to study GM paid off. The resulting book, *Concept of a Corporation*, became his landmark work and remained in print until 1993. Over the long term, it also established a market for business books, with more than 2,000 published annually today. For the project, Drucker visited every GM division and many plants east of the Mississippi; he was a fly on the wall at GM board meetings and had unfettered access to managers, executives, and workers. After 18 months of research and writing, he published the book in 1945.

Drucker developed two major themes in *Concept of a Corporation*. One was the elegance of GM's decentralized structure, which allowed it to turn on a dime to respond to the vagaries of demand. The other was a thinly veiled appeal for the automaker to begin treating its workers more humanely. While these themes appear obvious now, his findings resonated at the time as they continue to today. "[Drucker] puts the sensibilities of good management practices in words that make other people say, 'That really does make sense. I can do that,'" notes Wharton's Michael Useem. "His ideas are grounded in an exceptional grasp of the realities of daily managers."

When Sloan assumed control of GM in the 1920s, he decentralized the company's far-flung operations. Each division was granted significant autonomy from central management, which tended to deal with the larger issues, like negotiating labor contracts, providing capital, and setting car prices. This structure allowed the company, the world's largest at the time, to switch from

1939: Becomes a part-time teacher of economics at Sarah Lawrence College in Bronxville, New York, but is fired shortly after for refusing to sign a faculty petition in support of communism. States that he is unwilling to give in to the same kind of intolerance and close-mindedness he witnessed in Germany. Quickly finds a new position as professor of Politics and Philosophy at Bennington College in Vermont.

1942: Publishes his second book, *The Future of Industrial Man*, which is panned by academics. However, it captures the attention of Alfred Sloan, the legendary chief of General Motors (at the time the world's largest corporation), who invites Drucker to study GM, a study that forever changes Drucker's life.

1945: Publishes the seminal *Concept of the Corporation*, which draws a portrait of GM as both a social system and an economic organization. Book sets Drucker on a path from which he never strays—that of studying the insides of companies and organizations from the outside. While GM distances itself from the findings in the book, Henry Ford II reorganizes Ford Motor Company on the template Drucker created for GM. Book seals his reputation as a prescient thinker and consultant to major corporations.

1950: Drucker becomes professor of management at the Graduate Business School at New York University and remains on the faculty until 1971. During this decade, he consults for industry giants like General Electric and Sears Roebuck. GE leans heavily on the insights of *Concept of the Corporation* during its reorganization.

1950s: During the early part of the decade, is among the first to realize how computer technology will revolutionize business processes.

1954: Publishes *The Practice of Management.* The timing of the book is impeccable; it provides a text that explains how managers should run companies just as a fascination with management is about to explode. With the book's publication, Drucker is credited by many with transforming management into a discipline.

building cars during peace time to building tanks, guns, and planes during the war economy between 1941 and 1945.

While a decentralized structure created greater efficiencies at GM, Drucker concluded that the way the automaker treated workers reduced its effectiveness. GM was the paragon of assembly-line manufacturing. Drucker argued that the monotony of assembling only a small part of the finished product put a drag on the workers. Not only did the assembly line adopt the pace of the slowest member, but workers also had no sense of pride in the final product.

The book became an instant bestseller in the United States and Japan. While GM was slow to change its labor practices, many other companies began to implement the reforms that Drucker prescribed. Japanese automakers, especially, took to the team approach in their manufacturing processes. Over the next several decades, they became renowned for building less expensive but more reliable cars. Henry Ford II also acknowledged his debt to *Concept of a Corporation* as he reorganized Ford Motor Company on the decentralized model. By the 1980s, Drucker was credited for single-handedly moving the majority of the world's largest companies to "radical decentralization."

Not everyone, however, has been impressed by Drucker's decades-long track record. Many in the academic world see his work as the broad generalizations of a glib journalist rather than true scholarship. An academic discipline, they note, should be based on empirical studies and statistics. "This is an underestimation of [Drucker's] method," says Useem. "He doesn't just conjure up abstractly what he writes about but draws from experience. He has been looking inside companies and talking to managers. It is not statistics that communicate what management is about, but rather the ability to give a hands-on feel for the reality of managing."

Over the course of nearly a century, Drucker has succeeded in elevating management from the unknown to an art that has the potential to transform "a mob into an organization, and human effort into performance."

1966: Publishes *The Effective Executive.*

1975 to 1995: Writes monthly column for *The Wall Street Journal.*

1971 to present: Drucker is the Marie Clarke Professor of Social Science and Management at Claremont Graduate University in California. The university's Graduate Management School is renamed in 1984 as the Peter F. Drucker Graduate School of Management

Leadership Lesson

Adventures of a Bystander

Peter Drucker has made a nearly century-long career of articulating truths about business processes and customs that either eluded others or simply did not occur to them. His unique gift is that once he has expressed an idea, it makes others wonder why they did not think of it themselves. That may help explain why *Fortune* magazine dubbed him "the most prescient business-trend spotter of our time."

Since the early 1950s, Drucker has predicted how computer technology would someday transform the way businesses are run, and coined such terms as "privatization," "knowledge workers," and "management by objective." In 1999, *The Wall Street Journal* said that Drucker "has remained consistently fresh and ahead of the times."

Drucker is often viewed as the person who established the study of management as a discipline in the 1950s, though some argue that Marvin Bower, the legendary consultant who helped build McKinsey & Co. into a consulting powerhouse, shares at least part of the honor. Over the past decade, however, Drucker has focused on the emergence of the so-called knowledge worker—employees who create products and services based primarily on information and knowledge. The term, which he first used in the 1950s, is still in vogue today because it captures a major concern for companies struggling to work globally with a workforce that is designing products, conducting research, and processing data.

Drucker now teaches a course on increasing the productivity of knowledge workers. Here, he says, the emphasis is on managing relationships in "which you are not in command—alliances, partnerships, contracts, outsourcing. Such relationships are the way the world economy is going." Another course he teaches is designed to let executives harness the information they need to make their businesses succeed. He asserts that the way computers and data processing are used in the enterprise today means that executives have less information to work with than they used to. The course therefore concentrates "on the information they need and how to get it," says Drucker. "It focuses especially on how to organize the supply of a type of information that is totally absent today for executives—information about the world outside the company."

Drucker has fine-tuned his theories to address issues that he himself brought to light. Drucker says that today he teaches his management students subjects that he barely addressed 10 years ago, but barely touches the subjects he taught a decade ago. "I no longer teach the management of people at work, which was one of my most important courses, because I no longer think that learning how to manage other people, especially subordinates, is the most important thing for executives to learn," Drucker says. "I am teaching, above all, how to manage oneself."

At this stage, Drucker believes that as a business person you have to "know about yourself—how you have to learn, how to place yourself, how to take charge of your own work and your own career, how to make yourself productive, and so on."

Drucker was among the first to establish a connection between employees' productivity and the culture of their corporation. *Concept of a Corporation*, published in 1946, looked at the way people worked together rather than how a corporation makes a profit.

"All managers do the same things, whatever the purpose of the organization," wrote Drucker in an *Atlantic Monthly* article in 1994. "All of them have to bring people—each possessing different knowledge—together for joint performance. All of them have to make human strengths productive in performance and human weaknesses irrelevant. All of them have to think through what results are wanted in the organization—and have then to define objectives."

This humanistic approach laid the foundations for his management theory called "management by objective" which calls for employees to work with management to develop "meaningful objectives based on a thorough understanding of the work." These meaningful objectives underscore the need for the company to have a mission and to see what each employee can contribute to that mission.

Nearly all businesses today pay lip service to being customer-centric, while making a profit remains their highest goal. Drucker, on the other hand, has long held that businesses do not exist to "make and sell things" but rather to "meet human needs." Many of the most successful companies have taken his advice to heart.

1942: Born Sept. 14 in
Muskegon, Michigan. His
father was a management
consultant; his mother
taught home economics
before having children.

1964: Graduates from
Georgia Institute of
Technology with BS in
Industrial Engineering.

1966: Earns MBA from
Harvard Business School.

1966: Serves as special
assistant to the Secretary
of the Navy in the U.S.
Department of
Defense/Assistant to the
Comptroller.

1969: Joins the private
sector as director of
long-range planning for
Litton Microwave
Cooking Products.

1973-1978: Serves as
president of Litton
Microwave Cooking
Products.

1978: Joins Honeywell
as vice president of cor-
porate development.

1980: Promoted to
president of Honeywell
Europe.

1983: Promoted to
Honeywell's executive VP
of control systems.

1987: In January, named
Honeywell's EVP of
Industrial Automation
and Control; in May,
named president of
Honeywell's Industrial
Automation and Control;
in December, named
president of Space and
Aviation Systems.

WILLIAM GEORGE

The Challenge:

Managing a Critical Growth Stage

Most business executives might envy the challenge William George, former CEO and chairman
of Medtronic, says was the biggest one he confronted in his 30-year career.

With George at the helm, Medtronic—at the
time a $7.7 billion Minneapolis-based maker of
implantable biomedical devices—was on a wildly
successful run; its market capitalization had risen
nearly 2000% in seven years. But in 1998, the
company had reached a critical plateau. George's
decisions over the next three months would
either carry the company to the next level or
send it into a tailspin for the foreseeable future.
"On the surface, people might look back and say
things were fine, that the company was just kind
of all up, up and away," says George. "But in fact,
things were really turning sour."

After seven years of explosive growth in the
stock market, Medtronic had few prospects in
sight for short-term growth. Even worse, some of
its business units were in deep trouble. For example, Medtronic had acquired California-based
Micro Interventional Systems (MIS) for $73 mil-
lion in stock in 1995, but was now suing its
founders for securities fraud, charging that the
company had misled Medtronic about its financial
health. George moved aggressively to close the

operation and absorb its 100 employees. In addition, Medtronic's vascular business was showing disappointing results, forcing the company to lay off 600 workers. Altogether, Medtronic took a pretax $170 million restructuring charge for closing six vascular plants and shutting down the troubled MIS unit—the first time the company had taken a charge since 1985. Results for the quarter were a penny below analysts' expectations. The management team—built by George over nine years—was increasingly dispirited, battered by unrelenting pressure from Wall Street and investors to keep up the outstanding earnings growth.

To bring Medtronic out of its funk, George proposed making a series of acquisitions that he thought would transform the predominantly pacemaker company into the world's leading medical technology company with a diverse portfolio. Several board members disagreed with his assessment and challenged his leadership. Citing the MIS debacle, they believed that Medtronic should focus on effectively integrating the eight companies it had acquired since 1994. Some directors believed the solution was to pull back and hunker down to ride out the decline and announce Medtronic would not meet Wall Street's growth expectations.

"I could see years of good work going up in flames if we did that because people would lose confidence in us as a company," says George, adding that the retrenching would have also sent the share price tumbling. "People didn't realize that...you could lock the company in a box because you would lose the financial instrument of the stock to make acquisitions."

1988: As head of Space and Aviation, George uncovers accounting problems with a unit that predated Honeywell's acquisition in 1986. The accounting problems are tagged as the primary cause for Honeywell's $435 million loss that year.

1989: Despite being considered a leading candidate to succeed Honeywell CEO James Renier, George joins Medtronic as president and COO.

1991: Named CEO of Medtronic.

1996: Becomes chairman of the board of Medtronic.

1999: Joins the board of Novartis, a Swiss company that, before George's appointment, had directors only from Switzerland, Germany, and Austria.

2001: Retires as CEO of Medtronic but remains chairman of the board.

2001: Named "Executive of the Year—2001" by the Academy of Management.

2002: Named "Director of the Year—2001–02" by the National Association of Corporate Directors.

2002: Retires as chairman of Medtronic. Continues to serve on the boards of Novartis, Target, Goldman Sachs, and several non-profits and educational systems, including Harvard Business School, American Red Cross, Carnegie Endowment for International Peace, and Minneapolis Institute of Arts.

2003: Publishes book called *Authentic Leadership*. Writes an article in *Fortune* magazine, which begins: "Thank you, Enron and Arthur Andersen and WorldCom and HealthSouth. You woke us up. The business world has run off the rails, mistaking wealth for success and image for leadership. We're in danger of wrecking the very concept of the corporation…My generation of CEOs…began listening to the wrong people: Wall Street analysts, media pundits, economists, compensation consultants, public relations staffs, hedge funds, fellow CEOs—all the players in what I call the Game. The Game has stopped today's chief executives from focusing their energies on their company's customers, employees, and—ironically, since the Game is supposed to be all about them—shareholders."

Clearly, the decision to expand by buying more companies at this crucial time—given the failures of recent acquisitions—ran counter to expectations. "We had to strengthen our position with faster growth markets." After poring over analytical data and reevaluating his business strategy, George concluded that expanding the company into new markets was the right move. "I think, like all major decisions, it was intuitive," George says, stressing, however, the distinction between intuition and the old "gut feeling." Intuition, he says, is built on a vast base of knowledge and experience while a gut feeling may involve greater emotions or passion.

Before he could implement his plan, he had to weather some stiff opposition. Four members of the executive committee "were very opposed" to making these acquisitions. So over the course of three months, George lobbied those on the management team and the board who disagreed with his strategy and rallied those who stood by him. As the chief executive officer, he decided he not only had the duty to make the tough decisions but also the power and resolve to push through his agenda. The team slowly gave him its support.

With one battle behind him, George understood his leadership was at a critical juncture. "Leadership is about getting people to follow even though they have their own doubts and uncertainties," he says. "Military leaders do that…it's no different in business." But unlike the persuasive power of fear, such as the dread of being court-martialed in the military for disobeying orders, George used a softer touch to win the confidence of those who had questioned his strategy. "I did it by being open and straightforward, understanding their issues and concerns and expressing mine," he says. "This is where it is most difficult to be a leader. During those times when you are under the most pressure, you have to show a sincerity and commitment to get things done with a positive attitude."

And with that attitude, the plan was set in motion. Over the course of the next two years, Medtronic went on a buying spree, snapping up six companies for about $8 billion, mostly with Medtronic stock. Medtronic acquired Physio-Control International, a maker of cardiac defibrillators, for $500 million; Midas Rex, a powered surgical instruments maker, for $230 million; Sofamor Danek Group, which makes computer-assisted visualization products, for $3.6 billion; Arterial Vascular Engineering, a maker of vascular technology, for $3.7 billion; AVECOR Cardiovascular, which makes cardiopulmonary devices, for $91 million, and Xomed Surgical Products for $800 million.

George did not escape unscathed. Within weeks of closing the Arterial Vascular Engineering acquisition, Medtronic realized its new company's market share had dropped from the top spot to a distant third and was suffering from dwindling returns. George was forced to make a pre-announcement—the only one in 13 years with Medtronic. "I listened to 300 people beat me up on the phone, some of them even calling me a liar. That was very painful because I have always prided myself on my integrity."

The episode turned out to be a mere bump in the road. Over the next few years, the series of acquisitions helped transform the company, laying the groundwork for growth in the next decade. Medtronic's revenues doubled and its market capitalization surged from about $22 billion to $60 billion. The company that started in 1949 as a pacemaker manufacturer now included a diverse portfolio of businesses—from spinal surgery technology to external defibrillators and a greater presence in angioplasty.

Asked if he would have handled the challenge any differently, George noted that he would have been more aggressive about tempering Wall Street's expectations. He would have told them point blank that "not all these deals are going to work out. So just face it."

Looking back, the challenge also allowed George to examine his own leadership abilities. He discovered he possessed one particular quality that can be both an asset and a liability. "I learned that people would follow me if I had the courage to go forward with confidence," he says. "People realized I was decisive and strong-willed and if need be, I would make the decision and carry them with me." He added, however, that the same quality can also lead to trouble. "It's called hubris. There is that risk of having too much confidence in your ability, and going forward in spite of the wisdom of people telling you otherwise. So you have to make those tradeoffs."

In addition, lessons learned from one situation often don't transfer to others, yet there is that temptation to keep applying the same solution. "The biggest danger for leaders is they remember that they had great success and they try to replicate it," says George. "And it doesn't replicate well because conditions are never the same."

Leadership Lesson

In Search of Authentic Leadership

A crucial trait of successful leaders, as we noted earlier in this chapter, is their ability to detect humbug, or the absence of truth-telling. One occasion when William George demonstrated this ability was in 1998, when he met with a so-called superstar CEO to discuss Medtronic's possible acquisition of a medical equipment company. When the meeting began, the high-profile, charismatic CEO boasted about how his company paid no taxes in the U.S. because its headquarters were offshore, how he shut down all projects and investments that didn't pay back in one year, and so on. As George listened to the bragging, he realized something was wrong. At Medtronic, no project had ever paid back in a single year. After some 20 minutes, George left the meeting and walked away from the deal. "That's it," he said to himself. "We're not going to do any business with these people because we can't trust them." George's instinct was spot on: That superstar CEO was later indicted for fraud.

George, who retired from Medtronic in 2002, sees such incidents as part of a wider malaise that felled companies such as Enron, WorldCom, and Tyco. The remedy, he argues, lies in the development of authentic leadership, a concept that is closely related to truth-telling. Authentic leaders, says George, are "those who are committed to a purpose or a mission; people who live by their values every day and who know the true north of their moral compass. They lead with their heart, not just with their heads, and have compassion for the people they serve. They do so with the discipline and commitment to get great results, not just for their shareholders, but for all their stakeholders, including their customers, their employees, and the communities they serve. This sounds old fashioned and yet almost revolutionary." So strongly does George believe in the importance of these principles that he literally wrote the book on the subject, titled *Authentic Leadership*.

The need for authentic leadership has arisen, says George, because during the past few years both the values of corporations and the incentives by which CEOs are rewarded have gone awry. More and more companies have been focusing on shareholder returns as the yardstick for success, rather than considering the broader needs of other stakeholders, including customers and employees.

As George writes in the introduction to his book, in recent years "Instead of traditional measures such as growth, cash flow, and return on investment, the criterion for success became meeting the expectations of the security analysts. Investments were cut back to reach earnings targets, limiting the company's growth potential. Driven by speculators and security analysts, expectations kept rising, just as companies were struggling to make their numbers. Companies that met or exceeded the "magic" earnings number were handsomely rewarded with ever-rising stock prices. Those that fell short, even if they recorded substantial increases, were inordinately punished, and shareholders demanded replacement of the CEO. No wonder many CEOs went to extreme measures to satisfy shareholders!"

George argues that authentic leaders have character rather than charisma. Moreover, they breathe and live the five dimensions that endow leadership with authenticity. First, they are committed to a purpose. In his own case, George says, he knew from the time he left high school that he had to use his abilities to make a difference in the world, but "it took me 20 years to find out where and how. It wasn't until I got to Medtronic that I felt, 'Okay, I'm here.' This is the place I am meant to be." Second, authenticity requires that leaders live by their values—and not just pay lip-service to them. For example, former Tyco CEO Dennis Kozlowski, who has been charged with some associates of looting his company of $600 million, was once asked after a business-school speech what the source of his success was. "Integrity," he replied. "Almost every leader will say, 'We have really good values,'" George states. "But if you are going to proclaim a certain set of values, you better be darn well prepared to practice them. Above all, always be consistent with what you say you can do, even if sometimes you fall short or fail."

There have been times, George says, when he himself has fallen short of his values. For example, when he was at Medtronic, he once appointed a person to head the company's European operation. "I felt he was a really good businessman," George says, "and I didn't check out his values closely." Despite his colleagues' misgivings, George was adamant and went ahead with the appointment. "About four months later, I had the head of internal audit and general legal counsel in my office telling me this person was running a secret promotion fund on behalf of Italian doctors through a Swiss bank account. It became a very, very painful situation. I had to fire him the next day, but then we had a lot of recovery to do in Europe. It was all because I promoted the wrong person for the wrong reasons. I didn't check out his values closely enough."

Leading with the heart is the third dimension of authentic leadership, George says. "Too many leaders think they can lead strictly with their head." Their response to problems is to try and think them through. "They don't open themselves up to other people, and so they don't engender a sense of passion and response in other people. And because they are too cerebral, though they are really engaged, they don't express compassion for their employees, their colleagues or their customers. They are just too hardened. They lose a lot in their employees because they cannot express themselves." Leaders who lead from the heart, in contrast, engage with their constituents' hearts and minds, though they also make themselves more vulnerable by opening themselves up to their colleagues.

Fourth, George maintains that authentic leaders build deep relationships—not just casual, superficial ones but strong, long-lasting bonds. In his own case, he cites his relationship with the head of Medtronic's pacemaker business. "He called me one day from the hospital and told me that his estranged son, whom he hadn't seen for three years, had just shown up. He was at the hospital because his son had terminal stomach cancer. And so I went down to the hospital. I didn't tell him I was coming, I just got in my car and drove down there and met him. It was an extremely traumatic time in his life, but the interaction was a very intimate one. We hugged, and we talked about it. The fact that I did that when I had to be very demanding of him in the business carried a lot more weight than anything else I might have done."

The impact of all these attributes can be dashed unless leaders practice the fifth dimension of authentic leadership—self-discipline. "None of this matters unless we take our beliefs and philosophies and put them into action with discipline," says George. "That places a lot of pressure on us as leaders because we are always up on a pedestal. We have to demonstrate self-discipline in all our actions. If we don't, it becomes hypocritical. We end up saying one thing and doing another. Self discipline is about taking all these ideas and translating them into tangible results. If you don't do that, what good is it all?"

4

Identifying an Underserved Market

The most successful companies of the last 25 years haven't always been based on radically new products or technologies. Some have sprung from their leaders' ability to identify and cater to markets that were emerging but whose needs had not yet been identified. Vanguard Group founder Jack Bogle sold index funds directly to shareholders who previously had been charged high sales commissions and management fees; Charles Schwab, through his San Francisco-based discount brokerage, gave "Main Street access to Wall Street;" and Muhammad Yunus, founder of Grameen Bank, set out to "break the cycle of poverty" in his native Bangladesh by making loans to very poor villagers, thereby enabling them to become self-supporting entrepreneurs.

These leaders succeeded because the new markets they identified sustained demand for their product or service. Customers
whose needs had never been met began to thrive and prosper, as
did the companies serving them. The lesson that aspiring leaders
can learn from their example is not to focus just on the dominant
or most profitable markets of the day; these are obvious to all and
are likely to attract enormous competition. By identifying underserved markets (or niches) and customers (or segments) that no
one else is targeting, companies can enter new areas and develop
successful businesses long before their competitors.

JOHN BOGLE

The Challenge:

Setting Up a New Kind of Mutual Fund Company

During the stock market's go-go era in the 1960s, it seemed that investment managers could do no wrong. But the bubble popped in 1973 and stock prices fell by nearly 50%. Wellington Management Company, a mutual fund manager in Philadelphia, saw frightened investors withdraw $300 million as Wellington's share price plummeted. Early in 1974, the firm's board terminated its CEO, John Bogle.

"I think it's pretty clear that the biggest business challenge you can face is what to do when you are fired," Bogle says three decades later. His response: Use common sense and—as he puts it—a touch of "disingenuousness" to convince the board to form a new type of mutual fund company and to hand over control.

Bogle, who joined Wellington fresh out of Princeton in 1951, was named CEO in 1967. To broaden the company's offerings, he had engineered a 1966 merger with Thorndike, Doran, Paine and Lewis Inc., a Boston equities management firm. Now these partners had pushed him out. But Bogle was not entirely unemployed. In addition to running the management company, he was chairman of the Wellington Funds, the family of mutual funds run by Wellington Management. This job he kept.

1929: Born in Montclair, New Jersey. His father, William, was an executive with American Can Co., which had been co-founded by William's father, who also founded American Brick Corp. Bogle's mother, Josephine, was a home-maker. The 1929 crash destroyed the family's inheritance and Bogle relied on scholarships for prep school and college.

1949: As a Princeton student, Bogle becomes aware of the mutual fund industry after stumbling across an article in *Fortune* magazine.

1951: Bogle completes 140-page senior thesis, *The Economic Role of the Investment Company*, arguing fund companies must operate solely for the benefit of their investors, not the investment managers. He examines the benefits of index-style investing and keeping fund management costs low.

1951: Walter L. Morgan, founder of The Wellington Fund in 1928, reads Bogle's thesis and hires him upon graduation. Bogle rises in marketing and administration, not money management.

1956: A federal court ruling permits fund management firms to be bought, sold, or taken public. Bogle sees this as the beginning of the fund industry's decline from a customer-oriented profession to a profit-oriented business.

1960: Wellington Group goes public at $18 a share.

1965: At 35, Bogle becomes executive vice president of Wellington and heir apparent to Morgan.

1966: Bogle engineers merger of Wellington Management Company with Thorndike, Doran, Paine and Lewis, an aggressive stock management firm in Boston. The goal is to end Wellington's over-reliance on a single fund, find a way to offer an aggressive stock fund, and bring the firm greater investment management talent.

1967: Bogle becomes president and CEO of Wellington Management Company, which manages the Wellington Funds.

1971: Arguing that "a man cannot serve two masters," Bogle suggests Wellington Funds consider acquiring Wellington Management. Fund managers have a financial stake in seeing management fees rise, while fund investors benefit when they are low. The "mutualization" Bogle proposed would put managers under the fund investors' control. No action is taken on the proposal.

1973-1974: The go-go era ends and stock prices fall nearly 50%.

Since his college days, Bogle had been bothered by the conflict of interest inherent in many fund operations. Mutual funds are corporations owned by the ordinary people who buy fund shares to invest for retirement or college. But funds typically use outside money managers to select the stocks and bonds held by the fund. Those management companies also handle the administrative, marketing, and distribution functions for the funds they serve. Though the funds and their management companies are legally separate entities, in most cases, the fund company's board is dominated by executives from the management company. Income for the management companies comes from fees charged as a percentage of each fund's assets; the bigger the fee, the more it hurts investors' returns.

Bogle had long argued that funds and their management companies should have ethical standards like those of the legal and medical professions, based on an obligation to put the investors' interests first. Funds should constantly look for ways to reduce fees, not excuses to raise them. "All things considered, it is undesirable for professional enterprises to have public shareholders," he told the board in the early 1970s.

The day after being fired, Bogle formally proposed a change to the fund board that he had first suggested several years earlier. The funds should "mutualize" by purchasing the management company from the group of investors that owned it, he says. Because the funds themselves are owned by the people who invest in them, the management company would be owned by the funds' ordinary investors, eliminating the manager-investor conflict. Fund investors would be owners as well as customers.

The Wellington Funds board was less than enthusiastic about the proposal, but six months later, it gave Bogle part of what he wanted. A new company, The Vanguard Group, was formed as a wholly owned subsidiary of the Wellington Funds. Vanguard's only role, however, was mundane administrative chores, such as keeping records of customers' accounts. Asset management—the buying and selling of stocks and bonds for the funds—was forbidden. Vanguard was also barred from distribution—the selling of fund shares to investors. Those more essential duties remained with Wellington Management. "So I had lost," Bogle says. "I called it a Pyrrhic victory."

He didn't give up. "It was clear to me that what you need to build a fund company is control over how the funds invest—what kinds of funds you have, how they invest, and how they are distributed."

For more than two decades, Bogle had been intrigued by the idea of index funds. Instead of employing teams of expensive analysts and stock-pickers, an index fund would simply buy and hold the issues in a market gauge, such as the Standard & Poor's 500. Over time, the law of averages meant that few actively managed funds could out-perform the indexes. Indeed, the high fees and expenses incurred by managed funds typically caused them to trail the passively managed index by 2 to 3 percentage points a year. So a fund mod-eled on the index, and charging very low fees, could beat most managed competitors most of the time. It could offer investors far superior returns when that annual edge was compounded over many years.

1973: Wellington funds suffer cash outflows of $300 million, compared to $280 million inflow in 1967. Wellington Management's share price plummets.

1974: Bogle urges the funds board of directors to mutualize the funds by purchasing Wellington Management Company, which has a separate board. Fund directors ask for details. Bogle is fired as CEO of Wellington Management Company. Remains chairman of the Wellington Funds, which has a separate board. Bogle convinces funds to form Vanguard Group, but directors limit its role to administration, barring fund manage-ment and distribution.

1975: After receiving SEC approval, Vanguard begins operation as wholly owned subsidiary of Wellington Funds.

1976: Initial public offering completed for Vanguard's first index fund, which tracks the Standard & Poor's 500 stock index. Only $11 million is raised. Since index funds are not managed, the fund does not violate Vanguard's management prohibition, Bogle claims.

1977: Fund board accepts Bogle's recommendation to convert to a no-load system by ending distribution agreement with Wellington Management, eliminating sales charges and ceasing fund sales through brokers. Henceforth, investors can deal directly with Vanguard.

1980: Vanguard assets under management reach $3 billion.

1981: The SEC formally rules Vanguard can engage in distribution, ending four years of distribution under temporary permission. Vanguard takes over management of the bond and money market funds.

1985: Vanguard assets reach $15 billion.

1993: Vanguard assets reach $121 billion.

1996: Bogle steps down as Vanguard CEO. A month later receives a heart transplant.

1997: Vanguard assets reach $300 billion.

1999: Bogle retires from Vanguard's board of directors. After retiring, founds the Bogle Financial Markets Research Center. Bogle becomes a public speaker and writer, promoting low-cost, index investing and often criticizing fund-industry practices.

2000: The Vanguard 500 index fund, the company's first indexer, becomes the largest fund in the world.

Soon after Vanguard was formed, Bogle was back before the board asking it to create an S&P 500 index fund. "It seemed to me that would be a great entrée into investment management," Bogle says. "When the directors said I wasn't allowed to get into investment management, I argued the fund wouldn't be 'managed.'" Managed funds constantly seek new investments, and they typically change their entire portfolios every year. An index fund, he said, would just buy the stocks in the underlying index and hold them for the long term.

"This was a way to basically sneak into the field of investment management…They approved it. They didn't really want to, but they did because I persuaded them that it was not 'management,'" Bogle recalls.

Next, he went after the distribution operation. Ever since the Wellington Fund's founding in 1928, the funds had been sold to investors through stock brokers, often with "loads," or commissions, as high as 8%. After paying an upfront load, the investor started out in the red and had to earn that much just to break even. The alternative, still rare in the 1970s, was to bypass the brokers and sell directly to the public, charging no commission.

"I argued that we should go no-load, and Wellington Management didn't want to go no-load," Bogle says. Unfortunately, Wellington Management was still controlling distribution of the funds, and Vanguard was prohibited from that role. "I argued we weren't going into distribution, we were *eliminating* distribution," Bogle says. Again, the board acquiesced, and by the end of the summer in 1977, Vanguard had control of the fund management and the no-load distribution. "We were the full-fledged complex we are today," he notes.

Vanguard's S&P 500 index fund grew to become the largest fund in the world, with assets of about $96 billion early in 2004, and it inspired dozens of imitators. Vanguard and other companies also created a host of funds tracking other indexes. By 2004, Vanguard was the country's second largest fund complex, with some $700 billion under management in 161 funds and about 10,000 employees.

After retiring in 1999, Bogle devoted himself full-time to writing and speaking about conflicts of interest and excessive fees in the fund industry. "There's a tendency as we get older to lose our idealism," he says, "Don't do it. It's the most valuable characteristic you have...I think mine gets stronger all the time."

2002: Vanguard's weighted expense ratio—the portion of fund assets spent on management and other fees—falls to 0.26%, from 0.67% in 1975. Expense ratios for managed funds average about 1.3% throughout the industry.

2004: Vanguard funds assets total $700 billion, up from $1.4 billion in 1974. Vanguard is the second largest fund complex, behind Fidelity Investments of Boston. Vanguard's market share is 9.2%, up from 3.5% in 1974.

Leadership Lesson

An Index for Successful Investing

Ever since his undergraduate days at Princeton, Jack Bogle had been interested in research that showed the average money manager could not compile a portfolio that would consistently beat the overall market. If this were the case, the best mutual funds would be those that charged customers the lowest fees, because fees deducted from fund assets undermined performance. At the time Bogle formed the Vanguard Group in the mid-1970s, most funds were sold through stockbrokers who charged hefty upfront "loads" or sales commissions. In addition, the funds themselves charged substantial fees to pay their analysts and other employees, and to provide profit for the management company.

Bogle saw an underserved market: cost-conscious investors who might welcome the opportunity to buy index funds that would track the overall market and charge very low fees. To eliminate loads, Vanguard would sell funds directly to shareholders. Instead of outsourcing fund management to an expensive external management company, Vanguard would take over this role itself. Most fund companies are privately held or run as public companies beholden to shareholders. Vanguard would be owned by the people who invested in its funds, eliminating the conflict of interest between customers and owners. By making Vanguard a mutual company, owned by its investors, Bogle would be putting investors' interests first. "You can say that was callow college idealism. Or you can say it was vision that created Vanguard," says Bogle. "It's probably more of the former—idealism that just stuck with me all those years. It's also common sense."

To cater to underserved markets, Bogle had to come up with an innovative pricing strategy. Long before the Internet changed the way people shop, Bogle was thinking about price, value, and customer service. In the 1950s, '60s, and early '70s, experience and a study of the academic research confirmed his view that very few money managers were good enough to pick stocks that could consistently outperform the broad market. This fact formed the cornerstone of Bogle's low-price strategy at his mutual fund company, The Vanguard Group. "None of it required any particular brains," Bogle says. His approach, he adds, "took a little common sense, knowing that in the financial markets gross return minus cost is net return. Therefore, the lower your cost, the higher your net return."

In part, Bogle's strategy depended on his educating investors about the poor performance of the average, actively managed fund—then selling to this more knowledgeable class of buyers. It is a never-ending process because traditional, high-expense funds are always tempting customers with ads based on high, short-term performance. "Investors seem largely unaware of the substantial gap by which stock, bond, and money market funds lag the returns of the markets in which they invest," Bogle wrote in a July 8, 2003 op-ed piece for *The Wall Street Journal*. "While the Standard & Poor's 500 stock index has risen at a 12.2% average annual rate since 1984, for example, the average equity fund has grown at a 9.3% rate, only three-quarters of the stock market's return...What accounts for these shortfalls? They are largely created by the costs incurred by mutual funds."

"In 2002, the average expense ratio for equity funds reached an all-time high of 1.6% of fund assets," he wrote in the same article. Trading commissions and other costs related to the high level of buying and selling in actively managed funds increased expenses another 0.8 percentage points. With miscellaneous expenses included, total costs averaged nearly 3% of assets. However, at Vanguard's flagship S&P 500 index fund, the expense ratio was 0.18%—just over one-tenth that of the average stock fund industry-wide. Because index funds operate, essentially, on autopilot, with very little change in holdings, commissions and other expenses are low as well. Such funds also enjoy a tax advantage because there is little of the turnover that triggers capital gains taxes. To further minimize costs, Bogle decided the funds would be sold directly to investors without the "loads" or sales commissions, often as high as 5% of an investment, charged by funds sold through stockbrokers.

For Bogle, credibility is a big reason for Vanguard's success. "Create an identity, a company that stands for something...And when you make promises to the crew [Vanguard's term for its employees], deliver. When you make promises to investors, deliver. If people can trust you...you're never going to have trouble," he says.

Speaking at Vanguard's 25th anniversary ceremony on September 24, 1999, Bogle summarized the company's identity in a single word: "Stewardship: The one great idea that explains what Vanguard is, who it is, and what it does. Serving the shareholder first; acting as trustee, in a fiduciary capacity. Mutual funds of the investor, by the investor, for the investor." The same themes characterize Bogle's many public speeches, articles, and letters to newspaper editors—earning him the nickname "Saint Jack," which is not always used admiringly by his competitors. In retirement, he has carved out a role as fund industry gadfly. Most of his criticisms of the industry—that fees are too high, for example— serve to enhance Vanguard's brand as the low-cost leader.

"Bogle had this incredibly compelling vision that made such perfect sense in an industry that was so resistant to it," says Wharton's Peter Cappelli. What's astonishing, he adds, is that "nobody had tried this index approach before." Bogle pulled it off because he was "enough of an insider to be able to start an investment company and yet willing to be an outsider in his approach." In addition, Bogle brought science to this industry, Cappelli says, referring to research studies that show managed funds rarely beat index funds over long periods, and also to analyses of the corrosive effect of high fees on returns.

All of these cost savings are possible, Bogle says, because Vanguard is a mutual company owned by the people who invest in the Vanguard funds. "I guess the lesson would be to capitalize on your innate advantage," he suggests. "Make your product proprietary. Stake out some ground that other people can't afford to deal with. That's been a big part of Vanguard's success—we don't have low-cost competitors."

Bogle's strategy of long-term investing based on low costs helped the Vanguard Group build an image as the mutual fund industry's good guy—an image that can be especially valuable in periods of turmoil and scandal in the financial services industry. He constantly reminded his employees of the Vanguard mission, pounded away at the basic message in every public forum he could find, and reaffirmed the company's commitment to core principles in annual letters to investors. And when he felt that his peers had let him down, he didn't hesitate to castigate the offenders. "By our failure to act as good corporate citizens, this industry shares much of the responsibility for the great stock market bubble," Bogle wrote in a July 8, 2003 piece in *The Wall Street Journal*. "In the long run, this industry will grow only as fund shareholders are given a fair shake, not only in costs and disclosure, but also in having truly independent directors who place [investors'] interests first. Truth [be] told, this industry needs a change of heart."

CHARLES SCHWAB

The Challenge:

Getting Out from Under All the Paper

By the mid-1970s, Charles Schwab was best-known for chipping away at the dominance of button-down Wall Street investment houses with his discount brokerage firm. But it seemed that Charles Schwab & Co. would remain a small-time, regional broker, more of a nuisance than a challenge to the full-service brokerages. The problem? The company was getting buried—not by the competition—but by paper.

All brokerages faced a similar situation, although the established houses had legions of clerks sorting and managing transaction and order receipts. The highly regulated securities industry needed to fill out a form for every small or big trade order or transaction. The Securities and Exchange Commission (SEC) and the New York Stock Exchange (NYSE) mandated specific standards on how to record, manage, and archive the paper trail.

To keep up with trading volume, the Schwab offices were rigged with a three-track conveyor belt over which orders moved in one direction and confirmations moved in another. When trade orders poured in, the volume of paper sometimes clogged the belt and brought the office to a standstill. Schwab employees used something akin to a plunger to unplug the jam.

"We were just getting buried in paper," says Schwab, who hired Bill Pearson, a technology whiz, in 1975 to help overhaul how the company conducted its paper-intense business. "I realized we could never progress beyond that limitation without adopting a technology solution."

Against this backdrop, Schwab made a "bet-the-company" move to computerize the transaction order process—a step that helped grow the discount brokerage into a real threat to Wall Street and laid the foundation for the company's repeated success in harnessing new forms of technology. The move, however, was fraught with growing pains as glitches and technical problems made the company even more vulnerable.

Pearson "scoured the earth," says Schwab, to find a computer system that would allow a broker to make trades without generating the piles of paper needed to satisfy the SEC and the NYSE. Pearson found a software outfit in Milwaukee, Wisconsin, that had developed trading software that could be customized to fit Schwab's needs. This early back-office software, however, ran on mainframe computers, the giant systems that took up an entire room and cost a small fortune to buy. Schwab purchased a used IBM 360 mainframe computer and software for $500,000—"my entire net worth" at the time, says Schwab. "It was a giant step and a huge risk."

The new technology allowed Schwab's brokers to take orders over the phone and enter them directly into the computer using desktop terminals. The order would go off electronically to the stock exchange where it would be executed, eventually returning a confirmation to the broker who then relayed it to the client. The technology was revolutionary, allowing Schwab to broker higher and higher transaction volumes at a fraction of the paper-based cost. "Most firms didn't get there until 10 years later," he says.

1973: Schwab renames the venture Charles Schwab & Co. after buying out his partners and concluding that old banks and brokerage houses on Wall Street have widespread inefficiencies that they exploit to charge even higher commissions to their customers.

1974: Gets his big break when the SEC mandates a 13-month trial period for deregulating some brokerage transactions. Seizes the chance to build a new type of investment house: the discount brokerage.

1975: After 13-month trial period, the SEC approves a new commission structure, marking the official birth of the discount brokerage industry. Schwab awarded seat on The Pacific Coast Stock Exchange.

1976: Schwab becomes his own pitchman, posing in shirt and tie to represent the face of the discount broker. Begins to experiment with technology to smooth away some of the traditional inefficiencies. Implements the Bunker Ramo System 7 to deliver stock quotes directly to customers.

1979: Invests in the BETA mainframe system. The eventual success of this automated transaction and record-keeping system shows Schwab that technology will be the key growth driver.

1980: Schwab touts his company as "America's largest discount brokerage" with a "state of the art computer system." Now has 23 branches but still has trouble raising capital from banks and venture capital firms who see the company as a threat.

1981: Opens first office in Manhattan and becomes a member of the New York Stock Exchange.

1983: Still hard pressed for capital, agrees to sell to Bank of America, which pays $57 million for the company and its 500,000 accounts.

1984: Introduces the Equalizer, a DOS-based application online trading.

1985: With one million discount brokerage accounts, begins to challenge Wall Street closer to home by introducing VIP Services and Institutional Brokerage.

1987: Unhappy with Bank of America's bureaucracy, Schwab pays $280 million to buy back the company he started.

1987: Takes the company public, selling 8 million shares at $16.50 per share.

But the company didn't immediately realize any benefits from the purchase. The used IBM mainframe, for example, did not integrate well with the brokerage back-office software. "It was a mistake," says Schwab, who turned to IBM for assistance. The computing giant offered to lease Schwab a brand new IBM 370 mainframe computer and help integrate the software. The result was a more reliable system.

The company's difficulties in shifting to technology, however, were far from resolved. "We had a lot of hiccups," remembers Schwab. "It was a little like cell phones are today—the way they go down every few blocks." Schwab says his initiative may have been just a little ahead of its time because the existing telecommunications network was not built for this particular use. The glitches and customer complaints kept mounting. Whatever savings were generated by reducing paperwork were lost in reimbursing delayed trades and transactions.

The technology initiative even doomed Charles Schwab's chances of going public in the early '80s. At the time, the company was the largest discount broker in the country, with 20 branches and nearly 100,000 customers. Schwab was hoping to raise about $4.8 million for capital expansion by floating 1.2 million shares. When the company registered with the SEC in 1980, Wall Street became privy to the extent of trouble the discount brokerage had to put up with during its technology upgrade. The prospectus showed that in the first six months of 1980, the company had to fork over nearly 11%, or $1.1 million, of its total commission income of $10.4 million to cover bad debt and execution errors at a time when the average error rate for New York Stock Exchange members was a low 1.4% in comparison.

Charles Schwab's own books provided the full-service brokerages with the firepower to disparage discount services and warn clients to stick to Wall Street's reliability. In its prospectus, the company blamed its woes on the new electronic order processing system, which was constantly breaking down during periods of heavy trading. The error rate was pegged at 3.4% in 1978, rising to 5.4% in 1979 and soaring to 10.5% in the first half of 1980.

"It was a pretty painful three or four months. We had some bad publicity at the time," says Schwab, who traveled from office to office trying to instill a sense of confidence in his employees. "I became a cheerleader, assuring people that things would get better—and it did get better."

Having grown up on the West Coast, Schwab—a graduate of Stanford University, located in the heart of Silicon Valley—had an affinity for technology and sensed its immense possibilities. As an early adopter of technology, he knew he would be required to surmount obstacles not faced by others. "You're never going to introduce a perfect software solution. Any software or system you install will have setbacks and glitches," says Schwab. "You just get in and fix them."

Indeed the outlook began to improve as the company worked the kinks out of its Brokerage Execution and Transaction Analysis (BETA) system. Suddenly, each Schwab broker could handle a greater number of trade orders while the system did much of the background work, including checking open orders, calculating margin trades, and moving cash from trading accounts to money market funds. The company's costs fell while its efficiency and accuracy in processing trades rose.

1987: In October, stock market crashes. Customers struggle to dump stock through the company's trading system but fail to get through. Company survey finds that customers had come to think of the brokerage as a "cold transaction" company rather than the original friendly neighborhood brokerage. Schwab institutes a policy of surveying customers after each trade to determine their satisfaction, basing bonuses for brokers on the findings.

1993: Continues to experiment with the electronic world, replacing the Equalizer with StreetSmart online trading.

1995: Launches Schwab.com, pegging the company's future to online trading. Establishes a dedicated Electronic Brokerage Enterprise Group inside the company.

1997: Forms alliances with former competitors CS/First Boston, J.P. Morgan, and Chase H&Q to give Schwab customers access to IPOs. The company increasingly resembles its Wall Street competitors in market value and services.

1997: *Forbes* magazine names Schwab "King of Online Brokers."

1998: Schwab reaches a milestone. The discount broker's market capitalization exceeds that of Merrill Lynch at the end of trading on December 28, standing at $25.5 billion compared to Merrill Lynch's $25.4 billion.

1999: The company introduces Schwab Signature Services for active and affluent traders. It hopes to stop individuals from jumping to asset-management firms as their wealth grows and to attract wealthy clients, Schwab acquires U.S. Trust. Schwab now competing on two fronts, against the high-end asset management Wall Street firms and against the growing number of online trading firms that have slashed commissions to new lows.

2000: Company reaches $1 trillion in assets. At the height of the technology boom, Schwab introduces PocketBroker, a wireless investing service, hoping to capture traders when they are away from their desks. Company also acquires CyberTrader (formerly CyBerCorp) to serve its high volume online traders more effectively.

2001: When the stock market meltdown occurs, Schwab succeeds in handling the trading volume, but earnings begin to suffer as investors steer clear of the stock market. Company lays off 6,505 employees and re-evaluates its low commission, transaction-based model.

Wall Street nervously took notice and slapped the upstart with yet another major hurdle to its paper-less trade system. This time, the NYSE said BETA's paperless order tickets violated the exchange's rule requiring its member organizations to save paper tickets for seven years. Since there were no paper tickets generated by BETA, the NYSE refused to certify Schwab's system.

Schwab fought back by exploiting the wording of the regulation. The company insisted that the rules required the member firms to only *save* paper tickets but did not require them to *write* paper tickets. The NYSE had taken it for granted that brokers would have to write paper tickets while Schwab leapfrogged over the entire process. The exchange acquiesced and the orders began to flow into Charles Schwab's mainframe.

Sensing the inevitable—and watching as Schwab's trading volume soared while costs plummeted—other brokerage houses in the early 1980s also began migrating from their paper-based procedure to computerized systems. But Schwab had taken an early gamble that positioned his discount brokerage years ahead of his discount brokerage competitors as well as Wall Street. The move also established a technology paradigm—a comfort level with technology—within the company as well as for its clients. Schwab continued to seek ways of using existing and emerging technologies to revolutionize the securities industry. In the years ahead, he was among the first to give his clients the ability to bypass a broker completely by connecting directly to Schwab's systems to place trades—a precursor to Internet trading.

"This was *the* major stepping stone in the early days of the company," says Schwab. "If I had not taken a chance on technology, we would never have been able to create all the other technology-driven opportunities for our clients."

2003: Schwab resigns his post as co-CEO but remains chairman.

2004: During the first half of the year, company reports that net income rose 33% in 2003 to $472 million. Client assets rose to one trillion in February. However, trading volume, a barometer of overall well-being, continues to fall.

2004: By July, tumbling trading volume and intense competition from nimbler Internet-based rivals exacerbate company's financial outlook. Stock price continues to slip, dropping 27% for the year by mid-summer. Chief executive David Pottruck is ousted and Charles Schwab is drafted to rejuvenate the company he founded. With Schwab as CEO, company announces decision to close 53 branches (16% of total 339 branches) in effort to cut $150 million–$200 million in expenses.

Leadership Lesson

The Best at Fair Value

Charles Schwab, like Jack Bogle, was also out to shake up the financial services sector. Until the mid-1970s, there was really just one way to invest in the stock market: a broker at a full-service brokerage firm would recommend a stock to buy and would charge about $225 for the transaction as a commission. "Fundamentally, at that time, most people thought that individual investors were sold stocks; they didn't buy them," recalls Schwab. Wall Street, he adds, was in the business of generating commissions by "creating stories" to convince people to make these purchases.

In 1975, the Securities and Exchange Commission changed a long-standing law that had required Wall Street to charge fixed brokerage fees. Yet, while the revised law now allowed firms to offer discount fees, the securities industry had no intention of reducing commissions just because the law permitted it. Schwab, however, saw an opportunity to revolutionize the system by allowing investors themselves to choose stocks and buy them at a fraction of the cost charged by traditional brokers. Although he was not certain how much demand there would be for such a service, he speculated that there would be a "small sliver" of independent investors who based their decision to buy a stock on their own research and analysis. "I thought probably 3–4% of investors were in this category," including himself, he says. "I had deep empathy for what these people were looking for because I had grown up as a financial analyst and not as a stock salesman."

What Schwab could see was the "need for a very pure transactional firm that [would operate at] a much lower price" without "any so-called help or intimidation from the sales guys." So Charles Schwab & Co. charged $70 per trade. To his surprise, individual investors—about 10–15% of the individual investor population—took to the concept of discount investing immediately. Says Schwab: "I underestimated the size of the market."

Like Bogle, Schwab made sure that the organization he built to cater to this underserved market bought into his values. "When I started the company all those years ago as a pure discount broker, I weighed what I wanted to eliminate," says Schwab. He decided it was imperative to scrap the conflict of interest inherent in a broker receiving a commission for making a sale. "Imagine how you would feel if you knew your doctor was getting a commission for each drug he prescribed to you. You wouldn't feel too comfortable with that." Even as the company has added a multitude of financial products and services—like investment advisors, mutual funds, and instruments for high net worth individuals—Schwab says he has always "maintained its heart and soul." His employees, he adds, many of whom have come from traditional brokerage firms, express a sense of relief that they are not under a mandate to sell "the stock of the month," "make their commission quota," or "call clients to build book." "Yes, of course, we make money some place in the process from our clients, but our employees aren't incentivized to convince clients to be active," says Schwab. "It's a different culture here."

Price also plays an important part in the Schwab culture. The company never tried to position itself as the lowest priced service, he says. There were always discount brokers, and later, online trading firms that could undercut even his company. "That was not our mantra. I always tried to be what I considered the best at fair value. I wanted the best people working for me; I wanted the best computers, the best innovation. I didn't want our service to be 'cheapest' in any way…It's a ticklish balance and we certainly lead the conversation with price, but we finish it up with…superior service."

"King of Online Brokers"

Part of Schwab's vision hinged on discovering innovative uses of technology to introduce his clients to financial products. In 1979, he was among the first to harness the power of computers to scale his trading volume higher. Though the decision led to some early rough spots—trades that failed to be completed, a high error rate, and customer complaints—Schwab instilled in his company the importance of always being on the lookout for fresh opportunities.

In the 1980s, for example, new legislation had created a financial savings instrument called Individual Retirement Accounts (IRAs)—basically retirement mutual funds that grew on a tax-free basis. Schwab sensed that the demand for mutual funds was about to increase and quickly adapted his discount brokerage service to cater to the needs of individual investors hoping to take advantage of tax-free growth. "I decided that we needed to make it easier for people to buy a variety of no-load funds through a central account," says Schwab. The company created a mutual fund marketplace that revolutionized the mutual fund industry and helped companies like Vanguard and Fidelity gain greater traction.

Meanwhile, a part of Charles Schwab & Co. had morphed into a distribution vehicle. "Smaller, very effective money managers knew how to manage money. They didn't know much about distribution," says Schwab. "We essentially became their distributors by giving them a marketplace." By the mid-80s, this mutual fund marketplace allowed investors to buy and sell hundreds of different mutual funds in a single account. By 2000, Charles Schwab & Co. was pulling in about 10% of the net new money flowing into mutual funds.

During the 1990s, the company was again at the forefront by jumping onto the Internet before rivals even considered using the emerging networking technology. The company forged ahead despite the realization that online trading would cannibalize its broker-based transactions. David Pottruck, who later became co-CEO of Charles Schwab & Co., spearheaded the effort. While commissions on broker-assisted trades started at $39, Schwab charged $29.95. The company believed, correctly, that the growing number of online trades would make up for the revenue lost from its established business.

Again, Schwab had merged his readiness to innovate with his desire to offer more opportunities to average investors. The company's online trading system was considered the paragon for the medium. *Forbes* magazine even named Schwab the "King of Online Brokers." While the company's online trading business has slowed since the Internet bubble burst in 2001, at the height of the online trading frenzy between 1997 and 2000, the firm's profit rose 112%, driven by a 183% increase in daily trades.

MUHAMMAD YUNUS

My Greatest Challenge:

Using Microcredit to Lead Beggars into Business

Muhammad Yunus, founder and managing director of Bangladesh's Grameen Bank, has long focused on lending to the poor. As an innovator who recognized that lending need not be linked to collateral, he built Grameen by offering minuscule loans to very poor people, giving them the means to generate incomes and work their way out of poverty. Since its inception in 1976, Grameen has provided more than $4 billion in loans to some 3 million borrowers, the vast majority of whom are women.

Most observers have recognized Yunus's achievement in finding an innovative solution to perennial poverty—one that relies on the enterprise of the poor rather than on government aid or other kinds of charitable handouts. Lately, however, Grameen—and microcredit in general—have faced criticism for helping just the top tier of the poor, those who are able to use credit. The poorest of the poor, the argument goes, have no need for credit—they need water and food, and that can only be provided by charity.

A case in point: A recent report in *The New York Times* cited the example of Firuza Akhter, a young woman in the village of Gorma in Bangladesh, who borrowed small sums to invest in everything from cows and land to tutors for her children. The report said that while borrowers like Akhter may come

1940: Born on June 29 in Chittagong, Bangladesh, the third of nine surviving children. Five other siblings died at early ages. His father owned a jewelry store selling ornaments to Muslim customers; his mother occasionally worked on jewelry sold in the shop.

1953: Takes a train trip across India to the First Pakistan National Boy Scout Jamboree. Later credits the Boy Scout program with teaching him compassion and care for other people.

1965: Receives a Fulbright Scholarship and goes to the U.S. to study economics.

1969: Receives his Ph.D. in Economics from Vanderbilt University in Nashville, Tennessee. Becomes assistant professor of economics at Middle Tennessee State University.

1971: Bangladesh wins its independence from Pakistan.

1972: Returns to Bangladesh to become a member of the government planning commission. Finding the job "a bore, [with] nothing to do all day but read newspapers," he resigns to become head of the Economics department at Chittagong University.

1974: Devastating floods hit Bangladesh, causing widespread destruction of property and 1.5 million deaths. Worldwide press coverage inspires the famous Bangladesh concerts with late former Beatle George Harrison.

1976: Visits the village of Jobra, near his home of Chittagong. Lends $27 to 42 bamboo furniture makers in the village at a rate that allows them to make a profit and pay him back. This transaction signifies the informal beginning of the Grameen Bank project for the purpose of extending microcredit to the country's poorest citizens. Loans—as low as $1, at 20% interest rate—are made to villagers engaged in such enterprises as fish ponds, basket weaving, livestock rearing, and paddy cultivation. Grameen, which means "rural" in Bengali, will become the world's pioneer in microlending, and Yunus will become known as "banker to the poor."

1977: After studying how other loan programs are run, decides to do "exactly the opposite" of traditional banks with regards to setting up a credit program.

1979: Takes two-year leave of absence from University of Chittagong to officially join the Grameen Bank Project.

from "humble backgrounds," they "hovered at the upper fringe of poverty." Based in part on such arguments, the U.S. Congress has approved rules requiring that half of $2 billion in aid for such programs go to people earning less than $1 a day.

Yunus disagrees with this view, and he has often argued that microcredit benefits all layers of poor people, including those at the very bottom. Moreover, he is used to pushing forward in the face of opposition. He points out that skeptics abounded even when he was trying to get Grameen off the ground in the 1970s. "Things were always difficult for us, but I knew they would be because I was trying to do something that no one else believed in," he said in an interview from his office in Dhaka. Yunus had to develop Grameen's initial programs despite considerable opposition from bankers, who doubted that the initiative would work. In addition, he faced criticism from academic economists, who argued that microcredit could not foster true economic growth. Some religious leaders also opposed Grameen because its programs advocated giving loans to women. "There was opposition all around," Yunus says. "And it continues. Even today, there are lots of naysayers. I treat it as part of life. You just have to move on."

Moving on, for Yunus, means demonstrating what he believes is true, rather than just arguing his case. Faced with criticism that Grameen only reached the relatively better-off among the poor, Yunus was determined to show that microcredit could work for the poorest. To establish that, Yunus and Grameen launched a program in 2004 targeted at 10,000 beggars around Bangladesh. "We went to the beggars and told them, 'Look, when you go from house to house for begging, would you consider carrying some merchandise with you? Take some bangles, candles, cookies, or other kinds of food. Now you have a choice; you can beg, or you can sell. Maybe at some houses you could sell and at others you could beg."

Grameen Bank set up special rules to encourage beggars to join its program. For example, it clarified that the bank's rules would not apply to beggar members; they could make up their own rules. In addition, all loans would be interest-free, long-term, and have low repayment installments. (For a loan to buy a blanket, for instance, the repayment rate would be 3.4 cents a week.) All beggars are also covered by life insurance and loan insurance programs without having to pay premiums. The bank's website says, "The objective of the program is to provide financial services to the beggars to help them find a dignified livelihood, send their children to school, and graduate into becoming regular Grameen Bank members. We wish to make sure that no one in the Grameen Bank villages has to beg for survival."

Attracted by these terms, thousands of beggars in Bangladesh responded to Grameen's program. Following a modest beginning in January 2004, the program by April had signed on 8,000 beggars to sell simple products from house to house. Plans are afoot to increase the target to 25,000. Beggars who once sat under trees to beg could be seen selling Coke or Pepsi to thirsty customers. "As the beggars become successful, they remove their begging bowls and replace them with cash boxes," says Yunus. "The beggars become businesspeople. The next step is to put roofs over their heads and make them shopkeepers. It is working very well. We hope that in a year or so, many of them will stop begging."

1981: Ford Foundation provides Grameen with $800,000 as a guarantee fund for commercial bankers supporting Grameen. Rome-based International Fund for Agricultural Development provides a $3.4 million loan, which is matched by the Bangladesh Central Bank and is used to fund Grameen's expansion into five districts.

1983: Grameen Bank gets formal approval from government as a full-fledged private independent bank. Has 59,000 clients in 86 branches. Yunus tells his staff that anyone who asks for a loan is "a fake poor person. The person you are looking for will never come to you. When you find her, she will say, 'Oh, I don't need money.' When you hear that, you have found your person.'" Approximately 95% of the bank's borrowers are women, because they are more likely to spend profits on their families. The repayment rate is in the 90th percentile. Yunus states that the bank does not violate Islam's ban on charging interest because its borrowers own the bank.

1984: Applies for help introducing housing program to its borrowers under new Central Bank refinancing plan for housing loans in rural areas. Bank rejects application because size of loans that Grameen seeks is 'too small' to support real houses. Grameen resubmits application, this time for "shelter loans." Application rejected because such loans would be for "consumption items" (that is, shelter) rather than "productive activities." Grameen resubmits application for "factory loan," because the majority of its borrowers are women who work from the home. Application rejected again, but is eventually approved by Central Bank governor. Five years later, Grameen's housing program receives the Aga Khan International Award for Architecture. The houses are designed by the villagers themselves.

1985: Grameen pilot project—called Good Faith Fund—launched in Pine Bluff, Ark, with the support of then-governor Bill Clinton and wife Hillary. Other Grameen-style microcredit programs start in such places as Chicago, IL; Tulsa, OK; Dallas, TX; and Harlem, New York City.

1987: A Grameen pilot program is established in Malaysia. Three other pilot programs are launched in the Philippines, followed by programs in India, Nepal, Vietnam, China, Latin America, and Africa.

As such transformations occur, Yunus hopes they will help prove that programs motivated by charity, however well-intentioned, are less effective in reducing poverty than those that unleash the creativity and energy of the poor. In this regard, he believes that knowledge can play a critical role in ending poverty. "Knowledge is at the core of everything," he says. As a professor, he sometimes doubts whether traditional instruction helps students or merely molds them in their teachers' image. "Education shouldn't destroy the students' creativity and freshness," Yunus says. "Students are always imitating their professors, and imitation is dangerous." Knowledge should help students while allowing them to remain themselves.

Yunus believes the same approach should apply to anti-poverty programs. "People believe that a poor person can be helped through aid," he says. "He or she is not considered a creative person. This is wrong. A poor person is just as good a human being as anyone else in the world, but she is a victim of circumstances; the way in which she lives is only a reflection of the way in which society has rejected her. Instead of looking at her like a different kind of human being, we should be treating her as an equal, and extend to her the kinds of services that others enjoy. Once we do that, we will get out of the 'charitable' mode of thinking. We will get out of 'welfare system' mode." That, according to Yunus, is what will stimulate the creation of institutions that allow the poor themselves to develop their capabilities.

His ultimate vision is to build a world free of poverty. "We have created a slavery-free world, a smallpox-free world, an apartheid-free world," he wrote in *Banker to the Poor*. "Creating a poverty-free world would be greater than all these accomplishments while at the same time reinforcing them. This would be a world that we could all be proud to live in."

Leadership Lesson

The Poorest of the Poor

"Poverty," says Muhammad Yunus, "is…like a bonsai tree. You get only this little base to grow from. You are a stunted little thing. Maybe you could be a giant thing, but you never find out. That's poverty."

Thirty years ago, when Yunus was just beginning the journey that would lead to his founding of Grameen Bank, the rural poor in Bangladesh were a market that no one had clearly defined, let alone targeted as a constituency that could make a profit for a bank.

In 1974, a prolonged famine had devastated the residents of many of the country's small villages. Yunus, at that time an economics professor at Bangladesh's Chittagong University, first decided to enlist the media's help in calling attention to the rising number of starvation deaths, and then determined that he would focus his own efforts on trying to increase food production in one small village called Jobra, close to his home. Over the course of a year, he succeeded in helping farmers improve an irrigation system that would allow rice production on previously unused land.

That experience taught Yunus something that would prove instrumental to the future of microlending. He recognized that not all poor people are alike, that there are different levels of poverty depending on a person's individual circumstances. And yet, he said, government officials, economists, and social scientists failed to make these distinctions when they created programs to ease poverty. For these officials, the term

1990: Military government that ruled Bangladesh for nearly 10 years is toppled. Three months later, peaceful elections result in a victory for the Bangladesh Nationalist Party.

1990: Grameen and Yunus are subject of piece on CBS's *60 Minutes.*

1993: Grameen Uddog, a subsidiary, launched to help hand-loom weavers participate in the export market. New line of fabrics created called Grameen Check. Sales in three years reach $15 million. Eight years later, 8,000 hand-loom weavers produce Grameen Check fabrics for sale in Italy, France, the UK, and Germany.

1994: Grameen Trust receives close to $20 million from MacArthur Foundation, Rockefeller Foundation, World Bank, the U.S. government, the United Nations, and the German government to support 65 Grameen replication projects in 27 countries. Over the next eight years, these projects grant more than $444 million in loans to 1.14 million poor people.

1995: Grameen Bank for the first time makes enough profit to operate on a fully commercial basis without the need for preferential loans or grants.

1996: Grameen extends its one-billionth dollar in loans. Two years later, it lends its two billionth dollar.

1997: GrameenPhone Ltd., a rural cellular phone company that provides telephone service to village entrepreneurs, is launched; over the next seven years, the company makes loans to more than 43,000 villagers, allowing them to buy mobile phones. This venture is followed by Grameen Cybernet, a for-profit Internet service provider, and Grameen Communications, a nonprofit ISP. Eventually, there are more than two dozen organizations within the Grameen family of enterprises.

1997: Yunus leads the world's first microcredit summit, held in Washington, D.C. Participants pledge to get credit into the hands of 100 million of the poorest families by 2005.

1998: Unveils Grameen Investments where people can invest, rather than donate, capital for economic-development programs for the world's poor. First investor is Ted Turner.

1998: Grameen Textile Mills Ltd. starts production to sell flannel. Plans get underway to sell fabrics made from jute (a natural fiber) mixed with cotton or silk.

1999: Yunus receives the Indira Gandhi peace award for his microcredit initiative. It is one of numerous international awards and honors given to him.

2000: Grameen Communications establishes Internet kiosks in two villages.

"poor person" was a catch-all phrase that "could mean many things," Yunus wrote. "For some, the term referred to a jobless person, an illiterate person, a landless person, or a homeless person. For others, a poor person was one who could not produce enough food to feed his family. Still others thought a poor person was one who owned a thatched house with a rotten roof, who suffered from malnutrition, or who did not send his or her children to school. Such conceptual vagueness greatly damaged our efforts to alleviate poverty." Yunus noticed, also, that most definitions of poor people didn't include women and children.

He set about to establish different classifications of the poor based on such factors as region, occupation, ethnic background, gender, and age. At the end of this process, he had a definition of "poor" that differentiated, for example, between "marginal farmers" who were often the focus of international development programs, and the "really poor" who "had absolutely no chance of improving their economic base. Each one was stuck in poverty." This group of landless poor—who make up about 50 million of Bangladesh's 120 million inhabitants—would become the market that Grameen Bank would serve.

Yunus has repeated many times the story of how he first recognized the potential for growth inherent in poverty. On a visit to the same village of Jobra in 1976, Yunus met a 21-year-old woman making a bamboo stool in front of a run-down house with crumbling mud walls. This woman's daily profit, Yunus discovered after talking to her, was two cents, barely enough to feed one person, let alone feed, clothe, and shelter her three young children and send them to school. Consequently, these children, Yunus said, "were condemned to a life of penury, of hand-to-mouth survival, just as [their mother] had lived it before them, and as her parents did before her. I had never heard of anyone suffering" because she didn't have 22 cents.

Over the course of a week, Yunus and a university student made a list of other people in Jobra who had to depend on middlemen and money lenders for their subsistence work. The list had 42 people, who among them borrowed 856 taka—less than $27. "All this misery [exists] in all these families, all for the lack of $27," Yunus wrote in his book, *Banker to the Poor.*

With these insights, Yunus started up what eventually became the Grameen Bank—"an institution that would lend to those who had nothing," including no collateral and no credit history. The goal was to turn these villagers into entrepreneurs by giving them money to start their own small businesses, such as furniture making, egg production, basket weaving, commercial gardening, fish ponds, livestock rearing, and paddy cultivation. Loans—ranging from $1 to $100—were typically for a year, first at 16% interest and later at 20% interest. Recipients were required to start making payments the second week of the loan. Grameen only lent money to individual borrowers who had formed into groups of five. The idea was that peer pressure as well as peer support would help ensure that the individual loans were repaid.

2001: Grameen launches a program to convert its operational methodology into a new version called the Grameen Generalised System, (GGS, or Grameen Bank II).

2003: Grameen starts Struggling Members Programme, an initiative aimed at providing very small loans to beggars. Members are not required to give up begging, but are encouraged to sell small consumer items door to door, such as ribbons, fruit, or candles to generate income. By mid 2004, the program has signed up more than 8,000 beggars.

2004: Grameen bank has 1,195 branches, works in 43,681 villages, and has a staff of 11,855. Total amount of loans disbursed since inception is $4.18 billion, out of which $3.78 billion has been repaid, with a recovery rate of 99%. Of the 3.1 million borrowers, 95% are women. Borrowers of the bank own 93% of its total equity; 7% is owned by the government. The bank has made a profit every year since it started, except in 1983, when operations began, and 1991 and 1992, when the country was recovering from the effects of a cyclone that killed 150,000 people. The bank offers three loans: income-generating loans at 20% interest, housing loans at 8% interest, and higher education loans at 5% interest.

Grameen also lent mostly to women, reasoning that they are more reliable than men and more likely to spend profits on their families. And because Bangladesh is a country plagued by disasters—famines, floods, epidemics, tornadoes, and civil wars—the bank lent villagers new money to start up again if their means of production had been washed away, blown away, burned out, or destroyed. Old loans were not erased, but were converted into long-term loans that allowed individuals to pay them off more slowly.

When Yunus was asked why he charged these villagers any interest at all, his typical response was to challenge anyone to manage a bank for the poor that offers lower interest rates. Institutions such as his that are not self-sufficient, he added, will run into trouble because they will be dependent on politicians and government bureaucrats whose support is not always constant.

Indeed, from the beginning, Yunus was very clear what this market needed and didn't need. One thing it didn't need was government aid. "Our experience, in this region and everywhere else, has been that for the government to give credit—in rural areas, particularly, and credit as a whole—doesn't work," Yunus said in an interview in 1999. "Credit and government don't have a good chemistry. Government should distance itself from microcredit or, for that matter, any credit because it very quickly gets politicized."

Another approach that Yunus resisted was survival training. Yunus disagreed with those who claimed that before you loan poor people money, you should first teach them survival skills. For Yunus, the answer was "credit first." Poor people "do not need us to teach them how to survive; they already know how to do this...The fact that the poor are alive is clear proof of their ability," he said. By giving the poor access to credit, you "allow them to immediately put into practice the skills they already know...." Eventually, Grameen Bank made loans to villagers to help them build new houses or repair existing ones. The Bank also established Grameen Phone Ltd., a rural cellular phone company; Grameen Cybernet, a for-profit internet service provider; and Grameen Textile Mills, Ltd., among other ventures.

Yunus' trust in the creditworthiness of the village people seems to have paid off. By 2004, the Bank had loaned $4.18 billion, out of which $3.78 billion has been repaid, with a recovery rate of 99%. The microlending business that he started has spread far beyond Bangladesh.

An article in *US Banker*, written in August 2003, pointed to what it called "the consistently high profits of microfinance." Microloan borrowers, the article says, quoting Nancy Barry, president of Women's World Banking, a New York City-based non-governmental organization (NGO) with a microcredit arm, "are excellent credit risks." Barry pointed to the example of an Indonesian bank that had to "write off 100% of its corporate portfolio and 50% of its middle market loans during the 1988 financial crisis. But on-time repayment in its microfinance portfolio slid only 1%, to 97.5%. These borrowers are less risky than the Donald Trumps of the world," Barry said. "These borrowers have financial discipline. They know that if they screw up, they won't have access to lending."

Among our Top 25 leaders, Yunus is probably the only one who sincerely hopes that the market which has made him successful eventually disappears. His stated goal, he has said, is to halve the number of poor people by 2015.

5

Seeing the Invisible

When people say that "leadership involves vision," they generally refer to the ability of leaders to look into the future and articulate what they see in a way that is compelling to those around them. But for some leaders, it means something more: The ability to see what lies under everyone's noses, but what others, including some very smart people, cannot see. Call it seeing the invisible.

The way that Steve Jobs—co-founder and CEO of Apple Computer and CEO of Pixar—saw the potential of technology that later became the Macintosh computer offers a useful example. The story has long been part of Silicon Valley lore. It was November 1979, and Apple Computer was growing rapidly. With a few engineers, Jobs went to visit Xerox's famed Palo Alto

Research Center, the bastion of high-tech research. Scientists there had developed a computer called the Alto, and Jobs was very impressed—even excited—when he saw it. He later said in an interview that the "Alto had the world's first graphical user interface. It had windows. It had a crude menu system. It had crude panels and stuff. It didn't work right, but it basically was all there."

While Xerox researchers failed to recognize the potential of the Alto, Jobs could see it for what it was—technology that could allow ordinary people to work on computers through the use of graphic menus and a mouse rather than through arcane commands. This recognition enabled Apple Computer, under Jobs' leadership, initially to develop the Lisa, and then, more successfully, the Macintosh, one of its most popular and profitable products during the 1980s. Microsoft employed a similar graphic interface with its Windows software, which helped broaden the distribution of personal computers even further. In effect, these developments created the mass market for PCs.

Why was Jobs able to "see" what the Xerox researchers had missed? After all, they were brilliant scientists—and they had been clever enough to invent the technology in the first place. While endless speculation is possible over this question, part of the answer probably lies in the prevailing mindset of those times. During the late 1970s, though personal computers were starting to become popular, most people thought of computers as bulky mainframes. Hardly anyone believed that average people might have any use for personal computers; they were huge, lumbering devices that performed massive number-crunching exercises for big business or big government. Such impressions—which usually are habit-forming and can include preconceptions and sometimes prejudices—often blind observers to the potential value of a new technology. It takes a perceptive, intuitive outsider—like Jobs was at Xerox—to see the value and opportunities that lie latent in a new technology and the impact it can have if it is deployed.

That intuitive perception—and the corresponding ability to "see the invisible"—is a quality that many leaders have nurtured and used to their advantage during the past 25 years. Just as Jobs saw the value of Xerox's graphical user interface software for PCs, cable mogul Ted Turner—founder of Cable News Network and Turner Network Television—recognized the apparently invisible value that resided in old movies and TV programs. Financier George Soros, chairman of Soros Fund Management and the Open Society Institute, discerned economic trends long before they became apparent and used his insights to make investment decisions that garnered millions of dollars in profits.

What these examples show is that the ability to pierce through the superficial, sense-hidden signals and uncover hidden value can take many different forms. This is good news for those who want to cultivate their own leadership style and potential; it means they can choose from among a variety of models and nurture an approach to seeing the invisible that works best for them. It can also help them recognize that value can show up in the most unlikely places.

1955: Born in San Francisco, California, on February 24 and adopted soon after birth by Paul and Clara Jobs. His father, Paul, was a machinist whom Jobs was to describe as a "genius with his hands." When young Steve was five or six, Paul Jobs sawed off a part of his workbench and told him, "Steve, this is your workbench now." Jobs later credited his father for teaching him the rudiments of electronics.

1960: The family moves to Mountain View, California, a region where apricot and prune orchards abounded, which later became better known as Silicon Valley.

1972: Graduates from high school and enrolls in Reed College in Portland, Oregon. Jobs drops out after a semester.

1974: Returns to California and joins a computer hobbyists' club, where he befriends Stephen Wozniak. Jobs and Wozniak get jobs at Atari designing computer games.

1976: Co-founds Apple with Steve Wozniak in a garage in the Jobs' family home.

1977: Jobs and his colleagues launch Apple II.

STEVE JOBS

The Challenge:

Getting Creative in the Face of a Giant Competitor

It is an entrepreneur's worst nightmare: His or her company launches an innovative new product, it takes the market by storm, and then, drawn by that success, the industry behemoth decides to enter the fray. As the incumbent's massive marketing and financial muscle forces the David vs. Goliath mismatch towards an inevitable conclusion, how can the start-up survive? This scenario poses a crucial leadership test for new entrepreneurs. It is a trial by fire that either burns them out of existence or tempers them, like steel, and makes them stronger. That was the challenge that Steve Jobs, CEO of Apple and Pixar, faced in the early 1980s.

In 1976, Jobs, at age 21, had teamed up with his friend Steve Wozniak to launch Apple Computer in the family garage. (Some purists debate whether Apple Computer's first home was actually in a bedroom in the Jobs' family home, but by all accounts, the business did migrate to the garage and, eventually, out of it.)

In the mid 1970s, personal computing, like ham radio, appealed largely to hobbyists and techies. A handful of retailers sold kits with circuit boards and other components that had to be assembled before they could perform rudimentary tasks. Apple Computer's first products—Apple I computers—served the same demand; the Byte Shop, a retailer, ordered 50. Members of the Homebrew Computer Club in Palo Alto, to which Jobs and Wozniak belonged, also were among the initial customers. In 1977, along came Apple II, the product that put Apple Computer on the map and dramatically altered the shape of the personal computer industry. Unlike the Apple I machine, on which its technology was based, the Apple II had a beige case and featured colored graphics. Among its most popular features was its ability to run VisiCalc, an early spreadsheet that made it easy to perform complex calculations. Soon Mike Markkula, a former Intel executive, joined the company and helped bring in substantial capital. By the end of the 1970s, Apple II computers—priced around $1,200—were being sold in electronics stores around the country. The PC revolution had begun.

In its initial years, Apple Computer doubled in size annually, and in 1980, the company went public. Attracted by the potential of this rapidly growing market, IBM launched its own personal computer—the IBM 5150—in August 1981. Compared with puny Apple, IBM was a giant—that year it had 355,000 employees and $29 billion in revenues. IBM had been trying to make computers for personal use since the early 1970s. For example, after a six-month effort in 1973, the company's engineers had produced a prototype called "Special Computer, APL Machine Portable," or SCAMP, which could be used as a desktop calculator and perform a few other functions. Two years later, it produced the 5100 "portable computer," which weighed 50 lbs. and sold for between $9,000 and $20,000—and understandably failed to become a mass product. With the

1978–83: Apple has no competition, and the company grows at a compounded rate of 150% a year. In the early 1980s, IBM enters the PC market and overtakes Apple in just a couple of years.

1979: Visits Xerox's Palo Alto Research Center where he sees the Alto, a computer with a graphic user interface—including windows and a rudimentary menu system—and recognizes its market potential.

1980: Apple Computer goes public.

1983: Jobs recruits John Sculley, president of Pepsi-Cola USA, to become CEO of Apple Computer.

1984: Jobs, leading a team of 100, introduces the Macintosh. Launched with the famed "Big Brother" commercial on Superbowl Sunday, the Macintosh helps Jobs reinvent Apple as a revolutionary upstart fighting against a goliath-like IBM. The "Mac" helps kick off the phenomenon of desktop publishing.

1985: Jobs is ousted from Apple, following a boardroom coup led by Sculley. By then, Apple has grown to a $2 billion company. An angry Jobs, aged 30, leaves the company with $150 million.

1986: Jobs buys the computer graphics division of Lucasfilm for $10 million and establishes it as an independent company named Pixar. Ed Catmull, a vice president of LucasFilm, is the co-founder and becomes Pixar's chief technology officer.

1989: Jobs launches NeXT. The company focuses on object-oriented programming. Though Jobs struggles for the next eight years to create a second successful computer company, NeXT doesn't achieve that goal. Jobs later explains the reason for NeXT's failure was that it tried to copy the Apple model without realizing that the computer industry and the world had changed.

1993: As Apple's fortunes slide, the board lets Sculley go and brings in Michael Spindler as CEO. Spindler introduces the successful Power PC but has setbacks with the Newton, a personal digital assistant.

1995: Pixar goes public, raising $140 million and beating Netscape to become the biggest IPO of that year. *Toy Story*, which took four years to make, hits theaters, becoming the first fully computer-animated film, earning $342 million worldwide. It is the top box-office film that year.

IBM PC, however, Big Blue aimed directly at the mass market—and at Apple Computer. The IBM PC was priced at $1,565, and was able to run VisiCalc. In addition to being sold through the company's own product centers, it was distributed through retailers, such as Sears and ComputerLand. By 1983—the year John Akers became its president—IBM's PC had elbowed Apple aside to surpass it in sales. IBM had $40 billion in revenues and $5.4 billion in profits, and it wasn't about to let Apple Computer eat its lunch.

Jobs, and Apple, faced a critical question: When a giant forces you out of your game, what do you do? His response: Start a different game.

In November 1979, during a visit to Xerox's well-known Palo Alto Research Center, Jobs had seen computer technology that fascinated him. Unlike other computers, which ran on software that required users to know some programming, the Xerox machine, called the Alto, had a graphic interface with pop-up windows and drop-down menus that could be manipulated by a mouse. When he saw this, Jobs was so excited about the potential of this new technology that he began to jump up and down and shout, as Owen Linzmeyer notes in his book, *Apple Confidential: The Real Story of Apple Computer.* Jobs understood that if computers with such software were introduced, it would be easy for people to work with them. By making computing accessible to ordinary people, the mass market for personal computers would expand dramatically.

Years later, Jobs used an analogy from history to explain his thinking. When the telegraph was first introduced in the 19th century, the speed with which it made communication possible

between distant places turned it into a truly revolutionary technology. Soon demands were being
made that everyone should be required to learn
the Morse code because someday a telegraph
machine would sit on every desk. But then another revolutionary, distance-bridging invention
came along—the telephone—and the rest is history. The fact that anyone who could dial numbers and speak could use a telephone made it a
decisive winner over the telegraph as a personal
communication device. Jobs was convinced that
computers would follow the same path. Personal
computers that anyone could use almost intu-
itively, with little training, would have an advantage over those that required specialized knowledge.

Fired by this vision, Jobs brought together a
core team to create a new computer, the
Macintosh. Like the Alto, it had pop-up windows
and menus that could be operated with a mouse.
It had two times the memory of the IBM PC.
Remembering the experience of developing the
first "Mac," Jobs later said: "We worked like
maniacs. The greatest joy was that we felt we
were fashioning collective works of art."

The January 1984 launch of the Macintosh was
announced on Superbowl Sunday with the "Big
Brother" commercial that has become a legend
in the field of advertising. Directed by film maker
Ridley Scott and produced at a cost of $800,000,
it played off themes from George Orwell's novel
1984. Rows upon rows of bald, ashen-faced
drones file into a large hall where a giant face on
a screen addresses them. Suddenly a young, ath-
letic woman appears and runs down the hall, pursued by storm troopers; she carries a sledge

1995: During a vacation in Hawaii, Jobs and his friend Lawrence Ellison, billionaire software entrepreneur and chairman of Oracle, ponder taking over Apple.

1996: Spindler leaves Apple and is replaced by Gil Amelio, former CEO of National Semiconductor. Amelio tries to cut costs and begins to search for a new operating system. Jobs, who learns of this opportunity, calls Amelio to pitch NeXT's software solution. Amelio and Jobs begin negotiations, and in December Amelio announces Apple will buy NeXT for $400 million.

1997: Amelio and Jobs complete the deal for Apple to acquire NeXT, and Jobs returns to Apple. In July, Amelio leaves—critics say Jobs persuaded the board to fire him—and Jobs becomes the acting CEO. Journalist Alan Deutschman, who writes a book about Jobs, calls it *The Second Coming of Steve Jobs*.

1998: Apple launches the iMac, aimed at the education market, in an effort to return the company to its innovative roots.

2001: Pixar releases *Monsters, Inc.* The film rakes in more than $100 million in nine days, faster than any animated film had ever done.

2001: In January, Apple branches out into the music business by introducing iTunes, software that allows music lovers to download songs and burn their own CDs. Jobs announces that 275,000 songs are downloaded in the first week, making it a "huge hit with Mac users."

2001: In October, iPod, a portable music player, is introduced. Initially compatible only with Apple software, iTunes and iPod have a narrow market, but they attract attention because of their simplicity and elegance of design—and also because they offer a legal way to buy online music. "With iPod, listening to music will never be the same again," says Jobs, announcing the launch. "With iPod, Apple has invented a music player that lets you put your entire music collection in your pocket and listen to it wherever you go."

2002: In March, Apple announces the launch of the second generation of its iPod player, with a 10 gigabyte hard drive that lets users save up to 2,000 songs in its library.

2003: In May, Pixar releases *Finding Nemo*, which makes $70.2 million during its opening weekend. It becomes the highest grossing animated film worldwide, bringing in more than $800 million at the box office.

hammer, and wears red shorts and a tee-shirt with the Macintosh logo. Just before the troopers catch up with her, she spins around and hurls the hammer at the screen, shattering it as the giant head is proclaiming, "We shall prevail." The drones gasp, and the room is bathed in light. Then the message: "On January 24, Apple Computer will introduce the Macintosh. And you'll see why 1984 won't be like '1984.'"

The commercial was constantly played and re-played on news reports during the next few days, garnering millions of dollars in more publicity for the Macintosh. Although Apple Computer always denied that "Big Brother" represented IBM, the subtext was unmistakable in the minds of those who saw the commercial. The development and launch of the Macintosh allowed Jobs to reinvent Apple Computer as a revolutionary upstart con-fronting a domineering Goliath.

The Macintosh became one of Apple Computer's greatest successes during the 1980s, though the company ran into problems later when Microsoft introduced a similar interface with Windows. As Jobs said: "In doing the Macintosh, there was a core group of less than 100 people, and yet Apple shipped over ten mil-lion [computers]. Of course, everybody's copied it and it's hundreds of millions now. That's pretty large amplification, a million to one. It's not often in your life that you get that opportunity to amplify your values a hundred to one, let alone a million to one. That's really what we were doing…The contributions we tried to make embodied values not only of technical excellence and innovation—which I think we did our share of—but innovation of a more humanistic kind.

"The things I'm most proud about at Apple is where the technical and the humanistic came together, as it did in publishing. The Macintosh basically revolutionized publishing and printing. The typographic artistry coupled with the technical understanding and excellence to implement that electronically—those two things came together and empowered people to use the computer without having to understand arcane computer commands. It was the combination of those two things that I'm the most proud of."

2003: In October, a Windows version of iTunes appears, opening much larger markets for iPod and iTunes. In its first week, 1.5 million songs are downloaded from Apple's iTunes music store. Jobs boasts that this is five times the 300,000 songs that music fans downloaded from Napster in its first week of operation. By December, downloads from iTunes cross 25 million. *Time* magazine names it the "Coolest Invention of 2003."

2004: In January, Apple introduces a lightweight version of iPod, called iPod Mini. It is half the size of the iPod, weighs 3.6 ounces, and holds up to 1,000 songs. Jobs believes it will appeal to younger music lovers. In the same month, Apple announces a partnership with Hewlett-Packard to deliver digital music to HP's customers.

2004: In March, Apple delays the worldwide launch of iPod Minis to July because of extremely high demand in the U.S. On August 1, in an email sent to Apple employees, Jobs announces that he had emergency surgery for a form of pancreatic cancer, and that his plan is to be back at work in September.

Leadership Lesson

From Macs to Music

In Jobs' case, one of the hallmarks of his leadership style is his ability to see business opportunities in situations where others observe little more than chaos and confusion. His success in spotting consumer trends in the online music business and use that understanding to carve out a huge market for Apple's iPod music players and iTunes music store is a case in point.

Pandemonium reigned in the online music business in the late 1990s when Jobs decided to take the plunge. Ever since college students and others on the Internet took to swapping MP3s for free rather than paying for downloading songs, the music industry was in an uproar over piracy. After a bruising battle, the Recording Industry Association of America, which represents major music companies, succeeded in forcing Napster to shut down, but successors such as Kazaa, Morpheus, and Grokster were still around—and the industry reckoned it was losing $3.5 billion a year to piracy. The industry's response was two-fold: Erecting technological barriers to downloading, and filing lawsuits against downloaders and their enablers.

Jobs, however, recognized that both these so-called solutions were short-sighted and would end up alienating millions of consumers, the very people whose hearts and minds the music industry should be trying to win. He chose to pursue a third path: Creating user-friendly software and hand-held players that would let music lovers download their favorite songs for a small fee. That insight inspired Apple's foray into the iTunes music store and the stylish iPod players, which represent one of the company's biggest success stories in recent years.

In the spring of 2001, Apple Computer launched its iTunes online music service, initially just for Apple users. The economic model was simple: "Customers pay 99 cents to download each song. After that, it's almost like buying music on a CD, LP, or tape. The user can play it on the computer, burn it to a CD that can be played on any device, or transfer it to an MP3 player." One limitation was that each file had an embedded signal aimed at preventing the songs from being shared on Internet file-sharing services. The fact that Apple allowed customers to own digital music woke up the market.

Large as the market was when iTunes was available only for Apple users, it exploded when a Windows version was introduced in the spring of 2003. Jobs was delighted with the way the market responded to these initiatives. "The iTunes music store is changing the way people buy music," he said. "Selling five million songs in the first eight weeks has far surpassed our expectations and clearly illustrates that many customers are hungry for a legal way to acquire their music online." Commenting on this trend, Wharton Marketing Professor Peter Fader noted in Knowledge@Wharton in July 2003: "I think the success of Apple's iTunes service isn't the downloading per se, it's the interface—it's fun to use." iPod music players—which could store hours of music and were as small and easy to use as cell phones—added further to Apple's success in this business. Even people who found computers intimidating said they liked using iPods.

Jobs was repeating the Macintosh model all over again. By creating an innovative product that was fun and easy to use, he opened up a mass market for digital music. "iTunes sold 20 million tracks in its first seven months of operation...Between June and November 2003, music lovers bought 7.7 million songs online, but only 4 million single-song CDs at stores," according to a January 14, 2004, article in *Knowledge@Wharton*.

By the spring of 2004, Apple had emerged as the clear winner among online music services, with a reported 70% share of the market for legal music downloads and a 45% share of the MP3 market.

It is unclear how long Apple will be able to sustain its lead, considering that rivals Sony and Microsoft, among others, are planning major assaults on this market. But at the moment, Jobs' transformation of Apple has been impressive. Quoting a cultural historian who described Jobs as the "Henry J. Kaiser or Walt Disney of this era," *The New York Times* wrote, "Jobs has attained a level of influence over how life is lived in the digital age that is unmatched by even his most powerful computer industry rivals."

1938: Robert Edward "Ted" Turner III born Nov. 19 in Cincinnati, Ohio. Father ran a successful billboard advertising company; mother was a homemaker

1956: Entered Brown University. Started to study Classics, a subject his father ridiculed as worthless. Was expelled during his junior year for violating the rule against having girls in dorm rooms.

1961: Becomes an account executive at his father's company, Turner Advertising Co., in Atlanta, Georgia.

1962: His father pays $4 million for two divisions of rival General Outdoor Advertising, making Turner Advertising the billboard leader in the South.

1963: On March 5, Turner's father commits suicide at age 53 with a silver pistol. For years, Ted Turner keeps the gun in his office desk drawer.

1963: Becomes the company's president and COO.

1968: Purchases WAPO, a Chattanooga, Tennessee radio station, the first step in his dream of becoming a media mogul. Over the course of the next year, purchases two more radio stations in the South.

TED TURNER

The Challenge:

Keeping the Big Picture Clear

"I had to operate with gut feelings because there wasn't any precedent," says Ted Turner, founder of Cable News Network and Turner Network Television. "I was boldly going where no man had ever gone before."

Turner can be excused for quoting *Star Trek*, a popular science fiction series that began on network television in the 1960s but whose reruns are now shown on cable. After all, Turner almost single-handedly built a communications empire— including numerous cable stations—by recognizing the value of ideas that others criticized as ill-conceived or just plain wacky.

The biggest challenge along the way for Turner was figuring out how to capitalize on his insight that satellite-based broadcasting was the future of television, and to find enough good content to fill that future. There were "no blueprints" to give him guidance, he says. "So there wasn't any way to measure what was successful or not. There was nothing to measure against." The man known as "Captain Outrageous"—for blurting out off-the-cuff remarks without considering their ramifications—had strategies in place for each acquisition or entrepreneurial venture, but they were largely untested. His main criterion for gauging whether such ventures were going to be successful, he says, was "that I felt good about it."

Turner's first step into the media big league was the purchase in 1970 of Channel 17, a moribund Atlanta television station with a weak UHF signal. Industry experts said Turner had been hoodwinked and predicted that his plans would derail even before he got started. The station, however, would eventually benefit from Turner's embrace of a technology that few had thought would revolutionize the television industry, yet turned out to be the foundation for each of Turner's successes.

"I'm best known for CNN—that might have been my greatest impact. But the single biggest thing that I happened on was the communications satellite," he says. "The Russians had just [learned] how to put these satellites in a geostationary orbit. I tried to figure out how I could utilize [the technology] with my station in Atlanta."

His vision ran counter to accepted norms. Television broadcasters, including Turner's Channel 17, beamed microwave signals that were relayed beyond their range by bouncing them off transmission towers. Turner had already invested in a larger tower that extended his station's signal beyond its 40-mile broadcast range to five neighboring states. But the signal had reached its limit, weakening as it encountered geographic and man-made obstacles.

Satellite technology, however, would allow him to beam Channel 17's signal nationwide to various cable system providers that were starting up during the 1970s. When Turner transformed Atlanta's Channel 17 into a national cable network, he renamed it TBS, the Superstation. "I was the first commercial broadcaster to use satellite," he says. "Going into the satellite business, distributing our

1970: Turner Communications Group (formerly Turner Advertising) acquires its first television station, Atlanta's WJRJ Channel 17, a moribund station with a weak UHF signal. Renames TCG with lofty sounding name of Turner Broadcasting Systems (TBS).

1976: Turner begins transmitting WTBS via satellite to cable systems around the country. Overnight transforms a local station into a national one—an initial volley in the battle to chip away at the national dominance of major networks ABC, CBS, and NBC.

1976: TBS acquires Major League Baseball's Atlanta Braves. Decades before Disney purchases a major sports franchise to control more programming content, Turner transmits his team's games nationally over TBS. Cable, starved for content, looks toward TBS and Home Box Office to provide it.

1977: TBS buys the National Basketball Association's Atlanta Hawks. Adds more programming choices to TBS's growing stable of content.

1977: Turner captures yacht racing's prestigious America's Cup with his sailboat, Courageous.

1980: Launches Cable News Network (CNN), the first around-the-clock, all-news television station. Plagued by low production and editorial quality, the station is ridiculed by network news divisions as the "Chicken Noodle Network." Turner provides yet another source of cheap content to fill the void in cable programming.

1982: Starts *Headline News* offering updated newscasts on the half-hour. Format creates the template for competitors like *MSNBC* and *Fox News*, which don't appear until the 1990s.

1985: Launches *CNN International*, which provides global news service to 210 countries.

1985: Makes unsuccessful $5 billion bid to acquire CBS. Loews Corporation's Laurence Tisch gains control of the broadcaster with the support of CBS itself. Loss underscores Turner's alienation from the networks over past decade.

1986: First Goodwill Games held in Moscow. The Games, financed by Turner, show his evolution from an unsophisticated conservative Southerner to a man of international interests. They also provide cheap programming for his cable properties.

programming via satellite, was a huge risk at the time," especially given that the networks were busy lobbying federal regulators to squelch what they viewed as a threat to their dominance.

It was even riskier than he thought. In December 1979, the communications satellite that was supposed to be the new carrier of cable television programming, including Turner's CNN, got lost in orbit. RCA, which had launched the satellite, attempted to wriggle out of its commitment to provide Turner with a backup satellite. Turner sued RCA claiming, among other things, that the company was trying to keep CNN off the air to protect its subsidiary NBC. Turner won and CNN launched on schedule.

But even as Turner Broadcasting System (TBS) was expanding across the country, cable programming was proving to be a wasteland of old, second-rate shows. The industry, starved for content, was looking to HBO and TBS to provide it. Turner did his part: He bought the Atlanta Braves for $10 million to provide guaranteed baseball coverage. The team was so bad over the next few years that when they were mired in a 17-game losing streak, Turner tried his hand at coaching them. They still lost. "There were times when I was apprehensive; there were times when I was concerned, and there were times when I worried, but I never really had any serious doubts," says Turner. "My confidence in what I was doing was pretty strong." Turner went on to acquire basketball and ice hockey teams, and the Atlanta Braves made it to the World Series in 1991.

In 1985, Turner bought the entire library of the MGM movie studio for about $1.5 billion. At the time, industry followers believed Turner had significantly overpaid for the assets. Turner then acquired the library of the Hanna-Barbera animation studio, which had more than 3,000 half-hour cartoons. While these deals saddled TBS with even more debt in the short term and almost cost Turner control of his company (to a consortium of investors), he barreled ahead and spun out two more "crazy" ideas. One was a channel that showed nothing but cartoons, the Cartoon Network; and the other a channel that played nothing but classic movies, Turner Classic Movies.

Even though Turner was succeeding in making cable a viable threat to the networks, they still continued to ridicule him. As network-news divisions were shrinking their news bureaus and focusing on entertainment, however, Turner chose to take on greater and greater debt by expanding CNN's bureau presence around the world. "I gambled everything I had and really even resources that I didn't have," he says.

The dismantling of the Berlin Wall in 1989 and the 1991 Gulf War turned Turner into a legendary media figure for recognizing, and acting on, the public's untapped appetite for continuous news coverage. In reality, the lofty goal of raising the profile of news coincided with Turner's continuing effort to feed content into the cable system.

He didn't spend time thinking about his own strengths and weaknesses as a business leader, he says. "I was too busy. Whatever deficiencies I had, I was able to overcome....I am a generalist rather than a specialist," he adds. If he had spent his time becoming an expert in only technology or finance or business, "I would never have been able to see the big picture. Because I was learning a little bit about lots of different [things], I was able to connect the dots."

1986: TBS acquires the MGM library of film and television properties for $1.5 billion. Turner makes the decision to acquire the library without consulting his board and is criticized by industry watchers who claim he overpaid for the assets.

1988: Hoping to monetize the acquisition of the MGM properties, Turner launches TNT, a television station with an endless supply of already-paid-for programming.

1991: Acquires the rights and library of Hanna-Barbera Cartoons and its production facilities in yet another move to increase and own programming.

1991: After a decade of being on the brink of extinction, CNN comes of age during the 1991 Gulf War when Americans and people the world over are glued to real-time war footage. Turner is named *Time* magazine's "Man of the Year" for redefining news "from something that has happened to something that is happening at the very moment you are hearing of it."

1991: Marries actress Jane Fonda, his third marriage.

1992: Launches Cartoon Network, showcasing the Hanna-Barbera library.

1994: Turner Broadcasting acquires New Line Cinema, providing more film programming for his stations.

1994: Launches Turner Classic Movies (TCM) using films from the New Line Cinema collection and other properties.

1996: Time-Warner acquires Turner Broadcasting Systems for $7.6 billion. Turner becomes the merged company's vice chairman overseeing Time-Warner's cable properties, including TBS, CNN, HBO, and New Line Cinema.

1996: Launches CNNSI, a sports news channel.

1997: Launches CNN en Espanol.

1997: Turner pledges $1 billion to the United Nations over 10 years through establishment of UN Foundation.

2000: America Online acquires Time-Warner in January. Turner, one of the largest individual shareholders in Time-Warner, was not consulted on how the merged companies would operate.

2000: In May, Turner is officially named vice chairman and senior advisor of AOL Time Warner. Is stripped of his day-to-day control over Time Warner's Cable group—the company's fastest growing division, which includes CNN, HBO, and Turner Broadcasting Systems.

Leadership Lesson

Gold in Them Thar 'Toons

For a person who never watched television, Ted Turner always had a knack for savvy programming on his stations, in part because he was able to see what others didn't: the hidden value in old and well-worn television shows and movies. He realized early on that they would be a never-ending source of much-needed content for his burgeoning satellite-based cable empire.

At WTCG, the shaky precursor to TBS, Turner went against the conventional wisdom of the 1970s, which was to license films for a few showings. Instead, he chose to buy movies whenever they were available for purchase. He reasoned that instead of running them a few times on a rental basis, he could own them and run them as often as he liked. He also had the option of licensing his films and shows to others. Episodes of *Leave it to Beaver* and *I Love Lucy*, for example, ran constantly on WTCG. Turner not only promoted the shows themselves, but also the nostalgic family values that permeated them.

More than a decade later, Turner employed the same strategy to acquire even more valuable content. In 1985, he bought the entire library of the MGM movie studio for about $1.5 billion. It was an extraordinarily difficult deal to finance, because Wall Street considered the price too high and because Turner needed to rely on junk bonds to pay for the transaction. Commenting on the deal, *Forbes* magazine wrote: "It is no secret why Turner wants MGM. The only consistently profitable part of TBS is the Superstation, WTBS, which is beamed to 35.6 million TV homes in 205 markets, 24 hours a day. Sports fill about 25% of its time, and original programming another 15% or so, while just over 30% of its programming is syndicated reruns of TV shows and old movies, which Turner must buy from third parties. Back in the late 1970s, Turner could, and did, buy virtually all the programming he needed for peanuts. Today, of course, everyone is on to the game, and prices for old films and television series are reaching ridiculous heights. Turner, in effect, now finds himself in a position analogous to that of an oil refiner short of crude during OPEC's heyday."

Disregarding such criticism with his characteristic devil-may-care attitude, Turner pursued a similar transaction in 1991 with the Hanna-Barbera animation studio. At that time, he already owned 700 cartoons, which aired on his cable channels, but the Hanna-Barbera studio, with its archive of more than 3,000 half-hour programs of animated films featuring Yogi Bear, The Flintstones, the Jetsons, and Scooby Doo, would dramatically increase his content base. The acquisition price for Hanna-Barbera was in the $250 million to $300 million range, in part because Japan's Matsushita, the parent company of MCA, was also interested in buying Hanna-Barbera. But Turner teamed up with Leon Black, a former Drexel Burnham Lambert executive who had set up the Apollo Investment Fund, to finance the purchase.

While these deals saddled TBS with even more debt in the short term, Turner spun out two more "crazy" ideas. One was

2001: Turner and Fonda file for divorce. Turner calls his personal relationships with his wives "the biggest failures" in his life.

2002: Starts the first of 19 Ted's Montana Grills with restaurateur George McKerrow, Jr. Bison selected from Turner's ranches is main fare.

2003: Steps down as vice chairman of AOL Time-Warner. The decision comes after three years of watching his power and influence wane as he loses operational responsibilities.

2004: Turner asks the government to break up big media companies, saying they have become too powerful, that programming quality has suffered under them, and that they leave little room for diverse opinions.

a channel that showed nothing but cartoons, the Cartoon Network; the other was a channel that played nothing but classic movies, Turner Classic Movies. Cartoons, as Turner knew, are an immensely profitable business because kids will watch the same show over and over. By launching a 24-hour cartoon network and another for classic films, Turner was able to turn these acquisitions into money machines. In addition, they provided a launch pad for global expansion. In Asia, these days, TV viewers are treated to the joys of hearing Scooby Doo speak in Tamil.

In his early forays into television, Turner drummed up business—through the sheer force of his outrageous personality—from completely unlikely sources. When WTCG was struggling for survival in the mid-1970s, Turner tried to generate revenue by telling prospective advertisers that if they wanted their color ads to stand out, they should advertise on his cable channel. When asked why the ads would stand out, the reason was that all the "station's programming was in black and white!" Another gimmick was to inform advertisers that Turner's viewers were of above average intelligence. He had no evidence for this claim apart from telling them that it "takes a genius to figure out how to tune a UHF set."

Despite such antics, Turner slowly built an audience for his television properties on his way to becoming one of the most recognized and successful media moguls of his time.

GEORGE SOROS

The Challenge:

"It Is Hard to Do Good"

George Soros is the world's most famous specu-lator—and second most famous investor (after Warren Buffett). His Quantum Hedge Fund, start-ed in 1969, experienced average returns of 31% over the next 30 years, making billions for him and millions for his investors. His decision to short the British pound in 1992 and pocket a $1 billion profit earned him the title, "The Man Who Broke the Bank of England."

But one of his biggest challenges has not been making money; it has been finding meaningful ways to spend it. Unlike many wealthy donors, who direct their money to a specific medical cause, education-al institution, or arts group, Soros decided long ago to use his wealth to transform social orders. Over the past 25 years, he has given away close to $5 bil-lion to establish democratic "open societies" pri-marily in Central and Eastern Europe but also in Africa and Asia. In 1998 and 1999 alone, Soros reportedly donated $575 million and $570 million, respectively, to his various foundations and causes, solidifying a reputation as "the only U.S. citizen with his own foreign policy." Indeed, in some countries his donations have single-handedly exceeded the amount of aid given by the U.S. government.

The challenges of structuring donations of this size—and ensuring that they accomplish what the donor intends—are enormous. In Soros's case, he engages in the process with an inherent skepticism

1930: Born in Budapest, Hungary. His father is a lawyer, his mother a homemaker.

1936: Soros's father changes family name from Schwartz to Soros.

1944: Soros, his brother, mother, and father assume fake identities to escape arrest in Nazi-occupied Hungary.

1947: Leaves communist Hungary and his family to live in England.

1952: Graduates from London School of Economics.

1956: Moves to New York City, becomes arbitrage trader for brokerage firm F. M. Mayer.

1959: Hired by Wertheim & Co. as assistant to head of foreign trading department.

1963: Joins Arnhold & S. Bleichroeder, broker and asset management firm with emphasis on global research and trading.

1969: Sets up Double Eagle fund, a hedge fund later called the Quantum Fund, with $4 million from wealthy private investors. Between 1969 and 2000, Quantum Fund will return an average of 31% annually. A $1,000 investment in the Quantum Fund in 1969 will be worth $4 million in 2000.

1973: Leaves Arnhold & S. Bleichroeder and sets up Soros Fund Management with $12 million; Quantum is the flagship fund.

1979: Engages in first significant philanthropic venture—providing stipends for 80 black students to attend the University of Cape Town in apartheid South Africa. Unhappy with how the money is disbursed, Soros discontinues the project after its first year.

1980: Splits with business partner of 12 years, Jim Rogers.

1981: Cover story in *Institutional Investor* magazine calls Soros "The World's Greatest Money Manager." That same year, Quantum Fund suffers first major loss—down 22.9%.

1982: Fund recovers from previous year's loss: registers 56.9% growth.

1984: Quantum Fund rises 122% to slightly more than $1 billion; becomes first hedge fund to break billion-dollar barrier.

1984: Establishes the Soros Foundation in Hungary, the first of many Open Society foundations dedicated to promoting open and democratic societies throughout the world. In Hungary, the foundation provides books for libraries and educational institutions as well as hundreds of Xerox copiers for citizens, underscoring the right of citizens to access and share information.

of large, entrenched charities. During an interview with *The New Yorker* in 1995, he described traditional foundations as "too bureaucratic to respond in a timely way to real need, laden with overhead...and inherently corrupting." Consequently, during the 1980s, as he was establishing Open Society Foundations in places like Hungary, the Soviet Union, Poland, and Czechoslovakia, Soros set them up to be "short-lived...operated with minimal bureaucracy...and run only by local people," with Soros himself "maintaining a low profile and keeping his ego out of it."

With a vision this large, it is no surprise that his initiatives haven't always been successful, in part because he was dealing with countries in the midst of significant—sometimes revolutionary—transformations. Soros's legendary skills as a financier and speculator have been of limited use in helping him predict the impact that his huge philanthropic investments would have on emerging economies. As he told biographer Michael T. Kaufman, from 1979 to 1984 his philanthropic initiatives were a series of experiments—some of which failed. "I didn't know what the hell I was doing, and I made some wrong steps."

His first serious commitment occurred in 1979 when Soros provided stipends of $2,500 each for 80 black college students at the University of Capetown in South Africa. Instead of encouraging multiracial education, the program was met with hostility and the funds were diverted to other uses. As he notes in his book, *Soros on Soros*, the apartheid state was "so insidious that whatever I did made me an accomplice of the system." He abandoned the program within a year (although he established an Open Society Foundation in South Africa in 1993).

In China, he faced difficult challenges but met with a similar result. Soros had set up the Fund for the Reform and Opening of China in 1986 to provide grants to academics, journalists, scientists, and others who would help make China a more open society. But by 1988, he wrote, the fund had become "embroiled in the country's internal political struggle...In effect, the foundation was run by the secret police." Soros shut it down in 1989.

In Hungary, Soros's money had more impact. His foundation, set up in 1984, was able to supply educational institutions and libraries with 50,000 books from abroad and import hundreds of Xerox copiers for use in easily accessible public places. Soros saw the copiers as a "clear metaphor for the entire concept of an open society," in that they allowed people to freely gather and distribute information, and also "signified citizen involvement in finding data and passing it on." The project became one of Soros's greatest philanthropic successes.

In Russia, where Soros set up the Soviet Foundation in 1987, the results were mixed. The Moscow-based Cultural Initiative Foundation, as it was first called, "fell into the hands of a reform clique of Communist Youth League officials," whom Soros finally removed, and then was run by a man who "turned the foundation into his personal fiefdom." Soros got rid of him as well. Soros had to clean house again in 1994 after questionable financial transactions by the foundation administrators. "I learned from bitter experience how difficult it is to run a foundation in a revolutionary environment," he said a year later. A Russian journalist, commissioned to write a history of the Soros foundations, titled his piece, "It Is Hard to Do Good." Yet the foundation in

1986: Establishes Open Society Foundation in China; three years later, the Fund shuts down due to political party infighting.

1987: Writes *The Alchemy of Finance*, the first of eight books.

1987: Establishes Open Society Foundation in then-Soviet Union, later Russia.

1989: Berlin Wall falls, leading to collapse of communism and major upheaval in the former Soviet Union; Soros gives up day-to-day management of Quantum to Stanley Druckenmiller in order to concentrate on international philanthropy.

1990–1992: Establishes 16 more foundations in formerly Communist countries, including one in Ukraine in 1991. Number of foundations will eventually total 50.

1992: Establishes Central European University with its primary campus in Budapest, the only project for which Soros will set up a long-term endowment ($250 million).

1992: Shorts the British pound and makes profit of $1 billion when pound collapses. Earns title of "The Man Who Broke the Bank of England."

1992–93: Gives $50 million in aid to United Nations refugee agency to help refugees in Bosnia, $100 million to fund scientific research in former Soviet Union, $25 million to help Macedonian government service its debt, and $75 million to open foundations in central and Eastern Europe and South Africa.

1993: Creates Open Society Institute to support his foundations; OSI becomes headquarters for the Soros philanthropic network.

1994: Soros loses $600 million by betting wrong on the yen, makes it up by end of year. Quantum has second worst year of its history with return of 2.9%.

1995: Begins to emphasize philanthropy in U.S.; funds Project on Death in America to promote discussion about end-of-life care issues; pushes to allow the legal use of illegal drugs to ease suffering; sets up Emma Lazarus Fund to better the lives of immigrants, among other projects.

1997: Shorts Thailand's currency, the baht, and Malaysia's currency, the ringgit. Thailand subsequently devalues baht, setting off wave of devaluations in Malaysia and elsewhere that kicks off the Asian crisis; Malaysian Prime Minister Mahathir Mohamad accuses Soros of being a criminal.

Russia is also credited with a number of successful initiatives, such as funding scientific research (one year, Soros gave $500 each to 30,000 scientists), supporting the teaching of humanities and social sciences, and providing Internet access to regional universities.

In 1989, as the Berlin Wall fell and the Soviet Union was dismantled, Soros's approach to philanthropy changed dramatically. With his Quantum Fund now under the stewardship of Stanley Druckenmiller, Soros established 16 foundations in formerly communist countries between 1990 and 1992, seeing them as a way to help establish societies with free markets, free speech, the rule of law, and democratic governments. These years were also marked by the beginning of a new activism and visibility on Soros's part. While he preferred to play a low-key, behind-the-scenes role during the early years of his philanthropy, after 1989, he wanted his voice to be heard. "He thought he would be a market leader…as he had been so many times in the financial markets. The West would follow him…Soros could in some instances perhaps help decide who would be powerful—and he could shape these emerging societies not from the bottom but from the top."

Again, it was always more difficult than it seemed. Soros was accused of using his money to push his ideas on developing countries, of meddling in internal affairs, of blurring the line between philanthropy and investing. Responding to that last charge, Soros says: "To guard against [the accusation that I exploit my political influence for financial gain], I invest only on behalf of my foundations and not for profit whenever this possibility arises."

He has also been accused of playing by his own rules and changing them when it suits him, a charge he doesn't refute. "I do not accept the rules imposed by others. If I did, I would not be alive today," he says, referring to his days as a teenager in occupied Hungary when Soros, who is Jewish, and his family had to adopt false identities to escape capture by the Nazis.

Whatever the context, Soros's extraordinary level of philanthropy reflects his own view of himself as a "financial, philanthropic, and philosophical speculator." Descriptions of his business successes, for example, often refer to his ability to analyze huge amounts of information quickly and make decisive multimillion bets on currency or stock market swings. That same decisiveness has characterized his philanthropy. When big projects arose, Kaufman writes in his biography, Soros was the one who decided whether to get involved and how much to commit. "In philanthropy as in business, Soros was pulling the trigger."

As he still is. In a bid to help oust President George W. Bush from office in the 2004 presidential election, Soros gave more than $12 million to Democrats for political ads and other attack strategies. An article in the Feb. 5, 2004 issue of The Wall Street Journal describes Soros as "the most important money man in the Democratic Party this election year...but he isn't just writing checks; he is also imposing a business model on the notoriously unruly world of politics. He demands objective evidence of progress...and he is delivering his money in installments, giving him leverage if performance falters."

1998: Soros funds suffer $2 billion loss in Russia.

2000: Quantum Fund loses $3 billion following sell-off of tech stocks. Druckenmiller resigns and Quantum is renamed Quantum Endowment Fund, with new emphasis on safer investing to help fund Soros's philanthropic activities.

2002: French court fines Soros $2.8 million for insider trading, specifically for using privileged information to speculate in shares of French bank Société Générale during failed takeover bid in 1988. Soros appeals ruling.

2003: Gives $12.5 million to anti-Bush organizations, including $10 million to America Coming Together—a Democratic initiative aimed at get-out-the-vote efforts in 17 key states—and a web-based organization called MoveOn.org.

2003: Publishes The Bubble of American Supremacy: Correcting the Misuse of American Power, his eighth book.

2004: Soros Fund Management reported to have approximately $12 billion under management; Soros's projected worth is $7 billion; it is estimated that he has given away $4–$5 billion over the past 25 years.

Soros's attempts to affect today's "unruly world of politics" appear much in line with his attempts to alter the course of history after the fall of communism. He clearly remains confident in his ability to bring about change, perhaps because his enormous wealth affords him such unusual opportunity. Responding to a question several years ago about why he gave millions of dollars to Eastern Europe, he replied: "Because I care about the principles of open society and I can afford it. It is a unique combination."

Leadership Lesson

Hurricane from a Butterfly's Wings

George Soros was very much a behind-the-scenes investor during his early career. This changed in 1992, though, when he made a highly public, and spectacularly correct, bet against the British pound. He wagered 10 billion pounds—one and a half times the value of all his funds—that the pound would fall against the German mark. It did, and Soros made a billion-dollar profit.

In his book *Soros on Soros,* he says he was alerted to the pound's weakness by a remark by the German finance minister that "alluded to the Italian lira as a currency that was not too sound. I asked him after the speech whether he liked the ECU (European Currency Unit) as a currency, and he said he liked it as a concept but he didn't like the name. He would have preferred it if it were called the mark...I got the message. It encouraged us to short the Italian lira, and in fact, the Italian lira was forced out of the exchange rate mechanism shortly thereafter. That was a clear sign that sterling was also vulnerable."

This was just one example of Soros being able to read the "small signs" indicating that a so-called normal situation is turning into a "bubble, a boom/bust cycle or a crisis. We all know about the hurricane that begins with the flap of a butterfly's wings, but Soros is the rare person who is habitually willing to follow the implications. Very often those signs come from politics," noted a *Fortune* article in 2003.

Soros, by all accounts, has an uncanny ability to predict the future on the basis of seemingly random events or even random remarks that others typically ignore. "George's genius," says an employee of Soros Fund Management, "is in seeing the trend long before anyone else does. George realized what was going to happen practically from the moment the Berlin Wall came down. Because he thinks in such broad terms, he saw that German unification was going to be a lot more expensive than [Chancellor Helmut] Kohl was predicting, than anyone was predicting."

Getting predictions right has helped Soros's Quantum Fund make money by anticipating economic shifts around the world. The January 1995 issue of *The New Yorker* described Soros as excelling at "identifying those lacunae where perception lagged behind reality, leaving room for exploitation." Soros himself said that he was "particularly focusing on changes in the rules of the game, not in playing by one particular set of rules, but understanding when new rules came into being—and learning that before others did."

He explained his ideas further in *Soros on Soros*, noting, "The prevailing wisdom is that markets are always right. I take the opposite position. I assume that markets are always wrong. Even if my assumption is occasionally wrong, I use it as a working hypothesis...this line of reasoning leads me to look for the flaw in every investment thesis...I am ahead of the curve. I watch out for telltale signs that a trend may be exhausted. Then I disengage from the herd and look for a different investment thesis."

Michael T. Kaufman's biography of Soros, titled *Soros: The Life and Times of a Messianic Billionaire*, offers two examples of how Soros stayed ahead of the curve by seeing the invisible. During the conglomerate boom of the late 1960s, companies went on acquisition binges to spur growth. Many of these were high-tech firms that knew they could no longer count on defense contracts won during the height of the Cold War. When this strategy seemed successful, other companies also went on acquisition sprees. Imitative behavior intensified, acquirers became less discerning, and target companies were no longer judged on their merits. At the same time, "new accounting techniques enhanced the impact of acquisitions." Acquisitions had to get larger and larger in order to maintain the momentum. Soros saw what was happening and also where things were heading. He "rode the wave as acquisitions grew and then sold short as prices approached their crest."

Kaufman cites another instance, in 1972, when Soros began studying the banking industry. He decided that it was going to shift
from a dull, stodgy business to one with innovation and energy, in
part because business schools were graduating students who were
more interested in profits than their predecessors. So Soros bought
a number of bank stocks and "earned about 50% on those shares."
Even more importantly, his involvement helped him better understand, and benefit from, international currency markets "when the
old system of fixed exchange rates gave way to floating parities a
year later."

But seeing the invisible is worth little unless it is coupled with
the ability to act on what you see—in other words, to take big
risks. Much of Soros's success in the markets depended on his willingness to place the kind of bets that would cause ordinary
investors to break out in cold sweats. "What makes George so outstanding is his belief that if you like something, you buy it. I can't
tell you the number of times...when I would take a position that
I thought was quite daring and George's response would be, 'Why
so little?' That's the real key. When he thinks he's right, he'll bet
the ranch," said an employee of Soros Fund Management more
than a decade ago.

According to Stanley Druckenmiller, who ran Soros's Quantum
Fund for ten years, what gave Soros his competitive edge was "the
ability to compartmentalize, intelligence, coolness under pressure,
insight, a critical and analytical mind." But Druckenmiller also
repeatedly cited Soros's brilliance in 'pulling the trigger,' which, he
said, has little to do with analyzing or predicting trends, but is more
about "a sort of courage ...The ugly way to describe it would be
'balls.'" To Druckenmiller, that meant knowing when to bet it all.
"This is not something that can be learned. It is totally intuitive."

Soros himself thought of risk-taking as a way to clarify his analysis of what others might see as an ambiguous situation. "Going to
the brink...serves a purpose," he writes in *Soros on Soros*. "There is
nothing like danger to focus the mind, and I do need the excitement connected with taking risks in order to think clearly." When
you are a serious risk taker, he adds, "you need to be disciplined.
The discipline that I used was a profound sense of insecurity, which
helped alert me to problems before they got out of hand. If I gave

up that discipline, I would have to fall back on due diligence and other forms of routine, and routine is not my strong point...Once you take your success for granted, you let down your guard...That's when you have lost your ability to get out of trouble."

Using Price to Gain Competitive Advantage

Sam Walton was just plain cheap. He learned the value of a dollar early from his parents, who struggled to raise their family during the Great Depression. His father worked at a mortgage company and foreclosed on farms; his mother set up a family-run milk business. The two quarreled incessantly, except about one topic. "One thing my mom and dad shared completely was their approach to money: They just didn't spend it," Walton writes in his autobiography, *Sam Walton: Made in America.*

That devotion to a bargain became the foundation for Wal-Mart. Walton always resisted the temptation to move up profit margins at the expense of price; he lived by a simple formula: "Say I bought an item for 80 cents. I found that by pricing it at $1.00 I could sell three times more of it than by pricing it at $1.20.

I might make only half the profit per item, but because I was selling three times as many, the overall profit was much greater. Simple enough."

Walton is hardly alone. Many of the Top 25 leaders built enduring success for their organizations by managing their costs and prices to gain competitive advantage, though they did so in different ways. In Walton's case, his strategy was to buy low, sell at a discount, and make up for low margins by moving vast amounts of inventory. Wal-Mart, now the world's biggest company, has continued Walton's tradition by squeezing as much value as possible from its supply chain and passing along those savings to customers. Michael Dell's strategy has been similar. He, too, kept costs low by, in his case, using direct sales as his primary sales channel and integrating Dell's supply chain seamlessly with that of its suppliers. Jeff Bezos, CEO of Amazon.com, used technology and innovative sales discounting methods to grab market share from traditional bookstores as well as online rivals such as Barnesandnoble.com and Borders.com. In all three cases, balancing the cost-and-price equation was critical to these individuals' ability to build powerful companies.

SAM WALTON

The Challenge:

Wal-Mart Versus Kmart

The year was 1962. Downtown department stores in big cities still employed elevator operators wearing uniforms. In small towns, family variety stores sold everything from Easter finery to fishing rods, with first-name service.

Yet a revolution in retail was brewing as three merchants with national clout began to discount brand-name merchandise in big, suburban self-service stores. S. S. Kresge opened its first Kmart in Michigan that year. Dayton's of Minneapolis launched its first Target store. The nation's largest retailer, F. W. Woolworth, started Woolco.

In Rogers, Arkansas, Sam Walton drove from his office in nearby Bentonville and opened his first Wal-Mart. Over time, the family-owned discounter would eventually overtake the better-capitalized members of the Class of '62 with a small-town strategy that would make it the world's largest company. But that ending was far in the future. Walton was to experience a few ups and downs on his way to making a name for himself in the annals of business history. When the second Wal-Mart opened in Harrison, Arkansas, for example, David Glass, a drugstore retailer who would later succeed Walton as chief executive, attended the grand opening, which featured watermelon and donkey rides in the parking lot. "It was 115 degrees, and the watermelon began to pop and the donkeys began to do what donkeys

1918: Born in Kingfisher, Oklahoma. Father worked for a mortgage subsidiary of a large insurance company, and Sam often traveled with him as he repossessed hundreds of farms during the Depression. His mother ran a milk business.

1931: Becomes the youngest ever Eagle Scout in Missouri.

1936: Graduates high school in Columbia, Missouri, where he played on the state championship basketball and football teams. Voted Most Versatile Boy in his class.

1940: Earns business degree from the University of Missouri, moves to Des Moines, Iowa, and works as an $85-a-month management trainee at J.C. Penney.

1942: Drafted into the army, but because of a heart ailment is not sent to combat. Supervises security at aircraft plants and POW camps in California.

1945: Opens a Ben Franklin variety store in Newport, Arkansas, financed largely with loans from his father-in-law.

1950: Landlord refuses to renew the lease on the successful Ben Franklin store and puts his own son in business at the location. Walton relocates to Bentonville, Arkansas, and opens Walton's Five and Dime.

1960: Variety store chain grows to 15 stores with sales of $1.4 million.

1962: Opens first Wal-Mart discount store in Rogers, Arkansas.

1966: Attends classes held by IBM on using computers in retailing.

1969: Returns to Newport, Arkansas, with Wal-Mart's 18th store. Drives former landlord's son out of business.

1970: Initial public offering; opens first distribution center in Bentonville, Arkansas.

1971: Adds associates to profit-sharing plan enacted a year earlier for managers only.

1974: Thinking he would like more time to travel and play tennis, gives up CEO and chairman jobs but remains chairman of the executive committee.

1975: After being inspired by Korean workers, introduces a Wal-Mart cheer that begins, "Give Me a W" and ends, "What's that spell? Wal-Mart! Who's number one? The Customer!"

1976: Takes back chairman and CEO jobs after finding himself bored with retirement and concerned about a split developing in the company's management.

1977: Nationwide expansion speeds up with first acquisition, 16 Mohr-Value stores in Michigan and Illinois.

do and it all mixed together and ran all over the parking lot," Glass said. "And when you went inside the store, the mess just continued."

Walton eventually cleaned up his opening-day strategy and got on with the business of expansion. As he did, he became fixated on his biggest national competitor at the time—Kmart. Indeed, he considered his long struggle against the chain to be his company's greatest outside challenge. He would later write in his autobiography, *Sam Walton: Made in America*, that he "was in their stores constantly because they were the laboratory, and better than we were." Indeed, Walton went to Kmarts to do his own type of reconnaissance. "I spent a heck of a lot of time wandering through their stores talking to their people and trying to figure out how they did things. I've probably been in more Kmarts than anybody in the country."

After 10 years in business, Walton was running 50 Wal-Marts and 11 variety stores whose sales totaled $80 million a year. Kmart, which had 500 stores and $3 billion a year in sales, was still the leader. With its superior national distribution network, the Kmart chain was jumping across the country, planting its stores in highly populated urban centers and growing suburbs. Wal-Mart was plodding ahead with its strategy of saturating small-town America, county-by-county, with distribution centers ringed by stores.

Inevitably, those paths crossed. As Walton explained in *Made in America*, "For a long time, I had been itching to try our luck against them, and finally, in 1972, we saw a perfect opportunity in Hot Springs, Arkansas—a much larger city than we were accustomed to moving into but still close to home and full of customers we understood." The way Walton describes it, "We saw Kmart sitting there all alone, really having their way with the market. They had no competition, and their prices and margins were so high that they almost weren't even discounting. We got so much better so quickly you couldn't believe it."

Kmart retaliated by opening stores in four of Wal-Mart's better markets, Jefferson City and Poplar Bluff, Missouri and Fayetteville and Rogers, Arkansas. Walton would say later that Kmart's move into smaller towns led many back then to predict Wal-Mart's demise. Skirmishes continued throughout the South and Midwest into the late 1970s. As historian H.W. Brands relates, "Walton gave the order not to yield an inch. No matter how far Kmart dropped its price, Wal-Mart would not be undersold." A toothpaste war in North Little Rock, for example, found consumers happily paying just six cents a tube for Crest toothpaste. "Although Walton recognized that such extreme price-cutting couldn't last forever, in general he adopted the attitude that competition was healthy," Brand notes.

Wal-Mart's early underdog status forced it to find efficient ways to run the business, a discipline that eventually made the company stronger. For example, it focused on new distribution systems and cutting-edge technology to polish the operations side, because early on it had no distributors out in rural America. "Here we were in the boondocks," Walton said. "We didn't have distributors falling over themselves to serve us like competitors in larger towns. Our only alternative was to build our own warehouse so we could buy in volume at attractive prices and store the merchandise."

1979: Hits $1 billion in annual sales with 230 stores.

1983: Opens first Sam's Club warehouse stores; adds People Greeters—employees dressed in Wal-Mart vests smiling and welcoming customers at store entrance.

1984: Puts on grass skirt and dances the hula on the steps of Merrill Lynch's Wall Street offices after losing a bet that the company could not possibly hit a pre-tax profit of 8%.

1985: Named America's richest man by *Forbes* magazine.

1987: On a canoe trip with a Procter & Gamble vice president, decides the two companies should share information to improve inventory management at both companies, thereby breaking up the traditional reluctance of retailers and manufacturers to trade data about their businesses.

1988: Steps down again as CEO.

1990: Wal-Mart becomes the nation's largest retailer.

1991: First international store opens in Mexico City.

1992: Awarded the Medal of Freedom by President Bush on March 17. Dies of bone cancer at 74 on April 5. Later that year, his autobiography, *Sam Walton: Made in America*, is published.

1999: With 1.14 million workers, Wal-Mart is the world's largest employer.

2003: Wal-Mart tops Fortune 500 as both the world's largest and most-admired company.

2004: Wal-Mart tops Fortune 500 again as the world's largest company, but continues to encounter increasing resistance to its plans to build 'big box' shopping centers in large metro-politan areas. Opponents cite concerns over the company's labor practices, pay scales, and the impact its stores have on traffic congestion and local competitors. In addition, in the largest private civil rights case ever filed, 1.6 million current and former employees charge Wal-Mart with sex discrimination.

By 1981, Wal-Mart had saturated much of the nation's heartland but had little presence in the deep South. The company decided to buy the troubled Kuhn's Big K chain of 92 stores, even though Wal-Mart had only done one other acqui-sition and preferred to grow organically. The executive committee split down the middle on whether to go ahead with the purchase, reflect-ing Walton's own indecision over the deal. He eventually cast the deciding vote to go forward. The acquisition was a turning point. "We explod-ed from that point on," said Walton. "I think the Kuhn's deal gave us a new confidence that we could conquer anything."

In 1990, Wal-Mart at last overtook Kmart with sales of $32.6 billion. Five years later, Kmart's sales were a third of Wal-Mart's. "I don't know what would have happened to Wal-Mart if we had laid low and never stirred up the competition. My guess is that we would have remained a strictly regional operator," said Walton, adding that Wal-Mart would probably have ended up under the ownership of a national chain "looking for a quick way to expand into the heartland market. Maybe there would have been 100 to 150 Wal-Marts on the street for a while, but today they would all have Kmart or Target signs in front of them...We'll never know because we chose the other route."

In 2002, 40 years after the opening of its first store and 10 years after Walton's death, Wal-Mart surpassed Exxon to become the world's largest company. In January of the same year, Kmart filed for bankruptcy court protection. "If people believe in themselves," said Walton, "it's truly amazing what they can accomplish."

Leadership Lesson

The Hunt for Bargains

For Sam Walton, one way to keep prices down was by buying at a discount. When Walton was running his first business, a Ben Franklin variety store in Newport, Arkansas, he was always looking for suppliers that would charge less than distributors working with the Ben Franklin chain. He started driving into Tennessee to hunt for bargains. "I'd stuff that car and trailer with whatever I could get good deals on—usually on softlines [like] ladies' panties and nylons, men's shirts—and I'd bring them back, price them low, and just blow that stuff out the store."

One of the clerks from the first Wal-Mart store that opened in Bentonville in 1950 remembers Walton driving to New York to pick up a truck load of "zori sandals"—now known as flip-flops—which he tied together, dumped on a table, and sold for 19 cents a pair. The clerk, initially skeptical that this strange blister-causing footwear would sell at all, said that, on the contrary, they "sold like you wouldn't believe. I have never seen an item sell as fast, one after another, just piles of them. Everybody in town had a pair."

Walton's pricing strategy paid off. It helped him gain the loyalty of customers in small towns and rural communities, even though, ironically, his initial idea had been to go into business at a department store location in St. Louis, Missouri. His wife, Helen, however, balked at the idea of raising a family in a town with a population over 10,000, so he settled instead for Bentonville, Arkansas—population 3,000. Walton, too, believed in the American values embodied by small towns—family, church, and a loyal hunting dog in the back of the pickup. He also believed that rural communities were underserved by retailers, especially as national discount chains, including Kmart and Target, began to leapfrog from city to city, bypassing outlying areas when the population turned out to be too small to justify the chains' presence.

To attract attention to his low prices, Walton used some circus-like tricks. Indeed, his first business loan wasn't for real estate or inventory. He borrowed $1,800 to buy a soft-serve ice cream machine, which he put in front of that first store in Arkansas, next to the popcorn machine. This led to a strategy of filling his parking lots with sidewalk sales, bands, and small circuses—to spread the word about his business without having to spend money on advertising. But parking lot parties were also a way to connect with his customers, to give them something besides cheap motor oil and mattress pads. "Back then, we tried literally to create a carnival atmosphere in our stores," Walton later wrote. "We were only in small towns, and often there wasn't a whole lot else to do for entertainment that could beat going to the Wal-Mart."

Many Wal-Mart employees at Walton's stores came from these same small towns, which cemented even further Walton's connection to the local communities. Stores sponsored charity events—including kiss-the-pig contests—organized parades, and offered scholarships to help local kids attend college.

Walton's success in the execution of his pricing strategy was based on his ability to build an organization that acted in sync with his vision and values, one that emphasized homespun fun along with inexpensive marketing events. Wal-Mart employees in Nebraska, for example, formed a precision shopping-cart drill team to perform in local parades. In Georgia, Wal-Mart workers won first place in the Irwin County Sweet Potato Parade by dressing up as fruits and vegetables grown in the southern part of the state. In 1987, after losing a bet on a sales target, a Wal-Mart vice president put on pink tights and a blond wing and rode a white horse around the Bentonville, Arkansas town square.

"We're constantly doing crazy things to capture the attention of our folks and lead them to think up surprises of their own, things that are fun for the customers and fun for the [employees]," Walton said. "If you're committed to the Wal-Mart partnership and its core values, the culture encourages you to think up all sorts of [ways] to break the mold and fight monotony." All that fun, Walton believed, dropped down to the bottom line.

In the early days of the company, Walton admits he was chintzy with his employees. In 1970, when he began a profit-sharing program at Wal-Mart, he limited it to management only. A year later, at the urging of his wife and also because of union organizing at two Missouri stores, Walton reversed what he called his "single biggest business regret" and expanded the profit-sharing program to all employees. In another stroke of egalitarianism, he borrowed an idea from his first and only retail employer,

J.C. Penney, and began calling all Wal-Mart's employees "associates." "The truth is, once we started to experiment with this idea of treating our associates as partners, it didn't take long to realize the enormous potential it had for improving our business. And it didn't take the associates long to figure out how much better off they would be as the company did better."

Walton himself filled the role of cheerleader-in-chief, flying in to visit stores in the early part of the week and returning to Bentonville for managers' meetings on Fridays and Saturdays. "You gotta get out there. You have to talk to the people. You have to listen to them, mostly. You have to make them know this is a partnership. That's our secret. We have been able to motivate our people to a higher degree than most any other retail company."

Valuing a Dollar

Walton combined this penchant for discounting—he always insisted that the markup on any item be kept to 30%, no higher—with low overhead, to the point where some of the company's first stores were located in old cattle auction yards or former Coca-Cola bottling plants. His desire to keep operating costs low shows up in his book's first chapter titled, "Learning to Value a Dollar." In it he writes: "Every time Wal-Mart spends one dollar foolishly, it comes right out of our customers' pockets. Every time we save them a dollar, that puts us one more step ahead of the competition—which is where we always plan to be."

The rent Wal-Mart paid as late as the 1970s averaged less than one dollar per square foot. Walton's constant pressure to maintain low prices paid off in the crowds of people that overran Wal-Mart's stores, thrilled to have the same opportunity to buy discount goods as shoppers in bigger towns and cities. Heavy sales volume delivered the money Walton needed to continue expanding, and expand he did. Between 1976 and 1980 he opened 151 new stores, for a total of 276. During the 1970s and 1980s sales doubled about every three years. By 1990—five years after Walton had been named the richest man in America by *Forbes* magazine—sales rang up at $26 billion and profits totaled $1 billion.

Eventually, Walton would go head to head with chains like Kmart and other traditional retailers. Walton beat them all, not just through sheer size and relentless discounting, but also by his adoption of sophisticated technology that brought huge advantages in operational efficiency, including better inventory control, automated distribution centers, and satellite systems to collect, exchange, and store data. It's a competitive advantage the Wal-Mart empire still holds today.

Walton's timing also helped. Adrian Slywotsky, in his book *Value Migration*, writes about a "significant shift in the priorities of a large segment of American consumers" between 1970 and 1990. Consumers, he says, became increasingly price-sensitive, for good reason: "With tax, interest, medical, and social security payments growing from 25 percent of personal income in 1970 to 34 percent in 1990, the average middle-income family faced a real decline in its purchasing power." This was coupled with the shift of more women into the workforce and longer work weeks, all of which meant less time and money for the average woman to spend shopping.

Wal-Mart met the challenge. By discounting everything and piling it all into huge 100,000-square-foot stores, Wal-Mart "freed up 30–50% of [many consumers'] discretionary income...and trimmed an average of two hours a week off [their] shopping time." The company also opened the Sam's Clubs wholesale chain in 1983, a new business that sold goods in bulk and targeted customers who were even more price-conscious than the already price-conscious Wal-Mart shopper.

Walton never moved his company headquarters away from Bentonville, and he loudly disagreed with critics who suggested that by driving local stores out of business, he was destroying the very small towns he professed to believe in. "Of all the notions I've heard about Wal-Mart, none has baffled me more than this idea that we are somehow the enemy of small-town America," he said. Quite the contrary, Walton felt his stores were the salvation of many communities that were losing customers and jobs to larger towns nearby. A lot of these critics, Walton added, are probably "folks who grew up in small towns and then deserted them for the big cities decades ago. Now when they come home for a visit, it makes them sad that the old town square isn't exactly like it was when they left it back in 1954. It's almost like they want their hometown to be stuck in time, an old-fashioned place filled with old-fashioned people doing business the old-fashioned way."

Through much of the 1980s and into the 1990s, as Wal-Mart began its national expansion, analysts questioned whether the company would continue to flourish without Walton at the top (he died in 1992). According to William Cody, managing director of the Jay H. Baker Retailing Initiative at Wharton, "If you asked Walton, he would always downplay it, but now when you talk to anyone at Wal-Mart who worked for him, they still speak as if he's in the room. The culture that he gave that organization still pervades it 12 years after his death, although there are probably a lot more expensive cars in the parking lot than he would appreciate."

1965: Born the second of three sons in Houston; father is an orthodontist, mother a stockbroker.

1980: Buys first computer, an Apple II, then takes it apart to see how it works.

1982: Skips a week of high school to attend the National Computer Conference, the forerunner to Comdex, at the Astrodome.

1983: Starts selling upgraded PCs and components from his freshman dorm at the University of Texas; moves out of the dorm and into a condominium by the end of the school year.

1984: Leaves college, forms Dell Computer Corp. selling computers directly to customers, bypassing dealers.

1986: At Comdex unveils a 12 megahertz PC selling for $1,995 compared to IBM's 6 megahertz model selling for $3,995.

1987: Opens operations in the United Kingdom.

1988: Begins selling to large customers, including government agencies; raises $30 million in initial public offering.

1989: Gets caught with excess inventory of memory components and cancels overly ambitious Olympic program that combined desktop, workstation, and servers, but was more technology than consumers wanted.

MICHAEL DELL

The Challenge:

Managing Extraordinary Growth

Like the processing power of computer chips, for Michael Dell, founder and chairman of Dell Inc., business has grown at an exponential rate.

In its first year, the company moved four times, starting out in a 1,000 square-foot office and ending up in a 30,000-square-foot factory the size of a football field. Less than two years later, the company had to move again. In its first eight years, Dell's revenues grew about 80% a year, then nearly 60% for the next six years. "Our revenues are close to $50 billion and we are only 20 years old," Dell says. "If you look at most companies with those revenues, they have been around 50 or 100 years. The biggest challenge, by far, has been developing our organization to keep pace with the incredible growth of the business."

Such phenomenal expansion clearly came with some painful lessons for its youthful founder, who had spent his freshman year at the University of Texas at Austin running a business upgrading PCs. By the end of the year, sales were hitting $50,000 to $80,000 a month. His success inspired Dell to drop out of school and officially start Dell Computer Corp., the first company in the industry to sell custom-built computers directly to end users—thereby bypassing the then-current strategy of using computer resellers to sell mass-produced units.

In the early days, rapid growth fed the company's energetic can-do spirit. Engineers helped out on the assembly line. Salesmen stuffed RAM chips into tubes while taking orders on the phone. Dell pursued any and all opportunities for growth, including a new Olympic product line that encompassed desktop, workstation, and servers.

That was the problem. By the late 1980s, the company was big enough that when it stumbled, the mistake was obvious. In 1989, the company was caught with excess inventory in computer memory just as the industry was shifting from 256K to 1 megabyte. At the same time, the Olympic line proved itself to be a costly flop, in part because it overemphasized technology and "provided way more than what the customer wanted…" In short, Dell had taken its eye off the all-important end user.

Not one to touch a hot stove twice, Dell corrected those mistakes and enjoyed three years of growth that, looking back on them, once again set him up for a fall. The company strayed from its direct-selling model and entered the retail distribution chain in 1990. The move drove up sales, but turned out to be unprofitable. Then in 1992, Dell initiated price cuts in its assembled computers in order to head off competition. Sales grew from $890 million to $2 billion, severely straining the company's operations and management. "By the end of 1992, we still had the infrastructure of a $500 million company," Dell wrote in his book, *Direct from Dell: Strategies that Revolutionized an Industry.* "Just about every system we had installed a couple of years before was now unable to support our business," everything from the finance function to factory systems to the phone network.

1990: Begins selling through consumer stores such as CompUSA and Best Buy; opens manufacturing plant in Ireland to serve Europe.

1991: Converts product line to faster Intel 486 microprocessors.

1992: At 27, becomes youngest CEO of a Fortune 500 company.

1993: Posts quarterly loss due to exit from notebook and retail markets and restructuring in Europe. Cancels second public offering.

1994: Moves back into notebooks with Latitude line; opens first Asia-Pacific operations in Japan and Australia.

1996: Takes direct-order concept from telephone sales to the Internet at Dell.com.

1996: Enters the server market, triggering doubts by analysts that his PC company can sell the larger machines.

1997: Launches "The Soul of Dell" campaign to develop a culture within the company as it winds down from its early phase of rapid growth.

1998: Opens a sales and manufacturing center in China.

1999: Makes first acquisition, ConvergeNet, a storage-area equipment maker; opens plant in Brazil.

2000: Caught in the post-dot.com technology bust, Dell shares sink from $58 in March to $16 in December.

2001: First company layoffs; 1,700 employees, or 4.2% of its global workforce, are eliminated in response to slow PC sales.

2002: Ships first blade servers and enters the handheld market with Axim X5 PDA.

2003: Changes company name to Dell Inc., reflecting move into other electronics, including printers and television sets, after several years of slowing PC growth.

2004: Relinquishes CEO title to Kevin Rollins; remains chairman.

Dell knew he needed help. He brought in outside managers and introduced a strict profit & loss initiative that soon restored the company to profitability. By the end of 1993, *Upside* magazine named Dell turnaround CEO of the year, prompting him to comment: "I hope I don't ever win that award again."

For the most part, Dell has grown organically, with no big acquisitions or mergers to add instant employees, plants, or customers. To cope, Dell has tried to build a culture in which employees are equipped not just for their current job, but for new jobs ahead. "I see the rational kind of command and control structure—where everything is hierarchical—as working less and less well," says Dell. "What's really valued in leadership is not just execution, but also vision and inspiration and driving commitment."

The vision part was especially important. Every time the company entered a new geographic market, or offered a new product or service, it was met with skepticism, recalls Dell. "When the company was only three years old, we went outside the U.S. and all we heard was, 'It's not going to work here. Our country is different. You need to go back home. You're only 22 years old. Don't even try it here.'"

The same thing happened when the company began to offer notebooks and servers. Dell recalls a meeting with analysts in New York in 1996 as the company was entering the server market. "The reaction was, 'That's a bad idea. You guys are good at desktops and notebooks. You're going to waste a lot of money. We're not sure you have the technical capability.'" Dell, however, was looking one step ahead, arguing that if the company did not make this move, competitors would be able to charge high prices for their servers in order to subsidize their PC business and undercut Dell. "I never thought for a second that we weren't right. Not even for a nanosecond."

The doubts, according to Dell, have worked to his advantage. "Competitors believed the skepticism and massively underestimated the impact we would have on the system. Go back 10 or 15 years and they were saying, 'Oh well, Dell is selling to a small niche in the market; only a certain percentage of people will buy using that method.' Eventually, the niche becomes the whole market."

Meanwhile, with the explosive pace of growth an ongoing challenge, decision-making structures at the company evolved from a strategy of relying on in-house entrepreneurs to one that relied on outside advice, better long-term planning, and shared decision-making among top executives. In addition, while managers in most companies gain increasingly broad responsibilities as they move up the chain, at Dell, it works in reverse. Jobs continue to be segmented, with executives focusing more intensely on fewer aspects of the business at it grows.

Even Dell has phased himself out of a job several times, adding top executives to the "office of chairman." In 2004, he dropped the CEO title altogether to focus on long-range strategy and technology issues and leave day-to-day operations to Kevin Rollins, who had worked with Dell as an outside consultant. "We don't make any big decisions alone," says Dell. "We make them all together and our decision quality is far higher."

Despite the wild ride, Dell believes in rapid growth, even hypergrowth. Young companies, he suggests, need to stretch for seemingly impossible goals, as long as the company holds true to its place in the industry and adopts solid management disciplines.

Even Dell's youth and inexperience turned out to be assets. "They were helpful in the sense that I was naïve enough to think I could achieve these things," he says. "It was also helpful in that I was asking different questions and approaching the problems from a new perspective. That became part of our culture—to set extraordinary goals and learn by making mistakes."

Leadership Lesson

Cutting Out the Middleman

Walton believed that a bargain is a bargain anywhere—and that low prices are like magnets exerting an increasingly powerful pull on an ever-widening base of customers. At Dell, founder and chairman Michael Dell, too, says a low price translates into any language or culture. "The best value to the customer is an economic proposition that is valuable in Germany, France, Japan, or Norway. It doesn't matter. People have a sense of value that goes beyond a cultural affinity."

Michael Dell first experienced the PC business from the vantage point of a frustrated consumer. Buying a computer involved "incredible inefficiencies. It took way too long and it cost way too much money. And the level of service wasn't very good either," he says. Dell's idea was to cut out the middleman—computer dealers who sold machines manufactured by IBM and others—and eliminate the markups added at each level of distribution. Instead, the company would take an order directly from the consumer over the telephone or Internet, assemble the machine itself, and consolidate the markups into one ideal low price. Prices could decline even as profits rose. Manufacturers had relied on this model to sell to large industrial customers, but no one had yet seen the advantage of a similar approach with individual PC owners.

"There were obstacles," says Dell. "One of the earliest was, 'How do you convince people to buy a computer over the phone?'" The answer was to offer a 30-day money-back guarantee and on-site service. "We systematically eliminated the need for a store," says Dell. "We had to break the stereotype that this is a mail-order company. It's a computer manufacturer selling directly to customers."

Today, one of Dell's chief selling points—and strategic advantages—is low price driven by low costs. The company spends very little on innovating its own products; its research and development budget, for example, is less than 2% of revenues. Instead, Dell buys components from a handful of suppliers with whom it maintains close relationships, thereby guaranteeing continued high quality and reducing inventory throughout the entire chain through standardization. Dell can not only squeeze its own costs by ordering just the inventory it needs, but it also uses its data on customers' demand patterns to help suppliers better manage their own production. Taking orders for custom machines directly from customers also allows Dell an advanced look at what these customers want in the next generation of PCs. "Typically, manufacturers don't have a direct relationship with the customer," says Dell. "They are insulated. They let the dealer take care of that. We never had this history and it's a tremendous resource for us." The result has been "all kinds of efficiencies...and the ability to deliver lower prices and better value." Sharing these efficiencies with the customers and suppliers also ensures their loyalty in the future.

The Dell build-to-order model relies on other advantages that contribute to its ability to maintain low prices. Industry-standard technology, for example, is cheap and commoditized, thus adding to the ability to predict component costs and maintain certain price levels. Referring to what it calls Dell's "mastery of the computer industry's central dynamic: falling prices," a May 2004 article in *The Wall Street Journal* noted that technological advances "continually shrink the cost of disk drives, display screens, and computer chips. Each week, those costs fall by roughly 1%, causing PCs to lose value even as they sit in warehouses or showrooms." Dell's advantage, the article added, is that its "PCs are built only after a sale is made, with components procured at the cheapest prices available, a cost advantage over rivals of roughly 6% per unit, according to Dell estimates." Dell translates this cost advantage into a permanent price advantage by "adjusting prices minute-by-minute based on demand, costs, competition, and even type of customer."

That type of efficiency, and the price flexibility that it allows, has helped the company reach sales of $41 billion, gross margins of more than 18%, operating margins of more than 8%, and a reputation as the world's number one direct-sale computer vendor—achieving cost leadership and quality leadership at the same time, something many companies find hard to do.

So when the company wanted to expand its product lines in the mid 1990s, it turned to the business sector, selling network servers and entire systems to companies by using the same low-cost, direct-sales model that was effective in conquering the PC market. In the enterprise market, says David Croson, a former Wharton professor who is now at MIT, reliability matters more than anything else, so it wasn't a major jump for Dell to become a server name. "It was precisely the right strategy for Dell to try to leverage its brand name in the domestic household market to get more currency in the business market." In 2003, 76% of Dell's sales were generated by corporate customers.

Dell repeated that strategy again in the next decade when, after several years of anemic corporate spending on technology, the company decided that people's homes were the next frontier for its products. In 2003, Dell began to extend its brand into computer peripherals, most notably printers, whose sales topped one million the first year they were offered. Borrowing a play from its PC model, Dell partnered with other companies that make printers and printing components—with the exception of Hewlett-Packard and Canon, which have their own brands—and applied the Dell name the same way it had slapped its name on IBM clones with components made by Intel and Microsoft.

"I think we can save customers a lot of money there and deliver a lot of value," said Dell in a magazine interview, referring to the printer market. "There are [many] companies that have technology and intellectual property, but have no brand, no marketing, no distribution." Consequently, he predicted, the main players in the industry will see Dell "as a wonderful path to the market."

Dellevisions

After carving out space next to the desktop for its printers, Dell began to move into home entertainment. It introduced the Dell DJ—an MP3 player—and other consumer electronics, including liquid crystal display (LCD) televisions that became known as Dellevisions. "The PC is becoming more and more the center of the entertainment experience," Dell said at a conference on emerging technology at MIT in 2003. "The PC is not just a computing device—it's entertainment, it's music, it's videos, and it's television."

LCDs are another product that makes strategic sense, according to Dell. "We sell more LCD monitors than anyone in the world, so adding (television) tuners to them is a fairly obvious extension.

We're seeing a lot of customers use the monitor now. We started it in Japan, but it's taking off rapidly here. We have broadened [into] 17-, 23-, 30- [inch displays]. We will keep pushing those as well."

Dell has met some of the same resistance to selling its newer products over the telephone and Internet that it did when it first set out to sell computers direct to the public in the 1980s. "Printing is a good example. A lot of people said, 'Well, you can't sell printers. People have to see them.' We have sold way more printers than we thought we were going to," Dell says, adding that within six months the company had 12% of the all-in-one printer/fax/scanner market in the U.S. Monitors are another example. Again, industry wisdom said that customers had to see them before they would commit to a purchase. Again, that turned out to be untrue. Dell today has 18% market share.

But the move into consumer electronics brings the company into competition with an entirely new stable of competitors, including Sony, a consistently top-ranked global brand. Dell is undeterred. He sees competitors with margins that are at least fat enough to support dealers. "Look at the value chains in consumer electronics," he says. "They are really inefficient in terms of the dealers, the distributors, the cost structure. Take this 30-inch LCD that we just introduced for $3,299. It's at a much, much better price than any product out there—certainly than any product with a brand people would recognize."

Meanwhile, back on the personal computer front, Dell faces huge competition from Hewlett-Packard which, since it acquired Compaq Computer in 2002, has been challenging Dell's dominance in the market by selling PCs at prices so low that HP is barely making any money on the deals. Through its PC subsidization, HP hopes to attract new customers who will then purchase some of the company's higher-margin items, such as printers and consumer electronics.

According to Croson, Hewlett-Packard has chosen a strategy that would have "worked well when Dell was a PC-only company but that is suicidal in 2004. It has subsidized basic PCs, which are complements to Dell's entire non-PC product line...I'm sure that Dell would be delighted, on balance, if customers were to buy the zero-margin Compaq PC and then splurge on a $3,300 Dell LCD monitor. The Dell brand is placed on a dazzling display on the desktop and the HP/Compaq brand is attached to a piece of commodity hardware hidden under the desk."

In addition, Dell will say that while price is key to a brand, it's not everything. "We figured out a long time ago, if you just have a low price, that doesn't win. You've got to have some great value and satisfy customers to win over a long period of time." If the PC market is an indicator, Dell's strategy has built brand loyalty, ranking first among the major brands with a 77% repurchase rate, followed by Apple and Hewlett Packard/Compaq.

Dell is betting the formula will work with music and television. "We took that business model and applied it to adjacent products and services. Today we are enormous, but we still have only a 5% share in an $800 billion market. We have a long way to go."

JEFF BEZOS

The Challenge:

Raising Capital for Amazon.com

It's been a rough ride for Amazon.com since it raised $54 million in 1997 in one of the earliest blockbuster Internet initial public offerings. The e-commerce pioneer saw its market capitalization soar to $32.1 billion and then plummet to $8.9 billion when the Internet bubble burst; it watched brick-and-mortar retailers stream online to compete on its digital turf; and it lost billions of dollars over a span of six years, to the point where some dismissed the site as "Amazon.org" because, as the joke went, it appeared to be a not-for-profit company.

Yet according to Jeff Bezos, Amazon.com's 39-year-old founder and CEO, his biggest challenge came in 1995 when he tried to raise $1 million in seed capital to launch his company and keep it operating for at least two years. "There was a time there when the whole enterprise could have been extinguished before it had even started," he says.

During the now legendary trek from New York to California in 1994, Bezos's wife MacKenzie drove while he wrote a business plan on his laptop for a bookstore that would use the power of an emerging networking technology—the Internet—to revolutionize retailing.

If it had taken him just another year or two to reach Silicon Valley, he would have found investors clamoring to fund his idea, Bezos says. But the

1964: Born Jan. 12 in Albuquerque, New Mexico. His mother, Jacklyn Gise, marries Miguel Bezos, eventually an Exxon executive, who officially adopts him. He never knows his biological father.

1977: Bezos is profiled in a book, *Turning on Bright Minds: A Parent Looks at Gifted Education in Texas*. The book follows 12-year-old Jeff (renamed Tim to protect his privacy) through his school day in an advanced program at Houston's River Oaks Elementary School.

1982: Graduates from high school as the class valedictorian and enters Princeton with dreams of becoming a theoretical physicist. Surrounded by brilliant physics students, soon realizes that he has the potential to be a mediocre physicist at best. Switches majors and begins studying electrical engineering and computer science.

1986: Graduates summa cum laude, Phi Beta Kappa from Princeton with a bachelor of science in engineering. Becomes director of technology at Fitel, a startup with an ambitious plan to create a global equity trading network.

1988: After two years at Fitel, joins Bankers Trust looking for greater job security. Directs the bank's IT programs.

1990: At 26, becomes the youngest vice president in the history of Bankers Trust. Despite the honor, Bezos is bored and searches for a way to escape financial services. Decides his real ambition is to take advantage of the power of computers and automation to revolutionize business.

1990: Moves to another financial services firm, the hedge fund D.E. Shaw. Bezos is impressed with Shaw's intellect and creativity in developing new trading strategies.

1994: At D.E. Shaw, Bezos is told to explore new business opportunities in the suddenly exploding online world. Quickly realizes that selling books over the Internet makes the most sense given that book catalogues have been digitized for the past decade. Shaw is not prepared to delve into selling books over Internet.

1994: Quits his job and turns to his parents for seed money. To make sure he will always be welcome back home, he sets their expectations low by assuring them they will lose their entire $100,000 investment.

1994: Heads out West with his wife, MacKenzie Tuttle. Stops in Silicon Valley to enlist a handful of programmers and then heads to Seattle to set up a virtual bookshop.

investment frenzy that sparked the go-go days of the Internet bubble wouldn't kick in until 1997. Then, he adds, "people were raising $60 million with a single phone call."

Serial entrepreneurs—those who have a track record of starting up several companies—usually find venture capitalists' doors wide open, but Bezos had no such base from which to raise $1 million. The amount itself was too low to pique investors' interest. He did, however, have a $100,000 investment from his parents, the "classic seed round that comes from people who are betting on the entrepreneur rather than on the startup idea," Bezos notes.

Banking on a few contacts he had from his days working on Wall Street, Bezos managed to line up meetings with several angel investors in Silicon Valley. "I talked to all the people I knew who I thought could afford to invest $50,000," he says. Over a six-month period in early 1995, Bezos met with about 60 private investors. At the same time, he was also recruiting programmers to develop the website and working out the details of starting a company that, as yet, had no precedent. Raising the money "was more difficult than we expected," he says. "It is hard to get people to invest $50,000 because the worst-case outcome is not that unlikely; and the worst-case outcome is that you lose your entire investment."

Although no "capital crunch" existed in 1995, investors were still in the habit of carefully evaluating each business plan before opening their checkbooks. With little understanding or faith in the Internet's potential, they were skeptical. "We got the normal comments from well-meaning people who basically didn't believe the business plan; they just didn't think it would work," Bezos says. During his visits to investors, he recalled being told things like: "You can special order these books"…"Why would someone buy them online?"…"If you're successful, you're going to need a warehouse the size of the Library of Congress."

What made Bezos' challenge so difficult was that he needed to raise the entire $1 million at one time. He didn't have the luxury of getting $50,000 one week and then another $50,000 several weeks later. If somebody puts in $50,000, they worry that an entrepreneur might fritter away that money "before it could be combined with the rest for maximum benefit," Bezos says. "So toward the end of the process, it has to be synchronized."

Bezos never considered lowering the amount of capital he was seeking. "It wasn't a practical solution." If he had suddenly settled for $500,000, investors would have looked askance. "They would have said, 'What has changed so that now you only need $500,000, and is my $50,000 going to be at risk because you didn't raise the $1 million?'"

But a few prescient investors sensed that Bezos was ready to capitalize on a seismic shift that would revolutionize nearly every aspect of the business world. Other companies that would later attain legendary status—like Netscape, which created the web browser for non-technical Internet users, and Yahoo, which cataloged the exploding number of web sites—were appealing for seed money as well. The excitement about the web's potential was quietly beginning to percolate.

Bezos had more than just his persistence to help convince these wary private investors. Using

1995: Amazon.com launches in July. The Seattle yellow pages list a telephone number for Amazon.com resulting in a large number of people trying to place orders by phone. Bezos de-lists the company from the phone book, pushing to be an Internet-only retailer.

1997: Amazon.com begins trading on the NASDAQ as AMZN at split-adjusted price of $1.50.

1998: Amazon.com expands from being only a bookstore to selling music CDs.

1999: Amazon.com stock peaks at $113 per share, but the company has yet to turn a profit. Bezos remains focused on plowing all revenue back into expanding the company and establishing its brand name and reputation as the premier e-tailer.

1999: Expands to selling toys, electronics, software, and video games. Company also encroaches on eBay's territory by launching Amazon.com Auctions.

1999: Bezos ranks No. 19 on *Forbes* global rich list with a fortune in Amazon stock worth about $10 billion.

1999: Named *Time's* Person of the Year. *Time* noted that Bezos "not only changed the way we do things but helped pave the way for the future."

2001: After losing about $3 billion since its launch, Amazon.com finally turns a profit of $5 million in the 4th quarter.

2002: Bezos' fortune dwindles down to $1.5 billion in Amazon stock and he is now ranked No. 293 on *Forbes* global rich list. Amazon stock has gone from $1.50 per share at its IPO up to $115 and now sits at $12. Bezos says he has no interest in pushing the stock price higher in the short-term. Tells his employees to instead focus on customers as a long-term strategy rather than on competitors or stock prices.

2004: In January, Amazon reports its first full-year profit—earning $35 million for all of 2003—since its launch in 1995.

research from John S. Quarterman, one of the earliest people to collect Net usage data, Bezos reported to his investors that the web was growing at 2,300% a year. "Things growing at 2,300% are invisible today and everywhere tomorrow," he told them. The business plan he had typed on the cross-country drive envisioned an online retailer focused on selling books—a "bookstore with more than 10 times the selection of even the largest physical superstores." He explained that he was going to build something unique online that could not be replicated in the physical world or through catalogs.

Investors began to realize that he had planned well into the future. Bezos, for example, talked about connecting the power of the Internet with that of databases. He proposed a "personalization" service that could highlight products to a shopper based on his or her previous purchases. (This service launched in 2000.) "Ultimately that $1 million was raised, $50,000 at a time, with about 20 angel investors," Bezos says. A year later, venture capitalists began to line up outside Bezos' door. The blue chip venture capital firm Kleiner Perkins Caufield & Byers was among those that pumped $8 million into the company, a move that paid off handsomely when the e-tailer went public.

Looking back at the arduous process of raising seed capital, Bezos says he clearly benefited from the experience. "I don't think it should be easy. One of the things that happened to some of the companies who started during the bubble is that the money was too easy to raise." And so, he added, "it was not appropriately valued."

Leadership Lesson

Discount Warfare

What Dell did for PCs—cut costs and prices by eliminating distribution systems—Jeff Bezos, chairman and CEO of Amazon.com, did for books. He avoided the lavish office furniture, foosball tables, and sushi lunches that marked many dot-com start-ups in the 1990s. Instead, he prided himself on keeping expenses low. Even employee desktops were simply old doors. "It's a symbol," Bezos says, "of the fact that we spend money on things that matter to customers."

On the other hand, Amazon.com has never shied away from spending cash to gain market share. In May 1999, just as Barnesandnoble.com was preparing for its initial public offering, Bezos announced that his company would begin offering best-sellers at 50% off list price, undercutting all his competitors but at the same time guaranteeing that almost no one would make any money. "This is not a sale, this is not a promotion, this is everyday low pricing," said Bezos in a company statement at the time. Barnesandnoble.com and Borders.com responded by matching Amazon.com's prices, but the online retailer—which had already fine-tuned the act of squeezing out inefficiencies by harnessing web technologies and industrial automation processes—was several steps ahead of them.

In 2001, Borders.com threw in the towel and instead partnered with Amazon.com, which took on the job of managing and fulfilling orders placed on a co-branded site. Bezos had no intention of gloating over the victory. "The goal here is to provide an even better customer experience," he said at the time. The partnership offered customers the option of reserving books over the web, and picking them up or returning them at a Borders store. It also publicized invitations to author book readings.

To cut prices even further, Amazon.com in 2001 brought back a promotional stunt that was common during the Internet boom. The company offered free shipping for orders over $99, telling customers they no longer had to factor in shipping charges when considering an online purchase. Less than a week later, Barnesandnoble.com followed suit. The move didn't go over big on

Wall Street, which expected Internet companies to focus on making a profit rather than returning to the pre-bust days of offering freebies just to attract new customers.

Nevertheless, Bezos charged ahead. In June 2002, he slashed the order minimum for free shipping to $49, unconcerned over how the strategy would affect the bottom line over the next few quarters. "When you lower prices, it always hurts your results in the short term, always, because the additional volume that you ultimately get from having lower prices does not materialize in the short term," says Bezos. "They materialize in the long term. To be relentlessly focused on lowering prices as a part of our DNA requires a long-term focus."

Despite the burden of offering free shipping, Amazon managed to steadily increase its revenues. In a filing with the Securities and Exchange Commission in 2002, the company cited new efficiencies in logistics, based in part on the use of "injection shipping"—a process that sent large quantities of products destined for one area of the country to geographic hubs. Bezos was onto something. During the second quarter of 2002, the company recorded sales of $806 million, an increase of 21% from the same quarter a year earlier.

In August 2002, Amazon.com dropped the minimum order threshold to $25 for free shipping. "If we can get more productivity in our business and are able to lower our cost structure, we are determined to give that back to the customers in the form of lower prices," says Bezos. "Decisions like making shipping free on orders over $25 are extremely expensive; that one is well in excess of $100 million annually. But we know customers like it; we know we can afford it; and we know that in the long term, it will make our business stronger and more valuable."

Bezos, however, didn't think of price as the only way to serve his customers. He was also determined to let them rave or complain about Amazon.com's service. To make the point, he recounts receiving an email from a 80-year-old woman early in the company's history who told him she loved the service but had to wait for her son to visit to break open Amazon.com's packaging. Bezos admits that the packaging was effective in keeping books and compact discs in pristine condition, but it was like opening a vault. As a result of the woman's email, Bezos had the packaging redesigned.

"If there's one thing we've figured out," he says, "it's that Internet customers have more power. If we make customers happy, they can evangelize for us and tell 5,000 friends on newsgroups and so on. Likewise, if we make customers unhappy, in the old world they would have told a few friends. Now they can also tell 5,000 people how horrible we are."

This realization also led Amazon.com to cut short an experiment with television advertising in 2002. "If you use television advertising, you are building your brand based on what you say about yourself," says Bezos, who admits the strategy works successfully for many companies. Instead, Bezos says Amazon.com will continue to build its reputation by making promises to customers and then fulfilling them. "In our opinion, every time we make a promise and keep it, we gain brand reputation," he says. "We built our brand by doing things well for our customers and they learn out of experience what this means."

7

Managing the Brand

Brand is one of those intangible assets that are vital to a company but hard to measure, like customer satisfaction and good will. Yet a number of the Top 25 leaders have been extraordinarily successful in understanding the value of their brands and leveraging them in creative, profitable ways.

Based on her ability to establish an emotional connection with her audience, Oprah Winfrey, chairman of Harpo Inc. and its group of companies, recognized early on the importance of protecting her brand, which, in her case, is herself. She resisted attempts from outsiders to license her name on a wide variety of products, choosing instead to start up her own magazine and cable television channel, among other initiatives. Richard Branson realized that his success with Virgin Records paved the way to extending his brand into such non-related areas as discount air travel, clothing, and cell phones. Branson guessed that hip, young consumers already aware of the Virgin name would assume that his other products offered the same quality and distinction. Lee Iacocca, too, instinctively understood the power of personal branding when as CEO, he appeared in Chrysler commercials, reassuring potential customers about the quality of his company's cars. He laid his personal credibility on the line to build Chrysler's brand equity.

Depending on a brand for competitive success can, of course, be risky, as Coca-Cola found out when it tried—and failed—to introduce New Coke in the 1980s. The emotional loyalty consumers felt to the Coke brand didn't extend to the new product. But the effort can also be successful, as IBM found when it expanded its product line from mainframe computers to PCs and, finally, to comprehensive business solutions.

OPRAH WINFREY

The Challenge:

"The Ability to Be Myself"

To understand how hard Oprah Winfrey has had to work to become one of the most recognized and beloved celebrities in the U.S., it helps to remember where she came from.

Back in the mid-1970s, when she was 22 and her career as a television journalist was faltering, she moved from her hometown of Nashville, Tennessee to Baltimore, Maryland to be a reporter and co-anchor for a newly expanded hour-long evening news broadcast. The problem: Winfrey did not have the emotional distance and objectivity expected of traditional journalists.

"It was not good for a news reporter to be out covering a fire and crying with a woman who has lost her home…," she recalled. "It was very hard for me to all of a sudden become 'Ms. Broadcast Journalist' and not feel things. How do you *not* worry about a woman who has lost all seven children and everything she's owned in a fire? How do you *not* cry about that?"

Co-workers also considered her unprofessional for straying from her scripts, for not knowing the town, and for letting viewers see she was uncomfortable with her co-anchor. Station managers criticized her appearance and ordered a makeover that included new clothes and a treatment that made her hair fall out. A voice coach hired by the station told Winfrey she was too nice for TV news and needed to sound tougher. Nine

1954: Born in Kosciusko, Mississippi, illegitimate daughter of Vernita Lee, a domestic worker, and Vernon Winfrey, a soldier. Winfrey, unaware he has fathered a child, is not present. Her mother intends to name the baby Orpah, after a Biblical character, but a clerical error transforms the name to Oprah in the birth registry. Vernita Lee moves to Milwaukee to find work, leaving Oprah on a Mississippi pig farm with her grandmother Hattie Mae.

1960: Winfrey joins her mother and mother's boyfriend in Milwaukee.

1962: When Lee and her boyfriend break up, taking care of two daughters is too much for Lee, who keeps Oprah's younger half-sister Patricia and sends Oprah to Nashville to live with her father, Vernon, and his new wife Zelma. Now out of the Army, Vernon has one job cleaning floors and another washing dishes. At the end of the summer, Oprah returns to her mother in Milwaukee.

1968: By 14, she has been raped by one relative and sexually abused by another, and at one point has run away from home. Oprah, concealing a pregnancy, is sent back to Nashville by her mother to live with Vernon and Zelma. Oprah has a miscarriage. She will live with Vernon and Zelma until she is 22. Later, she credits the couple's strong discipline for straightening her out.

1971: Classmates at East Nashville High School name her "Most Popular." While collecting a pledge as a volunteer for The March of Dimes walkathon, she meets a local radio station manager who is looking for part-timers to read the news on weekends. Liking her voice, he asks her to audition, then gives the 17-year-old a $100-a-week job.

1972: Wins Miss Black Nashville title.

1973: Becomes reporter and anchor at WTVF-TV in Nashville. At 19, she is the youngest person ever to anchor in Nashville, and the first African-American woman.

1976: Moves to Baltimore to co-anchor the 6 p.m. news on WJZ-TV.

1977–1983: Hosts WJZ's *People Are Talking* with co-host Richard Sher.

1984–1985: Moves to Chicago's WLS-TV to host the morning talk show *AM Chicago*.

months after starting at the station, she was removed from the anchor desk.

Then Winfrey got a break. A recently hired manager took over and made her co-anchor of a new morning talk show that would compete with a similar and highly rated program hosted by Phil Donahue. The innovative show, *People are Talking*, had a relaxed, unscripted, conversational format with lots of interaction between the co-hosts, their guests, and the audience. Winfrey thrived, and stayed with the show for six years, consistently beating Donahue. Her approach was—as it still is—to forgo the reporter's standard questions and look for the personal details her audience wants to know.

"When Donahue interviews Dudley Moore, he asks about his next movie," writes biographer George Mair. "Oprah wants to know how such a short man can make love to all the very tall girlfriends Moore has had."

Winfrey, as chairman of her closely held company, Harpo Inc., now runs a sprawling media empire, much of it designed to promote her own brand of self-help advice. "My message is: You are responsible for your own life," she told *Fortune*. At its heart is the biggest revenue-generator, *The Oprah Winfrey Show*, reaching viewers in more than 100 countries and topping the U.S. ratings for nearly two decades. Then there is her magazine, *O, The Oprah Magazine*, with more than two million readers. *O* was widely proclaimed the most successful start-up magazine in history. Other Winfrey companies make movies and television specials and produce content for her website, Oprah.com.

Along the way, Winfrey has adhered to a simple strategy for her career and business: to follow her instincts. She recognizes that her audience is drawn to her natural personality, not a packaged product. Every cover of her magazine, for example, features a glossy photo of Winfrey herself, and she closely oversees all content, even though she had no magazine experience before launching the publication in 2000. She continually feeds her audience's desire to know her, openly discussing sexual abuse she suffered as a child and her ongoing struggle with her weight. Winfrey is not a distant celebrity; she's the wise, generous, next-door neighbor.

In one famous scene on her show, she wheeled 67 pounds of lard onto the set to proudly demonstrate her recent loss from an all-liquid diet—not a typical act for a CEO. Later, she openly addressed the unhappy aftermath. "By sharing her own setbacks, like her confidence-busting weight gain after a drastic liquid diet in 1988, she also signaled that it was all right to fail," *Newsweek* said.

Ironically, Winfrey doesn't think of herself as a businesswoman, according to a 2002 article in *Fortune*, her only extensive interview with a business publication. She said she could not read a balance sheet, had no business role models, and had declined seats on the boards of AT&T, Ralph Lauren, and Intel. With no squad of MBAs behind her, she claimed her business decisions were seat-of-the-pants "leaps of faith," adding: "If I called a strategic planning meeting, there would be dead silence, and then people would fall out of their chairs laughing."

And yet Oprah is nothing if not strategic. Recognizing that her identity is her brand, she is careful not to lose control of it—refusing, for example, to license her name for use on everyday products. In addition, she has steadfastly kept her

1985: Makes her acting debut as Sofia in Steven Spielberg's *The Color Purple* and receives Academy Award and Golden Globe nominations for the role. Her television program is renamed *The Oprah Winfrey Show*.

1986: Incorporates her privately held company, Harpo, Inc., using her name spelled backwards.

1986: Winfrey's show is syndicated.

1987: Establishes the Oprah Winfrey Foundation. By the end of 2003, she has given about $32 million to African and African-American causes.

1988: Incorporates Harpo Productions Inc., becoming the first black woman to own a production studio.

1995: Goes online with "Oprah" site on America Online.

1996: Begins Oprah's Book Club segment on the TV show, quickly gaining the power to turn obscure titles into bestsellers. Receives the George Foster Peabody Individual Achievement Award and IRTS Gold Medal Award.

1997: Establishes Oprah's Angel Network, a non-profit organization for the needy.

1998: *Time* magazine names her one of the most influential people of the 20th century. Winfrey receives the National Academy of Television Arts & Sciences Lifetime Achievement Award. She co-founds Oxygen Media, which in 2000 launches Oxygen Network, a cable TV channel aimed at women that is available in 48 million U.S. homes by 2004.

1999: Receives the National Book Foundation's 50th Anniversary Gold Medal. Winfrey removes herself from future Emmy consideration that year and the next year as well. Awards are not her goal, she explains.

1999–2000: With her long-time partner Stedman Graham, teaches a fall semester leadership course at Northwestern University's Kellogg School of Business.

2000: In a partnership with Hearst Magazines, launches the bimonthly publication, *O, The Oprah Magazine*. Hosts the first of a series of daylong, interactive workshops titled the "Live Your Best Life Tour," drawing sell-out crowds.

2001: Winfrey and Harpo Productions launch the syndicated TV show *Dr. Phil*, with Dr. Phil McGraw, a "life strategist" who appeared on The Oprah Winfrey Show from 1998 through 2002.

companies private, so she does not have to answer to shareholders or take on projects she would not feel comfortable with, however profitable they might be. She has a hand in everything her empire does.

"Winfrey is used to ironclad control," *Newsweek* said. "A shrewd businesswoman, she still signs all the checks of more than $1,000 for her Harpo Entertainment Group…She binds employees at all levels to strict, lifelong confidentiality agreements. And she guards her off-air ventures as fiercely."

"If I lost control of the business, I'd lose myself—or at least the ability to be myself," Winfrey said. "Owning myself is a way to be myself."

Leadership Lesson

Preaching to the Faithful

Early in her career, Oprah Winfrey realized that her business success depended in large part on her personality, an appealing, down-to-earth image she carefully presented to what would become millions of adoring fans. She translated that insight into a decision to maintain complete control of all that is Oprah. She has kept her companies private and preserved majority control—even though she might have become even richer by going public. Because employees are required to sign lifelong confidentiality agreements, there have been no kiss-and-tell books or interviews by past or present insiders that could tarnish the Oprah brand.

Winfrey is directly involved in planning her TV show and magazine contents. The magazine always displays a photo of Winfrey on its cover, making it clear this is her magazine, not just a publication authorized to use her name. "Food marketers, clothing designers, perfume manufacturers, book publishers, and innumerable pie-in-the-sky entrepreneurs have tried to persuade Oprah to license her name for their products," noted *Fortune* magazine in 2002. "...Oprah has steadfastly resisted these entreaties."

Winfrey's brand is a brilliant mix of spontaneity and careful planning. This is how *Essence* magazine described one of Oprah's four "Live Your Best Life" events in 2003: Oprah "bounds onto the stage as the theme music from her television show crescendos. 'Looking good, Philadelphia!' she whoops to the thunderous applause of

2002: Disbands the book club, saying it had become too hard to find a good new book every month.

2003: Becomes the first African-American woman on *Forbes* list of billionaires, ranking as 427th richest with a net worth estimated at $1 billion. Revives the book club with an emphasis on classics.

2004: With a net worth of $1.1 billion, ranks 514th on *Forbes* list of richest people. Signs three-year contract extension—from 2008 to 2011—for her daytime TV show.

the 2,800 faithful who are now standing, rocking to the music, pumping the air, and screaming for their girl, the mighty O. For the next several hours, as Oprah preaches and prances, jokes, quotes her favorite self-help sages...and recounts parts of her remarkable life story, her power is palpable and transforming. It's easy to be a true believer."

Two years earlier, *Newsweek* magazine described the typical Winfrey mix of substance and entertainment: During a business school course on leadership at Northwestern University, students were discussing the civil rights movement. "The night's topic is...heavy," the magazine wrote. "But Winfrey knows how to keep the three-hour class moving. When guest speaker Coretta Scott King talks earnestly of her late husband's belief in service as the key to leadership, Winfrey raises her hand, stands and asks, "I mean, on your first date was [the Reverend King] just sitting up talking to you about service?"

Winfrey's carefully chosen staff works together to create exactly the right product mix for her shows. "I surround myself with people who are smarter than I am...[then] I feel I can learn something," Winfrey says. "My whole team watches a lot of TV. They are very current and interested in keeping the show's finger on the pulse of what is happening in pop culture."

Part of Oprah's formula is to present something of interest to nearly everyone; in addition, many of her shows focus on success, often as a result of overcoming adversity. The list of topics from Winfrey's TV schedule in the first part of 2004 is typical. The last three shows in January included *Inside the Human Body*, *Live: Oprah's 50th Birthday Bash!*, and *Inside Detox*. A week in the middle of January included *Lisa Ling Investigates Dowry Deaths*, *Children Left Home Alone*, *Automatic Millionaire: How to Become One*, and *Randy Jackson: Inside Gastric Bypass*. Through the winter schedule, viewers could hear discussions about people in prison for having sex with teenagers, weight loss success stories, older women having affairs with younger men, what not to wear, and the gorgeous men of decorating.

In addition to providing a virtual tour of middle-class culture, Winfrey is brilliant at knowing what sells and how to sell it. Back when she became host of her own TV show in 1985, the main daytime fare for women was soap operas and talk shows hosted by men. Winfrey immediately recognized that women wanted their entertainment to offer both substance and empathy. A chief factor in her brand appeal was, and still is, her willingness to be open about herself, whether that means discussing weight-loss battles, sexual abuse as a young woman, or career setbacks. She comes across as honest, straightforward and accessible, not a distant celebrity. She asks questions she thinks women want answered that men are unlikely to ask; she doesn't tell women how to seek perfection, and she doesn't make them feel inadequate.

Having connected with her audience on TV, Winfrey has been able to find other ways to cement the bond. In 2000, with her magazine *O*, the strategy has been to talk frankly about issues that interest women and to give customers good value. For example, "*O*'s table of contents runs on page 2 instead of page 22, unusual in a women's magazine. Advertisers would prefer that readers wade through a bunch of ads as they search for the table of contents, but Oprah said, 'Let's put the readers first,' recalls Hearst's [magazine president] Cathleen Black."

The reviews of *O* were right on target. "Without a single guide to thin thighs or a saucier sex life, *O* is a glossy rendering of Winfrey's on-air motivational crusade, encouraging readers to revamp their souls...," gushed *Newsweek*. "*O* reflects Oprah's gift for balancing preachiness...with practicality. And she knew that balance would sell, since it's exactly what informs her TV shows, where one day she'll interview [actor] Jim Carrey and the next she'll tackle the troubles of oppressed women in Afghanistan," trumpeted *Fortune*. In 2001, Winfrey launched the syndicated TV show *Dr. Phil*, with "life strategist" Phil McGraw. Wharton marketing professor Barbara Kahn describes these ventures as examples of Winfrey's ability to identify and "take on causes or business endeavors that speak to her customers' needs."

They speak to her own needs as well. "You'd be hard pressed to find another American chief executive this disarming, this confessional. But it's oh-so-Oprah," according to *Fortune*. "Sitting in an overstuffed armchair in her office in Harpo Inc.'s Chicago headquarters...the chairman swears that if she is a businesswoman, it's in spite of herself." Oprah addresses, and dismisses, the idea that underneath all the empathy, she is the consummate marketer. "I really don't define my happiness by my business decisions," she says. "I don't care about being bigger, because I'm already bigger than I ever expected to be. My constant focus is on being better."

1924: Born Oct. 15 in Allentown, Pennsylvania, to Italian immigrant parents; his father, who ran restaurants and a car rental business, brought Lee's mother back to Pennsylvania from Italy as a 17-year-old bride.

1934: At age 10, helps family through Depression by pulling shoppers' groceries home with a wagon.

1945: Graduates from Lehigh University, classified 4F for military service because of rheumatic fever as a child.

1946: Earns M.E. from Princeton University, joins Ford Motor Co. as an engineer trainee in Dearborn, Michigan.

1947: Moves into sales and marketing at the company's district office in Chester, Pennsylvania.

1949: Appointed zone manager in Wilkes-Barre working with 18 dealers.

1953: Promoted to assistant manager in the Philadelphia district.

1956: Devises a marketing campaign "56 for '56" in which any customer who puts 20% down would have payments of $56 a month for three years. The promotion moves the Philadelphia district from last in sales to first.

1956: Moves back to Dearborn as national truck marketing manager.

1957: Promoted to car marketing manager of the Ford division.

LEE IACOCCA

The Challenge:

A Big Tune-Up for Chrysler

Lee Iacocca did all he could to turn around the financial disaster that was Chrysler.

After firing 33 of Chrysler's 35 vice presidents, he assembled a new management team, including defectors from Ford Motor Co. He convinced Chrysler's unions to cut their hourly wages. Twice. In 1980, the company slashed $500 million in costs and laid off more than 15,000 salaried workers. Finally, Iacocca went to Washington, D.C., and subjected himself to harsh Congressional hearings before receiving $1.5 billion in U.S. loan guarantees.

Still, the world's third-largest automaker was operating on pocket change. The company was down to just $1 million in cash on November 1, 1981. "All my life has been managing crisis," says Iacocca. "That was my defining moment. We were bankrupt. I just didn't tell anyone."

Iacocca came to Chrysler in 1978 after a story-book career at Ford. He developed the phenomenally successful 1964 Mustang and had risen to become president of the company. Ultimately, he clashed with family heir and chief executive Henry Ford II and was dismissed in a highly public firing. Months later, Iacocca took control of deeply troubled Chrysler.

Now a regular speaker on the lecture circuit, Iacocca says that after all his years at Ford and Chrysler, he believes business leadership boils down to two simple points: Hire good people and set priorities. "It's that simple," he says. "I get $75,000 to give speeches saying essentially that."

At Chrysler, the priorities were all too obvious. Cash, for example. "I was always looking at our cash. I looked at it daily, sometimes hourly," recalls Iacocca. Meanwhile, each day required sweeping decisions. Iacocca says he is all for research, and in fact did extensive studies when preparing to launch the Mustang. At Chrysler, however, there was rarely time to form a committee and order a research analysis. "Even people high up the ladder don't want to take undue risks. They want to know every fact before they make a decision. But sometimes, it's a leap of faith. Finally, you've got to do something. You can't just stand there."

To show his commitment to Chrysler, Iacocca agreed to an annual salary of just $1 plus stock options. "You've got to get everyone and say, 'Hey guys and gals, We're all in this together,'" says Iacocca. "It all turns around once you get them leading with the idea that we're all going down the chute together." Iacocca calls it equality of sacrifice. "If we're all sacrificing equally, people will move mountains for you."

He was always mindful of the world beyond his own company. Government, in particular, was an outside force that shaped his work, from safety and environmental regulations to interest-rate policy to trade relations with Japan, Detroit's nemesis at the time. "A lot of CEOs—and successful ones—don't want to get involved in politics," he says. "They want to stay below the radar screen. They don't want to go to Washington. But I had to go. I needed to get a billion dollars."

1960: Appointed vice president and general manager of the division, replacing Robert McNamara who had been promoted to president.

1964: Rolls out the Mustang pony car.

1965: Becomes vice president of car and truck group overseeing planning, production, and marketing of all cars and trucks in the Ford and Lincoln-Mercury Divisions.

1967: Oversees development of Mercury Cougar and Marquis.

1970: Named president of Ford.

1978: Fired by Henry Ford II with the words, "Sometimes you just don't like somebody." Chrysler hires him as chief operating officer.

1979: Becomes Chrysler's CEO and begins negotiations on a $1.5-billion federal loan guarantee.

1982: Heads restoration of the Statue of Liberty and Ellis Island.

1983: Chrysler begins paying back federal loans; launches K-cars.

1984: Chrysler minivan debuts; *Iacocca: An Autobiography* sells 7 million copies.

1986: Earns $20.5 million at Chrysler and is top-paid executive in America.

1987: Chrysler buys American Motors Corp.

1988: Decides against Democratic presidential nomination; second book, *Talking Straight*, becomes No. 1 bestseller.

1992: Turns down U.S. Senate seat in Pennsylvania; retires from Chrysler.

1993: Selected by President Clinton to promote the North American Free Trade Agreement.

1994: Forms an investment bank, with stakes in casino-gaming.

1995: Kirk Kerkorian, with Iacocca's support, launches unsuccessful takeover bid for Chrysler.

1998: Daimler-Benz AG buys Chrysler.

2000–01: Iacocca holds secret talks with Daimler-Chrysler CEO Juergen Schrempp about a possible return to Chrysler. Schrempp eventually rejects the idea.

2004: Iacocca promotes environmentally friendly vehicles through his entrepreneurial venture, EV Global Motor Works, which sells electric-powered bikes.

The government loan guarantees, and $655 million in concessions from 400 banks, only bought Chrysler time, says Iacocca. The company had been betting its turnaround on its new K-cars, the Aries and Reliant, but they debuted to mixed success in 1981.

Chrysler continued to bleed right down to that last $1 million in cash. Iacocca even proposed a merger with rival Ford, but was rebuffed. He dug back in. Chrysler went to its suppliers, who were carrying accounts receivable of about $800 million a month, and asked for payment extensions. Some refused and quit shipping, briefly causing the closure of several plants. Other major suppliers, including National Steel and Goodyear Tire, agreed to extend payment terms.

The company was able to ride out yet another crisis. "Most people don't focus and stay with it. To me, it just takes perseverance. Sometimes you don't even know your own strength," says Iacocca. Finally, in 1982, the U.S. economy and Chrysler began to recover. Iacocca never missed a payroll, and in 1983, with great fanfare, he repaid the government early. "In the end, at Chrysler, we finally turned it around by focusing on building good cars. Prior to that we were just messing around."

Even while Iacocca was slashing costs, he insisted on investing in new products. Without them, he argued, Chrysler would have nothing to sell if it did manage to survive. He spent $700 million to develop one particular product he had championed at Ford. Henry Ford II had shot the idea down.

And so it was that Chrysler introduced the minivan in 1983. "The Mustang was a great thing, but the homerun, the cash cow, was the minivan," says Iacocca. By the end of that year, the company was making money and Iacocca had become a folk-hero. His commercials for Chrysler, asking consumers to give his brand a try, made him a celebrity. "I didn't want to go on TV, but again it was a crisis. When you're dying, you don't need a celebrity," he says. "People like underdogs and here I was. They could see that I was the guy who had to go home and make sure the car didn't rattle or leak."

Through it all, Iacocca was driven by a passion for cars and the industry, even though vehicles are so complicated now he can no longer tinker under the hood. "You've got to love what you're doing, not just like it. You can even have some fun in big business if you do." Chrysler, Iacocca adds, was enough fun for one lifetime. "I wouldn't want to do it twice. It was that tough."

172 Lasting Leadership

Leadership Lesson

Follow Your Market

Although Lee Iacocca had trained as an engineer, he soon became a marketing whiz at Ford Motor Co. where he developed the smash-hit Mustang brand. After he moved to Chrysler in 1979, he would develop and market another brand: Lee Iacocca.

It was at Ford, however, where Iacocca learned that the success of any brand is rooted in the approval of customers. As he rose through the ranks in Detroit, he saw how that seemingly simple idea was sometimes overlooked as auto executives focused on finance, operations, and other concerns. "I was a dealer guy," Iacocca says. "I went to all the dealer meetings to find out if the public really liked our cars, and if not, why not."

In 1960, still at Ford (where he would remain for almost two more decades until Henry Ford II fired him in 1978), Iacocca had sensed a new optimism in the country and realized that it would coincide with the growing economic power of a younger generation. To appeal to that market, Iacocca promoted the sporty, inexpensive Mustang brand. It was an immediate sensation.

At Chrysler, 20 years later, he met that market again. By now, the members of the Mustang generation had married and were transporting children to soccer games. "I didn't really plan on soccer moms, but I said, 'Follow your market,'" Iacocca remembers. The original Mustang buyers were now 40 "and they had changed. They had gotten married, had a couple of children, and entered the minivan world, a phenomenon that blew me away...I got them with the Mustang and when they were 40, I got them again."

Iacocca says Ford was already working on a small car when he was made general manager of the Ford Division more than 40 years ago. "The Mustang was more of a gut feeling. What I did was get a designer to re-skin it—to get it a new dress." The minivan, however, was the result of intense research, first at Ford, then again at Chrysler. And what the research showed was that customers wanted the utility of a van, but wanted to be able to park it in a garage. "They also wanted to sit high up, especially the women, and they wanted access to the kids yelling in the back. They had to be able to walk through to the back." Iacocca said the minivan was an idea that was "followed up and executed well and we made a ton of money" on it.

Iacocca also acknowledges that successful branding decisions aren't always planned out in advance. In 1987, for example, Chrysler acquired American Motors, primarily because Iacocca liked the Jeep brand. "I didn't even know they were selling SUVs," he says. "If you had told me in 1987 that the market for SUVs in the U.S. alone would be 4.5 million, I would have said, 'You're wacky.'" Sometimes it's timing, he notes, "and sometimes it's luck. The minivan is something I can explain intelligently, but not the SUV phenomenon—that people would be driving SUVs, polluting the world more than they probably should."

Meanwhile, somewhere along the road to restoring Chrysler's reputation, Iacocca himself became a brand.

During the struggle to win approval for government loan guarantees to Chrysler, the blunt-talking CEO had emerged as a national celebrity. Once that battle was won and the company stabilized financially, Iacocca faced the challenge of rebuilding the company and its brands. Chrysler's advertising agency suggested that Iacocca had enough credibility to go on the air to promote Chrysler cars. Iacocca was reluctant. "Whenever I've seen a CEO pushing his own company, it's left a bad taste in my mouth," Iacocca wrote in *Iacocca: An Autobiography*. "I was concerned that my appearing in television commercials would be seen by the public as a final act of desperation that would cause the entire enterprise to backfire."

The agency, Kenyon & Eckhardt, persisted, arguing that Iacocca had to put himself on the line to convince consumers that Chrysler was now the brand to buy. Iacocca finally agreed, reasoning that at least he could get the new spokesman cheap. He eased into it gradually, delivering tag lines such as, "I'm not asking you to buy one of our cars on faith. I'm asking you to compare." Later, he grew more aggressive, eventually coming up with his own slogan: "If you can find a better car—buy it."

Ironically, Iacocca had struggled with public speaking until he took a Dale Carnegie course while a young executive at Ford. "I was not born with [public speaking ability]. I was a shrinking violet," he says. Over time, Iacocca developed a reputation for being brutally honest in his opinions—his second best-selling book was titled *Talking Straight*—which became the essence of the Iacocca brand. "I learned to communicate early. I do it in person. I don't do it in letter writing. I don't do it by position paper," he says. "You can talk to death, but in the end you have to ask the employees to do the job or the customers to try your car. You have to make sure you're credible."

In all, he did 61 Chrysler commercials. "Most CEOs want good PR, but they want it purchased for them by some flack," said Iacocca in *Talking Straight*. "If a chief executive delegates the company's image—how the public perceives it and why—to some PR guy, he must be nuts. Yet most of them do. They issue a command: 'Just make sure everybody says nice things about us, and when they don't, I'll buzz you.'"

The Iacocca brand became so strong that Iacocca was approached about running for president as a Democrat in 1988. He sought the advice of Thomas "Tip" O'Neill, the speaker of the U.S. House of Representatives, whom he had come to know well during the struggle for loan guarantees. O'Neill told Iacocca that he didn't have the temperament to live with the compromises of Washington.

Iacocca was again approached about a political job, this time in 1991 to replace Senator John Heinz of Pennsylvania, who had died in a helicopter/plane crash. Political strategist James Carville was working for the state Democratic party and met with Iacocca to lay out the future senator's stance on certain issues. "I said, 'You don't even know if I'm a Democrat or not,'" recalls Iacocca. "He said, 'A Democratic governor is appointing you. Here's what you have to do on jobs, abortion, the death penalty—we've done focus groups." Iacocca asked: "If I'm a senator, don't I have something to say?" The answer was 'No' and Iacocca, true to his strong sense of personal credibility, declined the offer.

RICHARD BRANSON

The Challenge:

Choosing Between Music and Air Travel

It was 1992. Richard Branson had spent 20 years building Virgin Music into a hip, successful brand, as evidenced by the latest group to sign on, the Rolling Stones. Indeed, music was the foundation of all that had gone into the Virgin empire. Yet Branson was overextended and bankers were breathing down his neck. Virgin Atlantic, the troubled trans-Atlantic airline he started in 1984, was financed with loans backed by the record company. He would have to choose between Virgin Music and Virgin Atlantic.

"I was caught in a horrible dilemma," Branson writes in his autobiography, *Losing My Virginity*. "I simply couldn't decide what to do about Virgin Music. If we agreed to sell it, I would be able to invest sufficient cash in Virgin Atlantic to survive the winter and see off what I was beginning to suspect was a concerted British Airways attack." But if Branson sold Virgin Music, "we would be selling the one thing that we had spent the best part of our lives building up."

With as many as 200 private companies linked through a web of partnerships and complex, tax-driven, cross-collateralizations, Branson has become a billionaire by using one business to fund and build the next venture that captures his fancy. Whether clothing, trains, credit cards, or cola, this

1950: Born Richard Charles Nicholas Branson, in Surrey, England, son of a third-generation lawyer and a former flight attendant.

1967: Leaves Stowe boys school at age 16 to found youth magazine *Student.*

1968: Living in a London commune with *Student* staff, opens Student Advisory Centre, a counseling service for troubled young people.

1969: Notes that records are selling at premium prices and decides to set up a distribution business to supplement money-losing *Student.* Names the company Virgin.

1971: Opens first Virgin record store in London; buys a country manor to house a recording studio.

1972: Expands into music publishing and recording.

1973: Virgin Records releases Mike Oldfield's *Tubular Bells.* The album is used in *The Exorcist* soundtrack and becomes Virgin's first big hit.

1977: After several years of missing out on contracts with bands, including the Rolling Stones, Virgin Records signs The Sex Pistols.

1979: Buys Necker Island in the British Virgin Islands for 180,000 pounds.

1982: Following a nearly 1 million pound loss two years earlier, Virgin recovers with signing of such names as Boy George, Phil Collins, Simple Minds, and The Human League.

1984: Over strong objections of top staff, starts Virgin Atlantic, a low-cost, cross-Atlantic airline.

1986: Aboard Virgin Atlantic Challenger II, records fastest sea-crossing of the Atlantic in 3 days, 8 hours, and 31 minutes after failing earlier attempt when boat sank with just 60 miles to go.

1987: Finances and rides in first hot-air balloon flight across the Atlantic.

1988: Takes shares private after they decline in value in 1987 stock crash.

1990: Turns 40, contemplates quitting business to study history or become a campaigner to tackle social issues such as homelessness and healthcare. Instead, turns back to business when Iraq invades Kuwait, creating crisis at the airline with soaring fuel prices and reluctant flyers. Negotiates Virgin flight into Baghdad to free British nationals held by Saddam Hussein before war breaks out.

1991: Finances, and with a pilot, makes first hot-air balloon flight across the Pacific.

seemingly eclectic portfolio is backed by the Virgin name and promoted by Branson's own outsized personality and penchant for publicity. From his high-altitude balloon exploits to his bitter competition with British Airways, Branson has made his business very public. At the same time, he has kept financial control private, allowing himself the freedom to buy and sell businesses as he pleases. "I have always lived my life by thriving on opportunism and adventure," Branson writes. "By nature I am curious about life and this extends to my business."

Branson, who spent the early days of his career working and living in a London commune, seems an unlikely tycoon. He dropped out of school to found a youth-oriented magazine, one that was constantly short of money. Early on, he had keyed into the post-war generation's passion for its music. Noting that stores in Britain were not discounting records, he decided to set up a mail-order record distribution company to raise money to support the magazine. Slipped Disc was the leading contender for the name of the new company, until one of the magazine staffers suggested the name Virgin, because the people running it would be virgins in business, if nothing else.

The mail-order company grew into a retail chain as well as a mail-order business, even as Branson had to constantly juggle finances to keep both businesses going. In 1971, he was arrested in a tax-evasion scheme and agreed to pay fines to avoid going to trial. "Incentives come in all shapes and sizes, ranging from a pat on the back to share options, but avoiding prison was the most persuasive incentive I've ever had," Branson writes.

Over the next two decades, he worked obsessively to build a wide-ranging music business, negotiating deals with artists, opening new retail outlets, and converting a country manor into a recording studio where famous English rockers, including Paul and Linda McCartney and The Rolling Stones, would record. The company's first big hit was the offbeat instrumental album *Tubular Bells*, which became part of the soundtrack of *The Exorcist.*

The rock-and-roll industry proved to be a wild ride, which suited Branson's adventurous streak. After suffering a loss of one million pounds in 1980, Virgin managers argued the company needed to rein in expenses. They suggested Virgin cut loose The Human League, an up-and-coming band.

Branson took the completely opposite path. "I felt that unless we did something dramatic, which meant spending money, we would never get out of trouble." The Human League stayed. Soon, the band was among a stable of cutting-edge Virgin artists driving strong sales. In 1986, the company went public and Branson began to think about buying the competing music label, Thorn EMI, three times the size of Virgin Music.

In the meantime, Branson had plunged into Virgin Atlantic, again over the strong objections of key advisors. Why would he bet so much on a high-risk business that had no connection to the company's core music business? "Come on," he told them. "It'll be fun."

Fun, Branson writes in all seriousness, is always a critical requirement for him in any business venture. "From the perspective of wanting to live life to the full, I felt that I had to attempt it," Branson writes of the decision to go ahead with Virgin

1992: Just after signing the Rolling Stones, is forced to sell Virgin Music to Thorn EMI for $1 billion to keep Virgin Atlantic in the air.

1995: Creates Virgin Direct financial services company.

1997: Takes over train routes from London to Scotland creating Virgin Rail, but is later so embarrassed by his own company's poor management that he declines offer of knighthood in 1999.

1998: Launches Virgin Cola by driving a tank into New York's Times Square. Leaves Morocco in an attempt to circumnavigate the world in a hot-air balloon and makes it as far as Hawaii.

2000: Virgin Rail turns around and Branson is knighted by Queen Elizabeth in a Millennium New Year's ceremony.

2001: Fails in bid to take over Britain's National Lottery.

2002: Drops off a crane platform into Times Square wearing only a flesh-colored bodysuit and a mobile phone taped to his crotch to promote Virgin Mobile cellular service.

2003: Unsuccessful in attempts to block British Airways from ending its Concorde flights.

2004: Considers a low-fare airline in the United States.

Atlantic. The airline struggled and Branson engaged in a long and protracted battle with British Airways over adding additional flights.

By 1992, Branson was faced with the choice of closing the airline or selling the record business for nearly $1 billion in the hope he could turn Virgin Atlantic around. In the end, he decided to move on and sold Virgin Music to Thorn EMI, reasoning that he could not sell the troubled airline as a going concern. The music business would fetch a good price that might keep the airline flying, give Branson a war chest for new ventures, and preserve Virgin's good name.

"Selling Virgin Music would save the airline and leave two strong companies," he said. "Closing down Virgin Atlantic would leave one strong company and one bust company with 2,500 [layoffs] and the Virgin Group's reputation as a company and a brand name in tatters." After announcing the sale to employees, Branson walked out of the London offices and ran for nearly a mile through the city streets, tears streaming down his face.

With the cash from that deal as a cushion, Branson was able to ride out a recession and shore up Virgin Atlantic. He has since opened budget airlines in Europe and Australia, and ventured into clothing, cosmetics, bridal wear, and mobile phones. "Back in the early 1970s, I spent my time juggling different banks and suppliers and creditors, playing one off against the other to stay solvent," he writes. "I'm still living the same way, but I'm now juggling bigger deals instead of banks."

Leadership Lesson

A Hip Style

Richard Branson forged the Virgin brand identity during his youthful days in swinging London when early management of the Virgin record business boiled its image down to a simple formula: No Andy Williams.

Slightly dyslexic, Branson, a high-school dropout at age 16, recognized early the importance of thinking up business ventures that would tie in with the persona of his money-losing *Student* magazine. "I didn't see *Student* just as an end in itself, a noun," Branson writes. "I saw it as the beginning of a whole range of services, effectively an adjective, a word that people would recognize as having certain key values." Later, the word would become Virgin and the Virgin brand would ultimately be extended to auto sales, film production, and clothing, among dozens of other products and services.

But back in 1971, Branson saw that young people's passion for music wasn't being served by the dull, formal, and expensive record stores peddling the day's popular artists. "None of that feeling of excitement or even vague interest filtered through to the shops that sold the records," he writes. "The dowdy staff registered no approval or interest if you bought the new Jefferson Airplane. They just rang it up on the till as if you had bought Mantovani or Perry Como." Branson proceeded to set up a store on Oxford Street in London catering to rock aesthetes during the early days of album rock. Virgin provided headphones, sofas, and beanbags for the customers, along with coffee and free copies of underground music magazines, and refused to sell teenybopper records recorded by the Osmonds or the Sweet, which at that time were big sellers; they didn't fit in with the store's seriously hip image.

"We wanted [customers] to stay longer, chat to the staff, and really get into the records they were going to buy," Branson writes. People take music far more seriously than many other things in life. It is part of the way in which they define themselves—like the car they drive, the films they watch, and the clothes they wear. Virgin's first record shop had to incorporate all these aspects of how music fits into people's lives. In exploring how to do this, I think we created the conceptual framework of what Virgin later became."

After building a successful music business, Branson used the same process to make the leap into air travel. In 1984, the only airline offering cheap flights across the Atlantic was People Express. Branson relates how he picked up the phone one day and tried to get through to the airline's reservation system. The line was busy and remained busy the entire day. "I reasoned that either People Express was very poorly managed, in which case they would be an easy target for new competition, or that they were so much in demand that there was room for new competition." Branson started Virgin Airways.

In typical Branson style, the inaugural flight was loaded with 70 cases of champagne and passengers danced in the aisles to Madonna's song "Like a Virgin." At the beginning of the flight, passengers were told they would get a special view of the cockpit on their movie screens. With the plane hurtling down the runway, however, the three-man crew appeared to be totally unconcerned about flying the plane. As the nose of the aircraft pulled up, one of the crew members pulled out a joint. The passengers grew hushed, until the crew turned toward the camera revealing themselves to be a pair of famous cricket players and Branson. The special view from the cockpit had been filmed earlier in a flight simulator.

Branson admits he is not an innovator of new products or services. He is, however, very astute at identifying a product or service that is overpriced, of poor quality, or lacking competition. He then makes it over in his own hip, forever-young image. His strategy, he explains on the Virgin Group's website, has always been to "look for opportunities where we can offer something better, fresher, and more valuable, and we seize them. We often move into areas where the customer has traditionally received a poor deal, and where the competition is complacent. And with our growing e-commerce activities, we also look to deliver 'old' products and services in new ways...Contrary to what some people may think, our constantly expanding and eclectic empire is neither random nor reckless. Each successive venture demonstrates our skill in picking the right market and the right opportunity."

Branson has also extended his brands to new geographic markets, taking a formula that has worked well in the UK and exporting it. In 1989, he made his move into Japan, starting Virgin Atlantic flights to Tokyo from London and then striking several deals to help Japanese retail and consumer-products firms expand in Europe. In 1990, he opened the first of what grew into a 30-store chain of Virgin "megastores" selling music, movies, software, and books in a joint venture with local Japanese retailer Marui. These were followed by a 20-screen cinema chain. He also operates low-cost airlines in Australia and Asia.

In 2002, Branson brought his youth-oriented branding to the United States with a new cellular phone service. Virgin Mobile offers phones with names such as the K7 Rave, the Super Model, and Party Animal. When subscribers phone in for help with their accounts, a throaty computerized voice "operator" calling itself Amber asks for the mobile phone number. Then she jokingly asks for the real number, "not the one you give out in the bar." Just 18 months after starting out, Virgin Mobile USA signed on 1.8 million subscribers, putting it in the top 10 U.S. mobile providers. Its reported 50% annual growth rate was, for a time, the fastest in the business.

"Virgin is not a one-product brand, like Nike or Coca-Cola," Branson said in 2002. "It is different and diverse, so there are opportunities to extend it across a wider range of marketing areas. I want to make Virgin the number-one brand in the world, instead of around 10th, which is where it is now. There is great scope for this globally, but I think we've probably gone as far as we can in the UK.'"

Who knows where Branson will land next? "In all ventures, Virgin is ultimately about service, value for money, and simple products," Branson writes in his autobiography. "The vision I have for Virgin does not run along the orthodox lines of building up a company with a vast head office and a pyramid of command from a central board of directors...My mind doesn't work like that. I am too informal, too restless, and I like to move on."

8

Fast Learners

Leadership and learning go hand in hand. This is hardly a new insight. In Plato's dialog, *The Republic*, he wrote that learning was crucial for the Guardians, who held the reins of power in the utopian city state. Plato prescribed a tough regimen of intellectual and physical education for them from childhood, so they could grow to become leaders. The reason is simple: Leaders cannot guide their constituents unless they deepen their own knowledge through learning.

To be true to their function, however, leaders must be fast learners—in a way that does not necessarily refer to formal education or bookish knowledge. The need for rapid learning arises because all leaders—regardless of their domain—deal with realities that are in ceaseless flux. Markets change, new sets of political or military circumstances appear, and it is often unclear whether previous strategies or tactics still apply or new ones must be formulated. When situations change, is the correct response to stay the course or to change direction? Each decision is a judgment call, and leaders constantly are required to make them. To do so, they must be fast learners, seeking out new knowledge and information as they need it.

Each of the Top 25 leaders profiled in this book is a fast learner. William (Bill) H. Gates, chairman and chief software architect of Microsoft, belongs at the top of the list. He was a fast learner long before he began to write software programs at age 13, but especially so after launching Microsoft in 1975—at age 20—with his childhood friend, Paul Allen. In some 30 years, the company has grown into a software giant with more than 56,000 employees and annual revenues of $32 billion—largely because of Gates's ability to rapidly learn—and get Microsoft to execute—what needs to be done to take the company to the next level.

Frederick Smith, founder, chairman and CEO of Federal Express, is another leader who has repeatedly demonstrated his ability to learn rapidly from observation and experience. The classic example, in Smith's case, was his ability to sense, before either his customers or competitors, the need for a tracking and tracing system for the packages and documents that FedEx delivers. As Smith says, this has enabled FedEx to set itself apart in a competitive field and to offer services that cannot easily be "commoditized."

Louis Gerstner, former chairman and CEO of IBM, is also a fast learner. Soon after joining the New York-based computer giant, he realized that a plan by the former leadership to break IBM into smaller Baby Blues would be disastrous, and he bet the company on pursuing the opposite strategy—one in which IBM would offer integrated solutions to companies with a vast range and variety of IT needs. This knowledge, combined with a sharp focus on performance, helped Gerstner engineer a massive turnaround at IBM.

Examples and insights from these leaders can be invaluable in helping executives see how fast learning is a critical attribute to develop their own leadership. A word of caution, however, might be in order. Fast learning, to be effective, must become a habit. Leaders who learn a few lessons rapidly, and then expect to replicate their successes by applying them over and over again, do so at great risk. Offering old solutions to new problems is often a prescription for failure.

WILLIAM H. GATES

The Challenge:

Keeping Microsoft's Regulators at Bay (on Both Sides of the Atlantic)

Success sometimes undermines itself. At Microsoft, Bill Gates's combativeness and relentless competitive drive helped propel the company to overwhelming dominance in the global software industry. This massive clout assured rising revenues and profitability for Microsoft and made Gates the world's richest man. Market dominance, though, has a flip side. It created the greatest challenge that Gates and Microsoft have faced: Retaining their grip on the market while fending off antitrust regulators in the U.S. and Europe. In 2000, regulators in the U.S. came close to breaking up Microsoft into two companies. Though that threat has now disappeared, regulators still impose big legal and administrative costs on the company and could affect how it does business in the future.

Muttering against Microsoft's monopolistic moves has been heard for more than a decade. A *BusinessWeek* article in November 1992 titled, "Does Bill Play Fair?" highlighted early concerns that the company, though just 17 years old, had grown too big too fast. The magazine noted that Microsoft's MS-DOS operating system at that time was installed on more than 80% of the PCs worldwide. Today, Microsoft's Windows operating system resides on more than 95% of the world's PCs. That,

1955: Born on October 28 in Seattle. His father, William H. Gates Jr., is a Seattle attorney; his late mother, Mary Gates, was a schoolteacher, University of Washington regent, and chairwoman of United Way International.

1967: Gates enters Lakeside, a private school where Seattle's privileged and wealthy denizens send their sons. Here, he encounters his first computer.

1968: At age 13, Gates discovers his interest in software and writes his first software program for playing tic tac toe. He later says the computer he used was "huge and cumbersome and slow and absolutely compelling."

1973: Enters Harvard University as a freshman, where he lives down the hall from Steve Ballmer, now Microsoft's CEO. While at Harvard, Gates develops a version of the BASIC (Beginner's All-purpose Symbolic Instruction Code) programming language for the MITS Altair computer. He later drops out of Harvard without graduating.

1975: Launches Microsoft with childhood friend Paul Allen. Their mission is to commercialize software for the personal computer. Microsoft has $16,000 in revenues in its first year.

1977: Microsoft, having landed software-programming projects for companies such as Commodore, Texas Instruments, and others, earns $112,000 in pre-tax profits on revenues of $381,715.

1979: Microsoft moves from Albuquerque, New Mexico, to Bellevue, Washington. The main motivation is a declining relationship with MITS and the difficulty of recruiting talented software programmers in New Mexico.

1980: Gates, Allen, and Ballmer meet with IBM executives who want to license Microsoft software to introduce a personal computer. Initially, talks center on software in BASIC and other languages, but eventually the discussions expand to include the operating system.

1981: Microsoft incorporates on June 25. On August 12 that year, IBM introduces its personal computer with Microsoft's 16-bit operating system, MS-DOS 1.0.

1983: Gates makes his first keynote speech at Comdex, a computer industry trade show. He announces plans for a new software program called Windows. Gates's father operates the slide projector during the presentation.

by itself, is not necessarily bad. In fact, to the degree that it establishes a uniform, global standard for computing, it helps consumers. The problem is that Microsoft does not just make operating systems; it also produces software applications and competes for market share with other software firms. That issue has disturbed regulators—and undoubtedly Gates's competitors. Critics allege that when confronted by a successful software rival, Gates and Microsoft seem to adopt a two-fold approach: Buy it or bury it. Both tactics have serious anti-competitive implications.

An example of Gates's "buy it" approach was the way he dealt with Intuit, which makes personal finance software programs such as Quicken and Quickbooks. When its own personal finance products failed to make a dent in Quicken's massive market share, Microsoft in 1994 tried to take over Intuit. Regulators soon intervened—the U.S. Justice Department sued Microsoft to prevent the merger—and by 1995, the deal was dead.

Critics also claim that when buying a potential rival seems unlikely, Gates and Microsoft turn to hardball. The "bury it" tactic typically consists of offering the Microsoft application as a free download or bundling it with the Windows operating system. More often than not, this continues until the competing application is no longer a threat. The best-known case in point: Netscape.

Launched in 1994, Netscape's Navigator browser rapidly became popular among non-technical users around the world who were just awakening to the power of the world wide web. By the time Netscape went public in 1995, the Navigator was the dominant browser among web users—the hype surrounding its IPO helped inflate the dot-com bubble. Microsoft, however, struck back with Internet Explorer, which it later claimed was an inseparable part of Windows. As a free add-on, the Internet Explorer gained steadily in popularity, while Netscape, whose revenue model suddenly became uncertain, was sold in 1998 to AOL Time-Warner.

Over the next few years, Internet Explorer continued to grow at the Navigator's expense. In May 2003, Microsoft signed an agreement with AOL Time-Warner, as part of which AOL agreed to use Internet Explorer as its primary browser for seven years. Some observers believe that was the final nail in the Navigator's coffin. CNET's News.com website noted that Netscape would move from "a neglected orphan of AOL Time-Warner to a candidate for euthanasia."

To deal with such issues, trustbusters at the U.S. Justice Department began looking into Microsoft. Following the lawsuit in Intuit's case, they struck a more decisive blow against the company in 2000 when Judge Thomas Penfield Jackson found Microsoft guilty of anti-competitive practices and described it as a "predatory monopoly." Jackson ordered that the company be broken into two: One company would make the operating system while the other made software applications. Microsoft, however, pushed back. It appealed; the decision was reversed, and a much gentler punishment, in the form of restrictions, was imposed. Today, the case to break up Microsoft is all but dead. As *The Economist* noted in 2004, it "produces occasional rumbles, like the death-rattle of a mortally wounded dragon, but it no longer poses a threat to the company's survival."

Still, Gates and his colleagues continued to face two other challenges. One was Microsoft's fight against Real Networks, whose Real Player

1986: In February, Microsoft moves to a corporate campus in Redmond, Washington. A month later, the company's stock goes public.

1990: Windows 3.0 is launched with great fanfare in May, after several underwhelming launches. According to one observer, this is the "biggest, splashiest software rollout yet concocted."

1993: The U.S. Justice Department launches a probe into Microsoft for monopolistic practices.

1994: On January 1, Gates marries Melinda French.

1994: In July, the U.S. Justice Department reaches a settlement with Microsoft.

1994: Gates attempts to acquire Intuit, a company that makes personal finance software programs such as Quicken and Quickbooks. Ignoring opposition from senior Intuit executives who are opposed to the merger, Gates negotiates with company founder Scott Cook to take over the company for $1.5 billion in Microsoft stock, a 40% premium over Intuit's value.

1995: The Justice Department files a lawsuit to block Microsoft's merger with Intuit; Gates withdraws the purchase offer.

1995: In August, Microsoft launches Windows 95.

1995: Gates writes *The Road Ahead*, a book in which he muses on the past and future of the digital age. It holds the No. 1 spot on *The New York Times* bestseller list for seven weeks.

1995: In December, Gates outlines Microsoft's commitment to supporting and enhancing the Internet.

1998: In June, Microsoft launches Windows 98.

1999: Gates writes *Business@The Speed of Thought*, in which he argues that computers can help solve business problems in new ways. The book makes the bestseller lists of *The New York Times, The Wall Street Journal, USA Today*, and Amazon.com.

2000: In January, the Bill and Melinda Gates Foundation is established, resulting from the merger of the Gates Learning Foundation, which worked to expand access to technology through public libraries, and the William H. Gates Foundation, which focused on improving global health. Led by Bill Gates's father, William H. Gates, Jr., and Patty Stonesifer, the Seattle-based foundation has an endowment of approximately $27 billion.

2000: In February, Microsoft launches Windows 2000.

software (which lets users access audio and video content on the Internet) competes with Microsoft's Media Player. The issue loomed large in the minds of regulators at the European Commission, who announced in March 2004, after a five-year investigation, that "Microsoft has abused its near-monopoly power in markets for PC operating systems which resulted in restricting the interoperability of Windows PCs with non-Microsoft servers. The company also broke the law by abusing its power in markets for the technology that allows people to play music and videos on their PCs," regulators said.

Wharton professor Eric Clemons thinks the EU's point was well taken. "Under any technical definition of antitrust, any technical definition of abuse of market power, it's self-evidently true that Microsoft has monopoly power and that it abuses it," Clemons states. "The classic definitions involve things like cross-subsidizing product lines. Any time you give away products free, then by definition you're overcharging for something else. You have to be. If you're overcharging for something else, then you're crushing competitors…[Microsoft] can charge whatever it wants for Windows, and it can give away Media Player. The fact that it gives away Media Player, under traditional antitrust law, [makes] it clear that it is overcharging for the operating system."

The second challenge involved Google, Microsoft's biggest rival in the Internet search field. Google, which went public in August 2004, is the most popular search engine—according to one estimate, it accounts for some 80% of all Internet searches—but its revenues, at $1 billion, are a fraction of Microsoft's. Microsoft, which offers searches through its MSN web portal, launched a "toolbar" plug-in that resembles Google's toolbar. "Initially, the MSN toolbar is a free optional download, as Microsoft's web browser and media player once were," noted *The Economist*. "The next step, inevitably, will be to integrate such search functions into Windows, on the grounds that it constitutes a core technology that should be part of the operating system...In other words, Microsoft is preparing to use its dominance in web-browser and operating-system software to promote itself in yet another separate market—search engines this time—at the expense of competitors."

What does all this have to do with Bill Gates's leadership? A great deal, because by all accounts, Microsoft's moves follow from the intensely competitive culture that Gates has built at the company since its inception. In the spring of 2004, however, some signs appeared that Microsoft may be mellowing. The company settled its long-standing dispute with Sun Microsystems, an old enemy. Microsoft also signed a major cross-licensing agreement with Siemens that allowed both companies access to one another's patents. Optimists might say that these are welcome signs that after years of brawling, Microsoft and its chairman are moving toward a more collabora-tive, or at least less confrontational, approach to leadership. Time will tell.

2000: In April, the Justice Department wins an antitrust court decision against Microsoft that finds the company guilty of anticompetitive practices. U.S. District Judge, Thomas Penfield Jackson, cites Microsoft's illegal monopoly in operating systems and orders the breakup of Microsoft into two companies.

2000: In June, Bill Gates and Steve Ballmer outline Microsoft's .NET strategy for web services. Gates notes, "You could say it's a bet-the-company thing. We are putting our resources behind .NET because we believe in this, and so our entire strategy is defined around this platform."

2001: Appeals court reverses Jackson's decision ordering Microsoft's breakup and imposes "behavioral remedies" instead.

2001: In May, Microsoft launches Office XP and in October that year, Windows XP.

2001: Microsoft enters the intensely competitive video games market, pitting its Xbox against Sony's PlayStation 2 and Nintendo's GameCube. In three years, Microsoft passes Nintendo to become Sony's primary contender in this market.

2002: In November, Microsoft and its partners launch Tablet PC, a computer on which users can write with a stylus.

2003: Microsoft has $32.19 billion in revenues for the fiscal year ending in June and 55,000 employees in 85 countries and regions around the world.

2004: In January, Buckingham Palace announces that Gates will receive honorary knighthood from Britain's Queen Elizabeth II.

2004: On March 24, after a five-year investigation, the European Commission in Brussels announces that Microsoft has abused its near-monopoly power for PC operating systems. This has made it difficult for Windows-based PCs to work with non-Microsoft servers. The EC fines Microsoft $613 million. Microsoft says in June that it will appeal.

2004: In April, Microsoft and Sun Microsystems settle their long-standing battle. The agreement calls for Microsoft to pay Sun $700 million to resolve antitrust issues and another $900 million to settle issues related to patents.

Leadership Lesson

Combining Agility and Ability

Bill Gates was an eighth grader at Seattle's prestigious Lakeside school when he found a new machine installed in the math and science building. As Stephen Manes and Paul Andrews write in their biography, *Gates: How Microsoft's Mogul Reinvented an Industry—and Made Himself the Richest Man in America*, it was an ASR 33 Teletype, an "ungainly electro-mechanical contraption combining a keyboard, a printer, a paper tape punch and reader, and a modem that could connect the unit via telephone to the outside world." Gates found it fascinating. He taught himself how to program it so fast that William Dougall, a teacher who had helped bring the computer to Lakeside, said, "It took him a week to pass me." With that introduction to software came the first indication what a fast learner Gates could be. It was no accident that one of his books would be titled, *Business @ The Speed of Thought*.

During his career, Gates repeatedly has shown he is a quick study who responds to and shapes emerging developments. Two examples stand out as being critical to Microsoft's emergence as the dominant company in global software, as well as Gates's personal development as a leader. They include the manner in which a fledgling Microsoft struck its deal with IBM to become the developer of the MS-DOS operating system for Big Blue's PCs; and the way that Microsoft, despite initially lagging behind Netscape, rapidly recognized and responded to the emergence of the Internet.

At least five years before starting work on the IBM PC, Gates, his friend Paul Allen, and other associates had developed a version of the BASIC programming language for the MITS Altair, one of the first personal computers. At that time, Gates was a student at Harvard. One of the earliest lessons Gates learned was to treat software as a business. In the hobbyist-driven culture of those times— and in an interesting foreshadowing of debates that would occur 20 years later about free versus paid content on the Internet—users were willing to pay for hardware, but they expected software to be provided free. Gates challenged that assumption, arguing that hardware without software was meaningless. As such, if a company hired and deployed full-time programmers to write software code, it would incur costs and expect to recover them by earning revenues and making a profit. Treating software as a commercial proposition from the beginning—a stance that made Gates unpopular among the "free software" crowd—Gates and Allen set up Microsoft in 1975. In their first year, they received some $16,000 in royalties for Altair BASIC from MITS. In 1979, the year the company moved into new digs in Bellevue, Washington, revenues crossed $1 million.

By the early 1980s, personal computers were widely recognized as a fast-growing market. The Apple II, made by Apple Computer, was going strong, as were other machines made by Commodore, Radio Shack, and other firms. IBM was impatient to launch its own personal computer and was looking for a partner whose software could drive the machines. After an expensive and disastrous attempt to develop its own version of BASIC, IBM executives approached Microsoft in the summer of 1980. Initially, nonplussed by Gates's youthful looks (he was 25 but looked 18), they were won over by his confidence and knowledge of software. Microsoft was soon ready to sign an agreement to write software in BASIC and other languages for the IBM PC—driven largely by Gates's belief that the company would do what it took to land IBM's business.

That, by itself, would have been a major coup for Microsoft— but a larger opportunity was in store. Many computers at the time used the CP/M operating system made by a company called Digital Research. Though Microsoft and Digital Research had a close relationship—and Gates recommended Digital's operating system for the PC—IBM and Digital were unable to arrive at an agreement. Determined not to let the transaction fall through, Gates cut a licensing deal with a company called Seattle Computer, which had developed a rudimentary operating system called QDOS (an acronym for "Quick and Dirty Operating System") to replace Digital. Before the IBM PC was launched, however, Gates played a masterstroke: Microsoft acquired the operating system— now renamed 86-OS—from Seattle Computer for $75,000.

As Manes and Andrews write: "It wasn't just a fair deal for Microsoft. It was the deal of the century." This acquisition ensured that when the IBM PC was launched in 1981, Microsoft owned— and had the licensing rights to—its software and operating system. It laid the foundation for Microsoft's operating systems— initially MS-DOS and then Windows—to become the prevailing standard in the PC industry. Today, some 95% of PCs around the world operate on Microsoft's operating system.

What has kept Microsoft at the top all through this period is Gates's agility and his ability to understand new market conditions and what they mean for Microsoft. In the 1990s, for example, Gates was quick to understand the impact of the Internet on business processes as well as on Microsoft. Gates explained his perspective at the Internet World Conference held in April 1996. "The Internet phenomenon is really unbelievable," he said. "It's the most fantastic thing to happen in the world of computing since the original PC."

According to Gates, in the two decades since its arrival, the PC brought about massive changes. For instance, it transformed the way documents are created—because now more than 90% of all documents are created electronically. Still, the distribution of many of those documents did not initially change because most people printed the documents and mailed them, just as they would if they had been type-written or handwritten. In other words, before the Internet came along, the PC was not a communications tool, in part because the cost of communications was high and, secondly, because there wasn't a large enough critical mass of people who might want to use the PC to communicate with one another.

Between 1994 and 1996, however, the situation changed. Several factors came together to allow the PC to become a powerful communications device. In addition to a decline in the cost of communications, the number of PCs and people connected to the Internet increased dramatically. Result: A critical mass of users emerged that could use their computers to communicate. "What's going on today is like the arrival of the printing press, or the telephone, or the radio," Gates said. "And these communications tools did have pervasive effects. They made the world a smaller place...Now the personal computer connected to the Internet is far more powerful in many ways than any of these other communications devices." What makes it more powerful, Gates added, is the fact that the Internet allows PC users to connect to one another— and the marginal cost of communicating in this environment is close to zero.

For Gates, it wasn't enough to rapidly learn how the Internet was transforming society; he also had to engage Microsoft in taking advantage of the opportunities it offered. Microsoft responded to the rise of the Internet in three ways.

First, Microsoft developed the Internet Explorer web browser, which it positioned directly against Netscape, the most popular web browser of the mid-1990s. Pursuing a tactic that it had repeatedly used against rivals, Microsoft bundled the Explorer browser with its Windows operating system. Gates and Microsoft bet on the fact that, although this aggressive move might backfire, the regulatory backlash wouldn't be strong enough to counter the business benefit of becoming the market leader in this product. That, after a lengthy battle with the Justice Department's trust-busters, is exactly what happened.

Second, Microsoft began to adapt existing products and develop new products centered on the Internet. According to Gates, "Group collaboration will become very strong on the web with the ability to not only have audio but also to share applications...The value of those systems is really hard to exaggerate." To cater to these needs, Microsoft deployed productivity software as well as authoring tools, both built upon the foundation of its existing products.

Third, when companies came along that had established a strong presence in a niche where Microsoft was lagging behind, Gates responded with another time-tested tactic: acquisition. Example: one of the fastest-growing areas during the dot-com boom years was email, as Gates had noted in his analysis of PCs becoming popular communications tools. Hotmail, an upstart provider of free email (supported by advertising) saw explosive growth in this domain and became a Microsoft acquisition target: It was taken over in 1998 for more than $400 million.

Such moves, based upon fast learning and faster action, enabled Gates to keep Microsoft moving onward and upward—and to keep his own leadership skills well honed.

FREDERICK WALLACE SMITH

The Challenge:

Overnight Innovation

Fred Smith had one big idea and it generated an entire industry, nearly overnight.

Smith founded Federal Express in 1971 and the company grew to become the world's first overnight delivery system, handling 5.4 million shipments a day in 210 countries. It wasn't easy, but Smith's toughest job was yet to come.

"This company was enormously successful in its first 20 years of existence largely because it filled an unmet need," says Smith. "As we entered into the 1990s, it became very obvious that this single line of business was simply not going to be viable by itself over the long haul. It was the classic case of great success potentially sowing the seeds of its own destruction."

Now known as FedEx, the company's purple and orange jets still ferry time-sensitive packages through the night skies. But Smith has recast FedEx as an information-technology firm that manages customers' internal supply chains as well as their shipments by air and truck, even whisking goods through customs.

In a sense, FedEx helped drive itself out of its original business. The company showed its customers how much more efficient they could be by cutting back on inventory and supplies, and shipping only what was needed, when it was needed.

1944: Born in Memphis, Tennessee. His father, a founder of the Greyhound bus lines and Toddle House restaurant chain, dies when Smith is four; his mother later marries a colonel in the National Guard who has an aviation business.

1959: At age 15, learns to fly, enters prep school, and starts a recording studio with friends.

1965: While an economics student at Yale, writes a paper about a hub and spoke system to deliver spare parts and supplies to companies overnight.

1967: Joins the Marine Corps, serves four years in Vietnam flying 230 combat missions, earns the Silver Star, Bronze Star, and two Purple Hearts.

1970: Takes over airplane repair shop in Little Rock owned by his stepfather and grows frustrated with problems getting parts.

1971: Incorporates Federal Express to move parts and documents for companies overnight by air.

1972: Federal Express moves to Memphis because of availability of National Guard hangars and land.

1973: With 33 Falcon jets and 389 employees, Federal Express moves 186 packages through Memphis to 25 cities on its first day in business.

1977: Helps lobby for airline deregulation, which would allow the company to expand with larger planes.

1978: Company lists on the New York Stock Exchange.

1979: Launches COSMOS, a centralized computer system to manage vehicles, people, packages, routes, and weather scenarios.

1980: Introduces the first PC-based automated shipping system, later named FedEx PowerShip.

1981: Starts first international service to Canada.

1983: Unveils Zapmail, a service in which customers could fax documents from one Federal Express office to another. Service flops by 1986 due to rapid expansion of office fax machines.

1984: Acquires Gelco Express, a Minneapolis package courier serving 84 countries. Also makes acquisitions in Holland, Britain, and the United Arab Emirates.

1986: Initiates use of SuperTracker, a hand-held bar-code scanner system used to capture package information.

1988: Creates White Glove Services for items that need special handling.

1989: Tiger International, Inc. acquired, adding operating rights to 21 countries as well as an additional fleet of Boeing 747s and 727s, and McDonnell Douglas DC-8s. The move generates friction with Federal Express's pilots over seniority rights with Flying Tiger pilots.

Once companies figured that out, there were fewer last-minute shipments that absolutely, positively had to get there with a premium payment to FedEx. Businesses are always "in the process of commoditization," says Smith. "You simply have to constantly look to where markets and needs are going and anticipate those needs."

In 1973, he established his now-famous hub-and-spoke system in Memphis. Initially, Smith wanted to provide overnight transport of checks for the Federal Reserve System; hence the name Federal Express. The Federal Reserve then backed out, but the company grew and enjoyed success through the late 1980s before hitting severe headwinds.

The problems stemmed in part from Smith's support for a project called Zapmail, a system that used fax machines at FedEx offices to transmit documents for clients in different cities. After being introduced in 1983, the service was soon eclipsed by the rise of fax machines priced cheaply enough that most offices could purchase their own. In addition, Zapmail was based on satellite technology, which needed the space shuttle to work effectively. But the space shuttle blew up, dealing a body blow to FedEx's plans. FedEx folded Zapmail in 1986, taking a costly write-off.

Innovation is not without risk. "There are lots of examples of that at companies," says Smith. "But on the other side of the coin, if you're too cautious and too late—that's the story of the dinosaur businesses. Navigating that fine line is very important."

With revenue-growth slowing as the company came into the 1990s, Smith looked for new markets overseas. His revolutionary overnight-delivery idea had worked well in the U.S., but by the time he arrived in Europe, imitators were already in place. Although FedEx spent $1.5 billion on a global expansion, by 1991 it was beaten back. Meanwhile at home, competitor UPS was gaining ground and FedEx was struggling with a difficult integration of the legendary Flying Tigers cargo carriers.

FedEx was forced to regroup. Smith determined future growth would take place through the acquisition of more diverse transit companies, including ground operations. The major thrust, however, would be to buy and develop information companies that would tie into the shipping business.

The company had always been ahead of the curve in information systems. In 1979, it created a central computer system to track everything from vehicles to weather scenarios. In 1986, it introduced a hand-held, bar-code scanner to track packages. And in 1994, it became the first large transportation company to make extensive use of the Internet.

"One of FedEx's biggest innovations, one that revolutionized our business but also revolutionized the whole world of business, was the development of a positive tracking and tracing capability for millions of discrete items in motion," says Smith. "We saw a need that nobody else had seen. It was the understanding that what customers really wanted was to manage their inventory when it's moving as well as at rest."

He met the challenge of remaking FedEx into an information trafficker by assembling a management team with legal and financial expertise because he knew he would have to shape the new company with acquisitions. Smith also stressed the need for executives to communicate with

1990: Federal Express wins U.S. Commerce Department's Malcolm Baldrige National Quality Award for service.

1992: Expansion in Europe fails after problems initiating the hub-and-spoke system and reluctance by regulators to let the new company into existing European markets. Company takes highest quarter loss and closes European courier operations, laying off 6,600 employees.

1994: First major transport firm to launch a website with tracking and tracing capability.

1997: UPS strike swells business with 800,000 additional packages a day. Employees volunteer to work extra hours in hubs. After the strike, Smith takes out full-page newspaper ads thanking employees and ending with the military phrase, "Bravo Zulu."

1998: FedEx acquires Caliber System Inc., the parents of RPS and Viking Freight, and creates FDX Corp., a $16-billion logistics and distribution company, which is later named FedEx Corp.

2000: Acquires Tower Group International, a transportation logistics company, forming the foundations for FedEx Trade Networks to provide international trade and transportation assistance, including customs services.

2001: Buys American Freightways, a trucking company that consolidates shipments that are less than a full truckload with service in 40 states.

2002: Announces a $1.8 billion, six-year expansion of FedEx Ground, the company's truck delivery system that will add 10 new hubs and nearly double capacity by 2009.

2004: Buys Kinko's, the office-service company, to add distribution outlets and tap the home office market.

employees, to let them know why the company needed to move in new directions.

"It took leadership and communication by the operating management to explain to our folks what we were doing and make them feel good about it," says Smith. "Finally, it required the development of an iron-clad, disciplined business plan to execute on the acquisitions of new product lines we were offering, and to make sure we supported our original employees. In essence, we turned the new people we acquired purple."

In the late 1990s, FedEx went on an acquisition binge that added new ground and freight capabilities as well as logistics and technology services. In 2004, it paid $2.4 billion for Kinko's, the printing and office services retailer. Kinko's had itself been migrating from a neighborhood copy shop to an information and document management company.

Smith says vision goes with his job title. "At the end of the day, that really is what the CEO job is all about. I don't think I have a lock on that particular skill. The common denominator for people that have vision, and one of the things I think I bring to the table is the ability to look at a broad range of issues and synthesize a product, or service, or business solution."

Leadership Lesson

Learning to Change Direction at Express Speed

Federal Express founder Fred Smith was not just a fast learner; he also was an early one. As noted previously, the idea that became FedEx began life as a term paper for an economics class when Smith was an undergraduate at Yale in 1965. The main point of his paper was simple: As machines replace human labor, productivity will rise, but so will the need to fix equipment quickly when it breaks down. This means a system must be found (or created) to ensure that organizations have rapid access to spare parts and materials when they are needed. From this seemingly obvious but revolutionary notion, Smith created a hub-and-spoke–based transportation system of rapidly moving inventory that not only revolutionized its own business but "revolutionized the whole world of business," Smith says.

Along the way, Smith had to quickly learn—and sometimes unlearn—lessons so he could change direction as needed to keep FedEx growing. For example, while serving as a marine in Vietnam, he noted how military supply chains worked to provide food, uniforms, and ordnance to soldiers, but he also recognized that these processes were too supplier-focused; they emphasized constantly pushing out items that the military had decided to distribute. In contrast, the logistical processes he wanted to set up had to be primarily customer-driven. He later applied these insights when developing a delivery system for FedEx.

After Smith laid out his framework for an overnight delivery system for high-priority documents and packages, he still had to change direction many times to keep the company aloft. Early on, an obscure airline regulation would have restricted the type of airplane he could fly. Smith went to Washington and got the rules changed so he could fly larger planes.

In 1997, the company used new computer technology to identify low-profit customers and weed them out for better overall returns. The company that was born to deliver overnight then slowed the pace, building a better network of ground transportation to deliver items that don't absolutely, positively have to be there overnight, but could get there in a few days.

One of the most important lessons Smith learned is that customers are keenly concerned about the status of their packages, not only when they are shipped and when they arrive, but also while they are in transit—an insight that spurred FedEx to pioneer the development of tracking and tracing capabilities. Having learned before its competitors that FedEx was not just in the business of transporting cargo but also of providing information about that cargo to clients, Smith led the company to invest in information technology. As *Fortune* magazine reported, Smith "stressed that knowledge about cargo's origin, present whereabouts, destination, estimated time of arrival, price, and cost of shipment was as important as its safe delivery. He...insisted that a network of state-of-the-art information systems—a sophisticated mélange of laser scanners, bar codes, software, and electronic connections—be erected alongside the air and vehicle networks."

Smith says the reason he created this information system was that "people who move things—whether it is an abstract for an engineering survey or a critical part for an airplane or a hospital—they all would like the same level of control when it's moving, as if it were in their hands or in their warehouse." This understanding, synthesized with where technology was going, allowed FedEx to capture and manipulate the data at a low cost. The resulting innovation "has now revolutionized the world of logistics. It is one of the greatest improvements in societal productivity you could name," says Smith.

"The simple system by which FedEx tracks and traces all the cargo it delivers has allowed all businesses to significantly improve the velocity of their supply chains. It has dampened business cycles. That's an example where you see a need that's not immediately apparent. I will assure you that not one in 100 of our customers would have said, 'I need a system like that.' They just couldn't envision that until we had it." Based on his ability to sense what his customers didn't know they needed, Smith has formulated his own definition of vision. He says, "It's simply a broad understanding of big needs and developments, and then understanding how you can do something about it."

In addition to speeding up the transportation process, Smith argues that these innovations have made the process more cost-effective. In 1980, logistics accounted for 16% of the cost of producing goods; now it is 10%, Smith notes.

FedEx has also had to adopt varying strategies in Europe, where its hub-and-spoke system did not play out so well in Brussels. By the time FedEx began moving into Europe in the mid-1980s, imitators had already set up systems similar to its own. Regulators blocked FedEx from flying into new markets. Later, expensive acquisitions were difficult to integrate. But Smith says the company has persevered, changing its game plan along the way.

"Being absolutely determined to accomplish something is a very, very important asset," Smith told *Investor's Business Daily* in 1998. "A lot of people are put off by adversity or mistakes. If you keep your eye very firmly focused on where you want to go, and you're determined to get there, that's worth a lot."

Smith says his greatest contribution to society is the development of FedEx, which he says has allowed businesses to become vastly more productive. "I love what I do because it's right in the middle of everything. We basically are the sinews that keep the economic body operating every day." In part, that goes back to his service in Vietnam. As he told *Fortune* in 1997: "I wanted to do something productive after blowing so many things up."

1942: Born March 1 in Minneola, New York. His father, a milk-truck driver, eventually becomes a dispatcher; his mother is a secretary and administrator.

1963: Graduates from Dartmouth College with a bachelor's degree in engineering science.

1965: Receives MBA from Harvard Business School.

1965: Joins McKinsey & Co. consulting firm. Credits time there with teaching him the detailed analytical process for understanding a company's foundations.

1970: Becomes a principal partner at age 28, the youngest in the firm.

1975: Becomes a director, again the youngest, at 33. Grows increasingly restless playing the role of an advisor to the decision-makers. Remembers thinking: "I no longer want to be the person who walks into the room and presents a report to a person sitting at the other end of the table; I want to be the person sitting in that chair—the one who makes the decisions and carries out the actions."

LOUIS V. GERSTNER, JR.

The Challenge:

Making Elephants Dance

"My friends, in the last three years we have lost $17 billion and half our market share. The media is writing our obituary and our competitors are laughing at us," Louis Gerstner recalls telling IBM employees in 1993, shortly after he undertook the monumental task of turning around this blue chip company in freefall. "Don't you think we ought to try something different?"

The turnaround, Gerstner concedes, did not hinge on developing some heretofore-unknown strategy. It depended, instead, on actually focusing on business fundamentals, such as consolidating the company's 266 bookkeeping systems, 128 chief information officers, and 339 surveys for measuring customer satisfaction. "IBM knew what directions it needed to take. I found thousands of pages of good strategic analysis in the file," says Gerstner. "But the company didn't execute on any of those strategies. Why? Because internally the culture was bound up in a strait jacket... [Managers] would have loved me to introduce a new strategy, so they could do what they did so well: discuss and debate abstract concepts."

IBM dominated the computing industry for decades with mainframe systems used by virtually every corporation and government agency. By the late 1980s, however, companies like Hitachi and Amdahl were offering mainframe alternatives at lower prices, while others like Dell and Compaq were encroaching on the personal computer business. In the process, IBM's stock value crashed to $12 per share in 1993, from $43 in 1987.

Gerstner, the first outsider to lead IBM, had only a few months to set Big Blue on the right track. He quickly put an end to any talk of breaking IBM into several little blues—the prevailing wisdom on how to harness the company's valuable assets. Instead, Gerstner moved to transform the company into an "integrator," which would build, run, and house systems for customers using its own components as well as those of its competitors. His decision ran counter to the trend of the day, which favored the idea of smaller, nimbler technology companies specializing in only a few products and transforming themselves quickly to meet market demands. "We were getting killed by these single-point competitors," says Gerstner. "The only way we would have a distinctive competence in the market place was to be an integrator."

After extensive talks with customers, Gerstner concluded that clients wanted companies like IBM to handle their complex computing tasks. He reasoned that the typical products delivered by the computer industry are overly complex—difficult to install, integrate, and operate. He realized that customers are concerned about what they need done while the computing industry thinks about components and systems. "When I was a customer, what I really wanted was someone to translate these components into solutions," says Gerstner. "So I made this decision basically from my gut, from having been a customer."

1978: Joins American Express as an executive vice president and heads its charge card business. Rises to president of American Express and chairman and CEO of its largest subsidiary, American Express Travel Related Services. Grows frustrated when he is no longer next in line to be AMEX's CEO.

1989: Joins RJR Nabisco as chairman and CEO. The company, created by a merger between consumer food maker Nabisco and tobacco giant R.J. Reynolds Tobacco Co., had been taken private through a leveraged buyout. Finds himself heading a company saddled by debt. Oversees the sale of $11 billion in assets to help reduce debt load. Learns that he prefers to build companies rather than take them apart.

1993: Recruited to head IBM, a company in trouble. General Electric's Jack Welch is among many candidates who declined the position. Gerstner, who initially said he wasn't interested, says later: "I guess I got somewhat motivated by the fact that no one else seemed to want the job."

1993: On April 1, begins Big Blue career. Within three months, axes former CEO John F. Akers' plan to split the company into several little blues. Gerstner argues that the company's size and product breadth are Its strength.

1994: Sweeps clean the board of directors and disbands the Management Committee, the beginning of huge cultural changes that will take place throughout the company.

2001: IBM dubbed as the "turnaround of the century." Annual net income rises to $7.7 billion in 2001 from a loss of $8.1 billion in 1993; revenue rises to $85.9 billion from $62.7 billion; stock price rises to $120.96 per share. About 100,000 new employees are added over a span of seven years.

2001: Queen Elizabeth II awards Gerstner the designation of honorary Knight of the British Empire for his efforts on behalf of public education as well as his business accomplishments.

2002: Retires from IBM in December. Publishes book called *Who Says Elephants Can't Dance? Inside IBM's Historic Turnaround*, about his efforts to restructure the company and its culture.

2003: Named chairman of The Carlyle Group, a global private equity firm with more than $13.9 billion under management.

None of the steps would have been successful without flushing out a calcified IBM culture composed of fiefdoms that were out of touch with each other and with their customers' needs—insidiously undermining performance. Gerstner describes the IBM of that era as suffering from "success syndrome," a disorder afflicting companies that have been successful for decades. This malady, he says, locks them into repeating what made them successful in the first place, even when the competitive environment changes and new steps are required to remain relevant.

Gerstner says he spent about 40% of his time during his first two years meeting IBM employees face-to-face, exhorting them, and filling them with a sense of urgency over a short-term plan that had to be executed. "I was very blunt, very direct, and very honest," Gerstner notes. "I appealed to their pride, their competitive juices, and their economic necessities." He told them it was time to get back to fundamentals like talking to customers and actually selling products rather than simply developing them. He essentially rebuilt the culture to focus on performance.

Along the way, Gerstner led the charge against a vast number of internal processes that would invariably derail any changes. For example, he revamped compensation, promotions, and training programs. "It takes an enormous amount of work to change the culture because the culture is embedded in everything. As a leader, you can't just get on a soap box and say, 'Let's do this, let's do that,' if every day when [managers] come to work, the processes and the systems in the company drive them in a different direction." The cultural revolution spearheaded by Gerstner at IBM invariably involved bloodletting. "Those people who could not adapt to that new culture left on their own volition or they left because we told them they had to leave."

Gerstner concedes he was never fully confident about the company's turn-around. "I was always convinced that we had gotten the strategy right or at least the direction we were going in right. My confidence was challenged by my sense of whether we could execute."

They could. Between 1993 and 2001 (Gerstner stepped down as CEO the following year), IBM's annual net income rose to $7.7 billion from a loss of $8.1 billion; revenues rose to $85.9 billion from $62.7 billion, and the stock price rose to $120.96 per share from $14.12 per share.

In his book, *Who Says Elephants Can't Dance? Inside IBM's Historic Turnaround*, published in 2002, Gerstner wrote that "changing the attitude and behavior of thousands of people is very, very hard to accomplish....You can't simply give a couple of speeches or write a new credo for the company and declare that a new culture has taken hold. You can't mandate it, can't engineer it. What you can do is create the conditions for transformation, provide incentives."

Gerstner seems to have done that. After his retirement, he noted that IBM, despite its insular culture, was rich with creative talent that only needed to be set loose. The head of every major business unit today, he said in his book, is a long-time IBMer, including his successor as CEO, Sam Palmisano.

Leadership Lesson

Life Lessons for Fast Learners

Imagine this: A young man or woman, about five years removed from an MBA, meets Louis Gerstner on an elevator, realizes he is the former CEO of IBM, and asks him how to become a successful leader. What would Gerstner's two-minute reply be? In the blunt manner that former associates at American Express, RJR Nabisco, and IBM have come to know well, he says: "Part of the problem with people coming out of business schools is that they want to be leaders immediately. Their attitude is, 'Make me the CEO.' But they've got to realize that before they can succeed as leaders, they must first become effective workers and managers."

Gerstner offers plenty of advice to fast learners who want to become effective workers and managers en route to the Holy Grail of lasting leadership. "First, find an industry that is growing," he says. "Remember Warren Buffett's statement that when an industry with a bad reputation needs an executive with a good reputation, it is the industry's reputation that stays intact. You've got to direct yourself to a profession in an industry that has prospects for growth." Having done that, Gerstner adds, for the first five years, no matter what job you are offered, just adopt the adage, "I'm going to do this job better than anyone has ever done it before." Focus on getting the job done better, not on who's on the fast track to being noticed. "Don't game it," he says. "Outperform. Believe me, people will notice you."

Gerstner contends that when you become a leader, the situation changes. "As a leader, you become a manager of many people. Then it is a question of whether you can communicate honestly," he says, explaining that leaders need to ask themselves several questions: "Can you provide people with an offensive direction that they can get excited about? Can you communicate honestly about where the company or the unit is? Can you be open about talking to your team members about their performance and how they need to get better? Can you develop a sense early on that your job is to make them successful and that their job is to make you successful? Because, at the end of the day, if you make them successful, they are going to make you triple successful." In a nutshell, Gerstner says, the critical task of becoming a leader is passing through the difficult time of understanding that a strategy has to be executed correctly, and that you have to depend on others to get the work done.

When Gerstner was in his late 20s and early 30s, he had a hard time recognizing this reality. "Too many young people, when there is a shortfall in an organization, simply say, 'Give me that, I will do it—I will write the memo, prepare the presentation, do the work.'" At some point on the way to becoming a leader, that mindset has to change. "Leaders recognize that they only succeed if their team succeeds. And for a team to succeed, you need straight talk, sharing, and openness."

Do different kinds of organizations differ in the kind of leadership they need? For example, did Gerstner need different leadership qualities at IBM than he did at American Express or RJR Nabisco? "First of all," Gerstner says, "IBM forced me to change not so much my leadership style but my managerial style to a certain extent." As president of American Express, Gerstner had been heavily involved in regular operational reviews of the business. "I reviewed every one of my businesses every month with a strong performance measurement system. I worked operations regularly with my division presidents and group executives. When I got to IBM, I realized there were so many businesses, group executives, and division presidents that if I started having monthly financial reviews with every one of them, I would spend all month doing it and then start all over again." As a result, he came up with a new system at IBM, one that relied more on other people to drive results. "So, this is the message I would give a young manager trying to become a leader. You will find yourself increasingly becoming dependent on others, and by the time you get to the top of an organization, your success will depend on your ability to select, motivate, and encourage the team working under you. That will account for 90% of your success."

The fact that at IBM Gerstner was much less involved with day-to-day operations helped him realize the importance of culture as the embodiment of what people do, what they think, and what they value in an institution. "I had viewed culture as one of the things that you, as a leader, need to understand, and manage, like you do finance, marketing, public relations, and so on," he says. "I finished my IBM career with the view that culture is not one of the things you do, it is everything. Everything resides in culture. It is the crucible. So if you think you are going to change a company's strategy, you had better understand before you even try whether the culture will support or fight that strategy."

"I heard someone say the other day that when strategy clashes with culture, culture always wins. Again, this is something that many people simply don't understand. At one level, culture seems theoretical and soft because it consists of values, attitudes, behavior. But those values and behavior are driven and reinforced every single day by the processes in the company."

Gerstner offers an example of the dissonance that can emerge within a company when culture is in conflict with operations. "I love CEOs who say, 'We believe in the long term and are building for the long term,' and then on the next day, a memo arrives from the CFO saying, 'I want you to cut your budgets by 5% for the next two quarters.' People respond to the CFO's message, because they have to do that. So the culture becomes short-term oriented, not long-term, even though the CEO is out there, pointing to the fences on long-term growth. Such mixed messages produce conflicts within organizations. That is why so many successful people in the last decade who have come from outside to run an organization get enormously frustrated. They feel that what they point to, and suggest, and argue for, and even demand, does not get done."

Managing Risk

Leadership involves coping with risk. It is no more possible to imagine a leader who shuns risk than it is to conceive of an innovator or entrepreneur who avoids it. Most leaders, however, are not uncontrolled gamblers (though some might be); they invoke factors that reduce the risks and make them manageable.

All businesses face uncertainty regarding the future because markets might be influenced by factors that are neither known in advance nor fully controllable. As such, tools like scenario planning have evolved, which let executives imagine alternate futures and develop strategies to deal with them. In no area of business, however, does risk management play such a crucial role as in finance. Banks confront market risk when they lend money to borrowers, and possibly even greater internal risk that their own executives might make decisions that jeopardize the enterprise. Insurance companies constantly evaluate and make decisions about risk ranging from natural hazards to other kinds of catastrophes. Venture capitalists routinely bet on start-ups, hoping that one or more will turn into a future eBay or Google.

The Top 25 leaders in this book are skilled at assessing and managing risk. Three of them, however, demonstrate an uncanny ability to deal with it. Warren Buffett, chairman and CEO of Berkshire Hathaway, has had a phenomenal track record in managing risk, not only in his ability to pick winners among investment options but also in the field of insurance, which forms the core of the company's business. While Buffett shows how leaders can manage risk by, for example, choosing appropriate investment targets, Alan Greenspan, who heads the U.S. Federal Reserve, has been a master at managing risks at a macro level, including those that erupt from convulsions in the global financial system—such as the Asian contagion in the 1990s—or from stock market meltdowns, such as the one that hit Wall Street in October 1987. Although Greenspan has erred in his judgment from time to time—his support of Charles Keating and the management team at Lincoln Savings and Loan comes to mind—he acknowledges and corrects his errors. As Paul Samuelson once said about him, "The thing about Greenspan is that he doesn't stay wrong."

Peter Lynch, vice chairman of Fidelity Management & Research Company, the investment advisory arm of Fidelity Investments, and member of the Fidelity Funds Board of Trustees, managed Fidelity's Magellan fund for 13 years from 1977 to 1990. He excels at managing the portfolio of risks that confront mutual funds. During his leadership of Magellan, it became the top equity mutual fund in the U.S. He has written about his investment philosophy in popular books such as *One Up on Wall Street* and *Beating the Street*—explaining that investors should do their homework and avoid faddish stocks that are hot today but that may well burn out tomorrow.

WARREN BUFFETT

The Challenge:

Investing for the Long Term

By 1999, Warren Buffett had long been an investing legend. The year before, Berkshire Hathaway's stock price had risen more than 50% in the second-best year since Buffett took control in 1965. But 1999 was terrible: a stock loss of nearly 20%, while the Standard & Poor's 500 was up nearly 21%.

"We had the worst absolute performance of my tenure and, compared to the S&P, the worst relative performance as well," Buffett confessed in his annual report to shareholders. Buffett didn't blame the market. How could he when most stocks were soaring?

Buffett goes on to say, "Even Inspector Clouseau could find last year's guilty party: your chairman. My performance reminds me of the quarterback whose report card showed four Fs and a D but who nonetheless had an understanding coach. 'Son,' he drawled, 'I think you're spending too much time on that one subject.' My 'one subject' is capital allocation, and my grade for 1999 most assuredly is a D. What most hurt us during the year was the inferior performance of Berkshire's equity portfolio—and responsibility for that portfolio...is entirely mine."

Shareholders could excuse a little levity. That had long been Buffett's style. And long-term investors had little to complain about, as annual returns since 1965 averaged a stunning 24%, more than double the return of the S&P 500.

1930: Born in Omaha, Nebraska. Family operated an Omaha grocery store from 1869 to 1969. Howard, his father, is a stockbroker and Republican congressman; his mother, Leila Stahl, is a homemaker.

1941: At 11 starts work in his father's brokerage and buys his first stock.

1945: Makes $175 per month delivering The Washington Post and buys 40 acres of Nebraska farmland for $1,200.

1947–1949: Studies at the University of Pennsylvania's Wharton School, transfers to the University of Nebraska to complete his undergraduate degree.

1950: Earns B.S. from University of Nebraska. As a senior, reads Benjamin Graham's The Intelligent Investor, which advises avoiding fads and seeking undervalued stocks. Is turned down at Harvard Business School and enrolls at Columbia University's business school to study with Graham.

1951: Graduates from Columbia and goes to work on Wall Street, against the advice of his father and Graham. Then returns to Omaha to become a stock broker at his father's firm and teach night business classes.

1952: Marries Susan Thompson, with whom he has three children.

1954: Takes a $12,000-a-year job in New York helping manage Graham's investment partnership.

1956: Graham retires and dissolves the partnership. Buffett returns to Omaha and forms Buffett Associates, Ltd. with $105,000 raised from seven family members and friends, plus his own contribution of $100. Later, he starts two additional partnerships. Eventually, the three partnerships are merged. His goal is to beat the Dow by 10 percentage points a year.

1958: Buys the $31,500 Omaha home he never leaves.

1959: Meets Charlie Munger, his lifelong partner and eventual vice-chairman of Berkshire Hathaway.

1962: The partnership that began five years earlier with $105,000 is worth $7.2 million and the Buffetts are worth more than $1 million. All the partnerships are merged into Buffett Partnerships, Ltd. Begins buying stock in Berkshire Hathaway, a troubled New Bedford, Mass. textile mill, at less than $7.60 a share. Buffett uses Berkshire capital to invest in other businesses, such as insurance.

1963: The Buffett Partnerships become Berkshire's largest shareholder.

Throughout his career, Buffett's strategy, whether buying a block of shares or an entire company, has been simple: Don't pursue the high-flyers, look for beaten-down companies with lots of value that other investors don't see. He seeks out companies with good managers who will stay, and he generally leaves them alone. While many money managers change their entire portfolio every year, Buffett intends to keep his purchases forever. He told his shareholders at one point: "If the choice is between a questionable business at a comfortable price or a comfortable business at a questionable price, we much prefer the latter. What really gets our attention, however, is a comfortable business at a comfortable price."

In 1999, the tech-stock bubble had driven the S&P 500 into the stratosphere. But despite some criticism, Buffett had resisted any temptation to jump on the tech bandwagon. He had long avoided investing in any business he could not understand. More importantly, he shunned companies whose future cash flow could not be forecast. Many of the hot tech companies had no earnings, little revenue, and no long-term track records.

"If we have a strength, it is in recognizing when we are operating well within our circle of competence and when we are approaching the perimeter," Buffett wrote. "Predicting the long-term economics of companies that operate in fast-changing industries is simply far beyond our perimeter."

Buffett had long favored straightforward, traditional businesses, and Berkshire had big holdings in American Express, The Coca-Cola Co., The Washington Post Co., Freddie Mac, Gillette, M&T Bank, and Wells Fargo. But the heart of Berkshire was its stable of insurance companies. The insurance "float"—cash collected in premiums and invested until it's paid out in claims—had been used to fund many Berkshire investments. In 1998, he made Berkshire's biggest purchase, paying $22 billion for General Reinsurance. Unfortunately, storms in Europe pushed insurance claims unusually high in 1999, while price competition undercut premiums, causing a $1.4 billion underwriting loss at the big insurer. Buffett watchers complained General Re management had lost cohesion and Buffett had erred in sticking with his practice of not interfering in the running of Berkshire's subsidiaries.

There also was trouble at some other holdings, including Coke. Starting in the late 1980s, Berkshire had acquired about 8% of Coca-Cola, paying an average of $10 per share and reasoning that the markets had not fully recognized the value of the brand, especially given the potential for expansion overseas. The stock soared to $87 in 1998, but then tumbled to the $50 range, cutting the value of Berkshire's holdings in Coke by $7 billion.

In a March 2000 article titled "The Sage Has Some Explaining To Do," *BusinessWeek* writer Anthony Bianco summed up the critics' view: "In loading up on Coke a decade ago, Buffett acted on one of the definitive insights of his career: the recognition that Wall Street was grossly underestimating the intrinsic value of great consumer brands. By now, though, Buffett's view has been so thoroughly assimilated that it's a cliché." With the value of the brand fully reflected in Coke's price, the stock might never again provide big returns, Bianco wrote. Buffett appeared to have erred by

1964: Begins buying inexpensive shares of American Express while the company is mired in a financial fraud scandal. Shares double by the end of 1965.

1965: Gains control of Berkshire Hathaway.

1966: Buffett's share of the partnership is worth more than $6.8 million.

1967: Buffet's net worth is more than $10 million. He tells his partners he sees no more bargains in the soaring stock market. Berkshire acquires National Indemnity insurance for $8.6 million.

1969: The partnership is dissolved after achieving a compounded annual return of 29.5%, versus 7.4% for the Dow. Buffett had concluded too many stocks were overpriced. Assets distributed to partners include shares of Berkshire Hathaway. Buffett is worth about $25 million. Single-handedly forces Omaha's premier country club to admit Jews.

1970: Buffett owns 29% of Berkshire, names himself chairman, and begins writing the annual letter to shareholders that becomes famous. Berkshire makes only $45,000 from textiles, $4.7 million from insurance, banking, and other investments.

1973: Berkshire begins buying The Washington Post Co. stock. Buffett becomes a director a year later. Becomes an influential advisor to *Post* publisher Katherine Graham.

1974: With stock prices plummeting, Buffett's net worth drops by half. The SEC investigates Buffett to determine if he had improperly influenced the price of stock in one of his holdings. After two years, the SEC takes no action against Buffett and names him to a blue ribbon panel on corporate disclosure practices.

1976: Berkshire begins massive investment in GEICO insurance stock. Berkshire has its best year, with a 59.3% gain in book value per share, beating the S&P 500 by 35.7 points.

1977: Susan Buffett leaves Warren's home and moves to San Francisco, though they remain close until her death in 2004. Berkshire purchases the *Buffalo Evening News.*

1979: With Berkshire at $290 a share, Buffett is worth $140 million. Berkshire begins to buy shares of ABC.

1983: Berkshire ends the year at $1,310 per share, and Buffett is worth $620 million. Berkshire purchases Nebraska Furniture Mart.

1985: Buffett shuts down Berkshire's money-losing textile mill. Engineers ABC-Capital Cities merger.

refusing to sell Berkshire's Coke holdings the year before in time to lock in his Coke gains. Some critics wondered whether his judgment was clouded by a conflict of interest: Buffett had joined Coke's board of directors in 1989, and a sale by Berkshire could have hurt Coke's share price. But Buffett had always thought of his acquisitions as permanent; he hated to sell.

And he stuck with that policy despite the bad results in 1999. "Several of our largest investees badly lagged the market in 1999 because they had disappointing operating results," Buffett said. "We still like these businesses and are content to have major investments in them. But their stumbles damaged our performance last year, and it's no sure thing that they will quickly regain their stride."

Buffett's stay-the-course approach was vindicated in 2000, when Berkshire shares rose 26.6%. The S&P 500 lost 9% as tech stocks collapsed and a bear market took hold. Avoiding tech had paid off; meanwhile, the turnaround strategy was in place at the insurance subsidiaries, where premiums had been raised.

Also, Berkshire made a number of acquisitions. Buffett told shareholders, "We have embraced the 21st century by entering such cutting-edge industries as brick, carpet, insulation, and paint. Try to control your excitement."

Leadership Lesson

The Noah Rule

Warren Buffett, arguably the most successful investor of our times, believes in taking risks—calculated risks. Whether the risk is worth taking or not depends, in part, upon the circumstances in question as well as the potential reward. An important aspect of Buffett's leadership lies in his ability to think about risk differently than most investors do. For example, when a company is being slammed in the media, most investors might think it is time to head for the exits. Not Buffett. Consider, for example, his approach to American Express when the company was in trouble in the fall of 1963.

As Roger Lowenstein narrates in *Buffett: The Making of an American Capitalist*, the problems at American Express had begun innocuously and unexpectedly. An oil refining company had supposedly stored tank loads of salad oil in a New Jersey warehouse owned by an American Express subsidiary. Then, armed with receipts issued by the warehouse, the refiner's executives had borrowed an estimated $150 million. It turned out, however, that the tanks contained very little oil; most of them were filled with sea water. Having defrauded its lenders, the oil refiner declared bankruptcy; later, so did the American Express subsidiary that owned the warehouse.

Who, then, should make good the losses? American Express CEO Howard Clark, who was concerned that the scandal might erode the public's trust in the company's

1986: Berkshire hits $3,000 per share.

1987: Berkshire buys a block of Salomon Brothers for $700 million. Berkshire loses 25% of its value in the October stock crash.

1988–1989: Spends about $1.3 billion to acquire a big share of Coca-Cola and joins the company's board. The $10-per-share investment soars to $87 a share in mid-1998. Berkshire shares rise to over $8,000, giving Buffett a net worth exceeding $3.8 billion.

1991: Steps in as chairman of Salomon Brothers during a Treasury bond trading scandal.

1995: Engineers the $19.5 billion sale of Cap Cities/ABC to Disney. Over the years, Berkshire earned a $2.5 billion profit on its Cap Cities/ABC investment. Because Disney paid for part of the purchase with Disney stock, it was also a chance for Berkshire to become a big shareholder in Disney, and to benefit from the synergies expected when Disney, the content provider, was combined with the network, a content distributor.

1998: Pays $22 billion for General Reinsurance.

1999: Berkshire has its worst year, with the share price down nearly 21%, even as most stock indexes soared. Buffett rejects pressure to jump into technology stocks and says he's happy with Berkshire's holdings.

2000: The tech bubble bursts and Berkshire shares soar nearly 27% while the S&P 500 loses 9%.

2003: Harshly criticizes President George Bush's proposed tax cuts as an unfair break for the wealthy. Surprises long-time Buffett watchers by becoming a financial and economic advisor to California gubernatorial candidate Arnold Schwarzenegger. Buffett has long believed Schwarzenegger has the leadership needed to tackle California's deep fiscal problems.

2004: In his annual letter to shareholders, he criticizes high pay for corporate executives and mutual fund directors who are not accountable to shareholders. *Forbes* magazine lists Buffett as the world's second richest person, with a net worth of $42.9 billion. (Microsoft's Bill Gates is the richest.)

name, accepted moral responsibility and offered to pay off the liabilities—at least to the tune of $60 million. American Express stock took a huge hit, a situation made worse by market turmoil that followed Kennedy's assassination at around the same time. As details of the fraud unfolded, American Express shares continued to fall; they dropped from 60 before the scandal to 35 in early 1964. Then shareholders sued the company, arguing that by offering to pay because of moral (rather than legal) considerations, Clark was squandering American Express assets. As the negative publicity went on, the stock price plunged further.

Most investors believed, at that time, that American Express would be buried by the scandal. The stock had become too risky to hold, so they began to dump their shares. Buffett, however, did something different. Instead of focusing on the negative news, he went to steakhouses and other restaurants, where he noted the fact that diners were continuing to pay for meals with American Express cards. He visited travel agencies, where he learned that tourists, unconcerned about the salad oil scandal, were continuing to buy American Express travelers' checks. In short, he realized that whatever the falling stock price might suggest about the perceived risk of owning American Express shares, customers trusted the company enough to keep using its products. Based on his investigation, Buffett concluded that American Express would bounce back. He began to buy American Express stock and even met Clark to congratulate him for dealing with the problem as honestly as he had. Eventually, American Express stock prices rose again. Panicky investors were proved wrong; Buffett's view was vindicated.

Buffett has used a similar approach to weigh risks and rewards in making several investment decisions. As he explained to an auditorium filled with Wharton students during a visit to the school in April 1999, he bases his investment philosophy on four principles:

1. Understand the business in which you are investing. "I look for businesses within my circle of competence," he said. Having a large circle of competence is less important than having one with a well-defined perimeter.

2. Look for sound fundamental economics. Investors should seek out companies that have a sustainable economic advantage—a phenomenon Buffett called "a castle with a moat around it." Consider Coca-Cola, for example. The company's brand name has represented enjoyment for generations, which no competitor can buy for millions of dollars. "Share of market follows share of mind," noted Buffett.

3. Find competent leadership. Companies with a sustainable economic advantage need honest, capable, and hardworking leaders to retain their lead. Berkshire Hathaway's managers have one instruction: Widen the moat. That keeps the castle valuable.

4. Buy at the right price. Purchases must be made at the right price if they are to pay off.

Buffett cited example after example to show how he used these principles to make investment decisions during his career. As a young investment manager, he took Moody's manuals and went through them page by page until he found the companies he sought. A bus company in Bedford, for example, had $100 a share in cash, but its stock was being traded at $40 a share. Buffett found such deals because he went looking for them. "No one will tell you about them," he said. "You only get told about things someone is pushing for some reason." Buffett invested in companies like Coca-Cola and The Washington Post Co. for similar reasons. Berkshire Hathaway built its empire on the success of these investments.

The core of Berkshire's business is insurance, where risk evaluation is crucial. In Buffett's letter to shareholders reporting the
2001 results—hurt by September 11 insurance losses—he noted
some key principles of risk control: For example, sound insurance
companies usually "ignore market-share considerations" and are
"sanguine about losing business to competitors that are offering
foolish prices or policy conditions." They also "ceaselessly search
for possible correlation among seemingly unrelated risks." A key
problem in risk evaluation is to avoid excessive reliance on past
patterns. "In short, all of us in the industry made a fundamental
underwriting mistake by focusing on experience, rather than exposure, thereby assuming a huge terrorism risk for which we received
no premium," he wrote.

When things go wrong in assessing risk, Buffett's style is to take
the blame himself and to credit others when they go right.
Explaining Berkshire's poor showing in 1999, he accepted the
responsibility personally. In fact, a major factor was a huge underwriting loss at the insurance unit General Re. Because it is impossible to forecast insurance claims perfectly, insurance is a volatile
business and losses in any one year can just as easily be the result
of bad luck as bad management. Another unavoidable factor in
General Re's 1999 troubles was an insurance-industry price war.
Instead of criticizing his managers, Buffett waxed eloquent about
their talents. "It's simply impossible to overstate Ajit {Jain}'s value
to Berkshire," Buffet wrote of his top General Re executive. Buffett
predicted—accurately, it turned out—that General Re would turn
around over the next few years and become a stellar holding.

In 2001, Berkshire's net worth fell by $3.77 billion, though the
company still did well relative to its benchmark, the Standard &
Poor's 500. "Though our corporate performance last year was satisfactory, *my* performance was anything but," Buffett wrote. "I
manage Berkshire's equity portfolio, and my results were poor,
just as they have been for several years. Of even more importance,
I allowed General Re to take on business without a safeguard I
knew was important, and on September 11, this error caught up
with us." The September 11 attacks cost General Re more than $2
billion. General Re, Buffett conceded, had violated two principles
of good insurance businesses: to take on only those risks that can
be properly evaluated and to limit exposure to huge losses from a

single event. "The events of September 11 made it clear that our
implementation of [those principles] at General Re had been dan-
gerously weak. In setting prices and also in evaluating aggregation
risk, we had either overlooked or dismissed the possibility of large-
scale terrorism losses... Why, you might ask, didn't I recognize the
above facts *before* September 11? The answer, sadly, is that I did—
but I didn't convert thought into action. I violated the Noah rule:
Predicting rain doesn't count; building arks does."

1926: Born in New York City to Herbert, a small businessman who later becomes a stockbroker and economic consultant, and Rose, a homemaker.

1931: His parents divorce. Alan and his mother move in with her parents in the Washington Heights neighborhood of New York, and she takes a job in a furniture store in the Bronx. Herbert and Alan remain distant for the rest of Herbert's life, visiting only occasionally.

1943: Graduates from George Washington High School as a member of the honor society and recipient of a special citation from the music department. Though a gifted mathematician, Greenspan's ambition is to become a professional jazz clarinetist. He begins studying at The Julliard School.

1944: Drops out of Julliard to tour with a jazz band, Henry Jerome and His Orchestra, earning $62 a week. Greenspan is not good enough for a prominent role in the band and remains a background musician. He does not join the band members' wild partying but does take over the band's accounting and starts reading economics.

ALAN GREENSPAN

The Challenge:

Dealing with Uncertainty

In August 1998, Russia became the latest victim of the "Asian Contagion" that had started the year before with traders pulling money out of risky bets in Thailand. Russian officials defaulted on government bond payments and panicky traders dumped bonds all over the world, causing prices to plummet and interest rates to soar. Soon the stock markets were infected, and the Dow Jones Industrial Average dropped 6% on August 31. A Greenwich, Connecticut, hedge fund called Long-Term Capital Management (LTCM) had made enormous, leveraged bets on interest rate movements, which were now going the opposite way from what LTCM had predicted. The hedge fund could be wiped out, threatening to take down many big Wall Street firms that had lent it billions.

For Federal Reserve Chairman Alan Greenspan, the threat of a worldwide meltdown in the financial markets was reminiscent of the 1987 stock crash he had handled so deftly. What should he do this time?

A big part of the problem was psychological. If lenders worried that borrowers could not repay, lenders would refuse to make loans even if borrowers *could* repay. And with interest rates soaring, companies and individuals were reluctant to borrow anyway. The economic system might freeze up like an engine running without oil—or it might not.

"In practice, one is never quite sure what type of uncertainty one is dealing with in real time, and it may be best to think of a continuum ranging from well-defined risks to the truly unknown," Greenspan said in a 2004 speech reviewing his monetary policy since becoming Fed chairman in 1987. "As a consequence, the conduct of monetary policy in the United States has come to involve, at its core, crucial elements of risk management."

Greenspan had long believed no rigid set of rules could dictate Fed policy: Key decisions were judgment calls that, to be effective, had to be implemented well before a problem was clearly evident. This sometimes led to criticism, as Greenspan and his Federal Open Market Committee (FOMC) raised interest rates to head off inflation that had not yet arrived, or lowered rates to stimulate an economy that still appeared healthy.

At times, dealing with uncertainty meant making a decision that looked wrong. "Following the Russian debt default in the autumn of 1998, for example, the FOMC eased policy [lowered rates] despite our perception that the economy was expanding at a satisfactory pace and that, even without a policy initiative, it was likely to continue doing so," Greenspan said. "We eased policy because we were concerned about the low-probability risk that the default might trigger events that would severely disrupt domestic and international financial markets, with outsized adverse feedback to the performance of the U.S. economy."

In other words, the worst case wasn't likely, but it would be so devastating if it did happen that something had to be done.

1945: Greenspan realizes he doesn't have the talent to be a professional musician. Enrolls in NYU's School of Commerce, later known as the Stern School of Business, and joins a select group of students studying economics. (Greenspan has a 4-F medical deferment from the military because of a spot on one lung, though he later turns out to be in good health.)

1948: Graduates summa cum laude with a B.S. in economics. Begins graduate studies in economics at Columbia University. Greenspan gradually gives up his earlier view that government should closely regulate the economy and adopts a more laissez-faire perspective emphasizing free markets and deregulation.

1952: Marries Joan Mitchell, a Canadian in New York to study art history. Short of tuition money, Greenspan drops out of Columbia and takes a job with the National Industrial Conference Board, later called the Conference Board, a non-profit business-research organization.

1953: Greenspan and Mitchell have their marriage annulled but remain close friends for many years. Mitchell introduces Greenspan to writer and philosopher Ayn Rand and her circle of objectivists.

1953: While at the Conference Board, begins outside consulting, then joins one of his clients, William Townsend, to found the five-person economics consulting firm Townsend-Greenspan, which initially specializes in serving the steel industry. Leaves the Conference Board.

1958: Townsend, 70, dies of a heart attack. Greenspan, 32, keeps the firm going and, by the late 1960s, is a millionaire.

1966: Collaborates with a *Fortune* magazine economist to produce an influential cover story that shows the Vietnam War would cost $9 billion more than President Johnson had called for in his 1967 budget.

1968: Joins the Nixon presidential campaign as coordinator of domestic-policy research. Invited by old friends Leonard Garment, a former bandmate who had joined Nixon's law firm, and economist Arthur Burns, Greenspan's mentor at Columbia.

1969: Serves as Nixon's chief of budget liaison on the presidential transition team. Turns down Nixon's offer to be budget director and returns to Townsend-Greenspan. Greenspan does, however, serve on a variety of government commissions during the Nixon administration.

First, the Fed organized a consortium of 16 Wall Street firms that had lent some $20 billion to LTCM. The firms agreed to pool another $3.6 billion to keep the hedge fund afloat, thus averting the LTCM collapse that could set off a vicious cycle of fire sales in bonds. Brokering a bailout for a single player in the market was an unusual move for the Fed and put its reputation at risk; critics could claim this was a case of powerful people helping out their rich friends. But there was no public money involved, and Greenspan reluctantly backed the New York Fed official who had organized the rescue.

Then at the end of September, the FOMC cut the Fed Funds rate a quarter-point to $5\frac{1}{4}\%$. The cut was designed to assure the markets that the Fed would step in to guarantee liquidity—the availability of money—so the system would not freeze up. Fed rate-cutting could also help reverse the rise in rates that had swept the bond markets. Some FOMC members said another quarter-point cut was needed to ram the message home, but Greenspan held off the second cut until October 15. Success was immediate: Bond prices soared and interest rates dropped, and the next day the Dow scored its third largest point gain in history. The markets had gotten the message— the Fed had the situation under control. In mid-November, Greenspan convinced the committee to cut another quarter point as insurance.

As in 1987, Greenspan had been leery of moving too fast. Since the start of his career in the early 1950s, he had believed that, in most cases, regulators should let the markets sort themselves out. But he was nonetheless the pragmatist. "I often come out almost ad nauseam with free market solutions not because I have an ideology, but because I believe it works," he said. "Where it doesn't, I recognize that it doesn't."

Despite its power and the enormous stature Greenspan had attained, the Fed has very limited tools—primarily its control of two short-term interest rates affecting loans to and between institutions. The long-term rates that affect the markets most, such as those on bonds and mortgages, are set by forces of supply and demand that the Fed cannot directly control. But the Fed can influence those rates by sending signals about whether it is likely to raise or lower short-term rates in the future. Piloting the economy takes deft, gentle, and minimal adjustments to the throttle, else it would careen between excessive, inflation-producing growth and recessions that undermine corporate profits and drive up unemployment.

Under Greenspan, the Fed has adopted ever more elaborate ways to evaluate the economy to get an early read on the risk of overheating versus slowdown. The Fed does not provide details of the data and computer models it uses, but Greenspan has long been known for wringing insight from obscure signs.

"People who worked for him over the years were driven to distraction by the ever-increasing amount of data he would track," wrote biographer Justin Martin. As a consultant, for example, Greenspan had become enamored of paperboard, a ubiquitous packaging material. "If demand for paperboard was up, Greenspan took it as a signal that economic activity was on the increase... Greenspan was forever adding to his toolbox of indicators."

1970: The growing Townsend-Greenspan company moves to larger quarters in New York's financial district. In the 1970s, Greenspan serves as consultant to the Council of Economic Advisors.

1971: With inflation rising to 5%, Nixon imposes a 90-day freeze on wages and prices. Greenspan criticizes the move as inappropriate government fine-tuning. After the controls are lifted in 1974, pent up forces trigger the double-digit inflation of the mid-70s.

1974: Accepts Nixon's offer to be chairman of the Council of Economic Advisers, which advises the president on economic policy. Nixon resigns before Greenspan is confirmed. President Ford sticks with Greenspan, who is quickly approved by the Senate. Inflation is running at 12% and, by the end of the year, unemployment has gone to 8%, up from 3.4% in 1969—an unusual combination dubbed "stagflation."

1975: Though he doesn't believe in economic fine tuning, Greenspan urges Ford to cut taxes to stimulate the economy, making the attack on unemployment a higher priority than fighting inflation. The economic turnaround begins several months later. Recommends Ford resist any federal bailout of New York City, mired in a fiscal crisis, but later orchestrates a federal loan to the city.

1976: Over objections from Ford and Greenspan, Congress passes the Humphrey-Hawkins bill aimed at cutting employment to 3%, from the current level over 7%, within three years. Ford loses his reelection bid to Jimmy Carter. Greenspan steps down as CEA chair and returns to New York.

1977: Completes his Ph.D. at NYU after taking courses off and on for three decades.

1980: Becomes economic adviser to Ronald Reagan's presidential campaign.

1981: Heads Reagan's National Commission on Social Security Reform, which in 1982, recommends increasing the payroll tax, increasing the level of earnings subject to the tax, and taxing Social Security benefits. The recommendations became part of a law signed in 1983.

Because the Fed's arsenal is so limited, its success often hinges on the stature of its chairman, and Greenspan is considered a master politician. In his appearances before Congress and in public statements issued by the Fed, he tries to reassure. But he stops short of offering guarantees about the course of the economy lest otherwise unexpected results undermine his credibility and effectiveness.

"Policymakers often have to act, or choose not to act, even though we may not fully understand the full range of possible outcomes, let alone each possible outcome's likelihood," he said. "As the transcripts of FOMC meetings attest, making monetary policy is an especially humbling activity. In hindsight, the paths of inflation, real output, stock prices, and exchange rates may have seemed preordained, but no such insight existed as we experienced it at the time. In fact, uncertainty characterized virtually every meeting."

Leadership Lesson

The Limits of Risk Management

If Buffett did not foresee September 11 coming, Greenspan didn't realize when he moved into his job at the helm of the Federal Reserve that he would soon preside over an economy confronted by the biggest stock market meltdown in recent memory. Greenspan took office on August 11, 1987, "with much to learn and more to prove. A few days into his new job, Greenspan told a colleague that he felt like a VCR on fast for-ward...Parachuting into the top job at the Federal Reserve is preposterously difficult. Greenspan scrambled to make sense of the Fed's awesome capabilities. One thing he quickly grew to love was the massive research machine now at his disposal... Only a few weeks into his tenure, Greenspan began to see mounting signs that the economy was overheating," notes author Justin Martin in his book, *The Man Behind the Money*.

Just 24 days into his term, Greenspan raised the discount rate a half percentage point to 6% to head off inflation. There were numerous signs of trouble: a record trade deficit, an economic-policy fight with Germany, a huge federal budget deficit, a rise in interest rates that had taken the 30-year Treasury bond from 8.8% when Greenspan took office to 10%. Fear was in the air. Soon, the panic began to spread to Wall Street.

Stocks started to plunge on October 12. A week later, on October 19—which was to become known as "Black Monday" Greenspan was scheduled to fly from Washington to Dallas to speak to the American Bankers Association convention in his first public

1987: Reagan names Greenspan Federal Reserve Chairman. Greenspan closes Townsend-Greenspan in July and is sworn in as the Fed's 13th chairman on August 11. In September he raises short-term rates ½% to 6%, worried the strong economic expansion will lead to inflation. The stock-market crash hits in mid-October, with the Dow Jones Industrial Average falling 22.6% on October 19. Greenspan issues a statement that the Fed will pump extra money into the system to avert a banking collapse. The markets soon turn around.

1988: Fed returns to tightening mode. With the stock market crisis over, attention is focused on the superheated economy, which had grown at an annual rate of 7.2% in the fourth quarter of 1987. The move is unpopular with some Reagan officials who want a loose policy during the election year.

1989: George H.W. Bush becomes president, presiding over an economic decline, a savings and loan crisis, and recession. Greenspan and Bush have an uncomfortable relationship throughout Bush's term.

1990: The economy slips into recession. Greenspan is late in recognizing the situation.

1991: Unemployment rises to 7% and Greenspan comes under growing criticism, some from Bush, for not cutting interest rates. The Gulf War begins in January and the recession ends in March. After failing to find an alternative, Bush nominates Greenspan for another term.

1992: With the recovery limping along, the Bush administration, facing a reelection battle, pushes for bigger rate cuts than Greenspan is willing to make, though the Fed Funds rate is slashed to a 30-year low of 3% by September. Bush loses the election and blames Greenspan.

1993: Bill Clinton becomes president. He and Greenspan make a priority of reducing the federal budget deficit. Clinton pushes through a $241 billion tax increase.

1994: Worried that the Fed Funds rate had stood at 3% for 18 months, making inflation a threat, the Fed begins a series of moves to raise the rate to 6% by February 1995. Greenspan is widely criticized, since there was little sign of inflation and the rate hike causes deep losses in the bond market.

appearance since becoming Fed chairman. "Greenspan felt strongly that he should go to Dallas. His colleagues agreed. Canceling the address might send an unsettling signal to the markets. As a student of economic history, with 20-plus years in grad school and countless hours debating the topic with [Ayn] Rand's collective, Greenspan knew the value of appearing blasé in the face of a mounting financial crisis," says Martin.

He left for Dallas at 1:45 p.m. with the Dow down 200 points. Arriving at 5:45, he asked about the market close and was told it was "down five-oh-eight," which he interpreted as 5.08, before realizing an instant later it meant 508, a record one-day loss of 22.6%. The big worry was not so much the stock decline as the potential for a panic that would cause a credit crisis. Businesses that needed to borrow would fail if they were denied loans, as had happened in 1929 and in the 1930s, when Fed chairmen mistakenly raised interest rates. Greenspan and his assistants debated issuing a statement pledging the Fed to maintaining liquidity. Some thought this would worsen the crisis; others insisted a statement was needed. "Greenspan weighed in decisively; he felt that a statement was absolutely necessary. Striking a rare blow for brevity, he also insisted that it should be concise and to the point....

"People who dealt with him during this crisis were awestruck—a bit spooked even—by his calm. Here he was, just weeks into his tenure and the stock market had imploded. Although his reaction seemed odd, it was typical Greenspan. Calm and cautious were his natural states—bolstered in this instance by his age, his experience, and his knowledge of economic history," Martin notes. He did cancel his speech and flew back to Washington on Tuesday. Early Tuesday, he issued a one-sentence statement saying the Fed "affirmed today its readiness to serve as a source of liquidity to support the economic and financial system." The Fed was willing to lend money to keep banks operating, allowing them to lend money to brokerages and other businesses hit hard by the crash. "The Fed was delivering a one-two punch. First, it issued a statement about flooding the markets with liquidity. Then, [New York Fed President E. Gerald] Corrigan followed up with the banks, did a bit of canny arm twisting, made sure they actually made the loans available," writes Martin. Later on Tuesday, Greenspan and other officials met with President Ronald Reagan to urge efforts to rein in the deficit. Though little was ultimately done, Reagan issued a statement indicating a willingness to entertain proposals, and that helped calm the markets.

Greenspan's tactics worked and the markets quickly recovered. Some critics did argue his September rate hike helped unsettle the markets. "But mostly, Greenspan received praise for reacting quickly and decisively. By issuing its liquidity statement and backing it up by encouraging banks to lend, the Fed insured that 1987 did not become another 1929," concludes Martin.

Greenspan's leadership during the 1987 stock collapse revealed his ability to manage risk to the U.S. economy during times of uncertainty. Over the course of his

1996: Greenspan begins his third term. Clinton reelected. In a December speech, Greenspan says the stock market boom may be the result of "irrational exuberance." The preemptive strike against inflation works, with the rate dropping to 2.7%. The economy grows at a healthy rate of about 3.7% in the late 1990s.

1997: The Thai baht collapses, setting off the "Asian Contagion," Russian bond default, and collapse of Long-Term Capital Management hedge fund. The Fed responds by cutting interest rates and organizing a consortium of investors to keep the hedge fund afloat.

1997: Marries NBC political correspondent Andrea Mitchell.

2000: George W. Bush becomes president. The stock bubble of the late 1990s bursts and a bear market begins. Fed begins a series of cuts that will take the Fed Funds rate from 6% to 1%.

2001: Greenspan warns that too large a federal budget surplus could hurt the economy. Endorses large tax cuts.

2002–2003: Greenspan wrestles with the "jobless recovery" as economic growth improves and stocks begin to rise again but employers refuse to resume hiring.

2004: Greenspan warns
that the growing federal
budget deficit presents a
serious long-term
problem. Greenspan had
supported the tax cuts
implemented in 2001 but
said they should take
effect only if the
projected budget
surpluses actually
materialized, a condition
not included in the final
package. In 2004, says the
tax cuts should be made
permanent only if there
are offsetting budget cuts
to reduce the deficit.
Amidst worries that
American jobs are
moving overseas, says job
growth should
nonetheless come soon,
and hiring does pick up
in the first half of the
year.

tenure as Fed chairman, he has often shown this ability. His sure hand in leading the Fed—and also the U.S. economy—during such crises as the Asian contagion and September 11 helped him develop his own rules of thumb about risk management, which he explained in early 2004.

In managing risk, Greenspan recognizes there are limits to what he can do. In a speech titled, "Risk and Uncertainty in Monetary Policy" delivered on January 3, 2004, to the American Economic Association in San Diego, he said that "despite extensive efforts to capture and quantify what we perceive as the key macroeconomic relationships, our knowledge about many of the important linkages is far from complete and, in all likelihood, will always remain so. Every model, no matter how detailed or how well designed, conceptually and empirically, is a vastly simplified representation of the world that we experience with all its intricacies on a day-to-day basis."

Greenspan believes that some hazards cannot be avoided, so Fed policy should aim at reducing their consequences. Critics have argued, for example, that monetary tightening and other techniques, such as limiting margin lending, might have prevented the stock bubble of the late 1990s. Greenspan believes, however, that history offers numerous instances of tightening followed by stock gains and that the Fed should focus on the economy and not try to manage the stock market. "Instead of trying to contain a putative bubble by drastic actions with largely unpredictable consequences, we chose, as we noted in our mid-1999 congressional testimony, to

focus on policies to mitigate the fallout when it occurs and, hope-
fully, ease the transition to the next expansion."

The stock-market bubble burst in 2001, and the economy and
markets were hit by the September 11 attacks. During this period,
the Fed reacted by lowering the federal funds rate 5½ percentage
points to a 45-year low of 1%. "There appears to be enough evidence, at least tentatively, to conclude that our strategy of add
ressing the bubble's consequences rather than the bubble itself has
been successful," he said, pointing to the unusually mild recession
that followed the bubble's burst.

1944: Born in Boston. Father, Thomas, a math professor and employee of John Hancock insurance, dies when he is 10. Mother, Esther, is a homemaker. Lynch first started hearing about stocks while caddying for Fidelity President D. George Sullivan.

1963: As a college sophomore, buys his first stock, Flying Tiger Airlines, on what he later said was a faulty premise—that the airline was promising because the air freight business would grow. The stock rose fivefold, but for another reason—a contract ferrying American troops to Vietnam. The Flying Tiger profits helped pay Lynch's graduate school expenses.

1965: Graduates from Boston College with a bachelor of science degree and starts graduate studies at The Wharton School.

1966: Works as a summer intern at Fidelity, researching the paper and publishing industries by traveling the country by bus because of an airline strike.

PETER LYNCH

The Challenge:

Picking the Winners

In 1982, Chrysler Corp. was bankrupt. The stock price had nose-dived as investors raced to the exits to avoid further losses. No one, it seemed, wanted to own the legendary automaker. Almost no one.

Peter Lynch, manager of the Fidelity Magellan Fund, started to wonder whether the common wisdom about Chrysler was wrong. Ultimately, Chrysler was one among many, a prime example of the chief challenge of Lynch's career: to find the moment to go against the herd and bet huge sums on the belief that he was right and nearly everyone else was wrong. "I figured if *I* was wrong, I would lose all my money," Lynch says. "The stock market is kind of counter-intuitive. When the headlines are terrible, that's really when you ought to start buying."

While most Wall Street analysts and investors had been focusing on Chrysler's huge losses, Lynch focused on the fact that the losses were getting smaller. An improvement on the same scale would have excited investors had the company gone from small profits to bigger ones, and Lynch reasoned that a diminishing loss was just as positive. The market, he believed, had overlooked this point.

Also, the company had in hand a $1.5 billion dollar federal loan guarantee it had yet to tap. Chrysler "had this cushion of money it hadn't taken down yet," Lynch recalls. The unions had agreed to let the company outsource some of its parts orders, giving Chrysler a cost-cutting advantage over the other big auto makers—Ford and General Motors. While unions were playing hardball with the others, they had softened their stance with Chrysler, so it wouldn't go under and put them all out of work.

Meanwhile, the country was in a recession, with high interest rates, inflation, and unemployment all cutting deeply into auto sales. But Lynch realized that 49 states had auto-inspection programs that forced people to replace older cars. Many purchasers took out car loans for three or four years; after making their last payment, they could take on new loans for replacement vehicles without increasing their cost of living. "They could get another car and their payment would be the same." After more than three years of weak auto sales, there must be a pent-up need to buy cars, Lynch figured at the time, noting there had never been four consecutive years of falling sales. If the recession were to break, Americans would rush to the showrooms.

Lynch went to Detroit and met with Chrysler CEO Lee Iacocca and a number of his top executives. "They were a bunch of really great auto guys who knew the industry," he recalls, "and they had a lot of good things on the drawing board, like the minivan."

So Lynch started to buy Chrysler stock. By mid-1982, it represented 3% of Magellan Fund assets and the price began to rise. By the end of the year, 5% of Magellan was invested in Chrysler. It was a very big bet. "I was just hoping the auto industry would go from miserable to okay, and that [Chrysler] would get into the black," he says.

1967: Graduates from Wharton near the top of his class, having developed a deep mistrust of academic market theory. Comes to believe the worldly traders at Fidelity have better insight into the financial markets than academics do. Marries Carolyn Hoff, a physical therapist. They have three daughters. Carolyn later becomes president of the Lynch Foundation. Begins two years in the Army as a lieutenant in the artillery, stationed in Texas and Korea.

1969: Joins Fidelity as a metals analyst.

1974: Becomes Fidelity's director of research.

1977: Takes over management of the Magellan Fund on May 31, when the fund had $20 million in assets and only about 40 stocks. Begins to buy many additional stocks, at one point owning 150 in the savings and loan industry alone. Fund returns 11.6% by the end of the year, versus a loss of 4.38% for the Standard & Poor's 500. Fund assets: $22.2 million as of December 31.

1978: Magellan returns 31.7%, the S&P 500 6.6%. Assets: $26.4 million. Lynch first hears about La Quinta Motor Inns, which will become one of his favorite investments. His first tip: a Holiday Inn executive told him La Quinta was killing Holiday Inn in Houston. Lynch is impressed that La Quinta offered rooms comparable to Holiday Inn's, but for 30% less.

1979: Magellan returns 51.7%, the S&P 500 18.6%. Assets: $35.1 million.

1980: Magellan returns 69.9%, the S&P 500 32.3%. Assets: $53.5 million.

1981: Magellan returns 16.5%, the S&P 500 loses 5.0%. Assets: $107.3 million.

1982: Magellan returns 48.1%, the S&P 500 21.4%. Assets: $458.4 million. Lynch becomes interested in Ford Motor Company, then trading around $4 a share, because the company has $8.35 billion in cash, over and above its long-term debt—a very positive sign. By 1988, Lynch has bought Magellan more than five million Ford shares, realizing an enormous paper profit when the price rises to $38. While many analysts think it is time to unload Ford, Lynch holds on, again attracted by the company's enormous cash reserves. The stock rises another 40%. Also invests heavily in Chrysler Corp., betting the money-losing company will emerge from bankruptcy with greater operating efficiency and attractive new vehicle models such as the minivan. The prediction holds true and Chrysler becomes one of his best investments.

That fall, Lynch appeared on the television show *Wall Street Week*, which had earlier interviewed an analyst who insisted it was time to dump Chrysler to capture recent gains. The stock would go no higher, the guest said. Lynch disagreed. "When I did *Wall Street Week* and said I thought Chrysler was attractive, some of my relatives called me up and said, 'You don't know? Chrysler is bankrupt!'"

Over the next five years, Lynch's counterintuitive bet on Chrysler paid off. Auto sales rebounded and the public embraced Chrysler products. With its costs slashed, the company started making money. Many of the shares Lynch acquired for Magellan in 1982 returned more than 1,000%. Lynch calls that a "10-bagger"—two home runs and a double.

Running against the herd as he did with Chrysler required two things: hard work and the ability to resist the doubts that come with being alone. "When I think of my best ideas—Taco Bell, Chrysler, Fannie Mae, La Quinta—I think if 100 people had done the work, 99 would have bought them," says Lynch. "They just didn't do the work." He didn't delegate; he spent eight or nine days a month on the road closely studying hundreds of companies a year. "You had to go visit the company or talk to them. You had to get the story. You had to understand the industry."

Ultimately, the story—the reason the company was likely to do well—had to be simple enough to explain to a 12-year-old, he says. "What's the basic hypothesis? It's usually the fundamentals of the company…You have a very good idea what McDonald's does. You don't have any idea what Dow Chemical does. It's a pain in the neck…but you've got to learn it." According to Lynch, some of the most valuable insights are found talking to a company's competitors. "People always dump on the competition. If they ever say anything *positive* about it, you know it's true."

At Fidelity, fund managers were given a great deal of freedom to make their own decisions, and the company and fellow managers avoided the second-guessing and sniping that can undermine a manager's confidence, Lynch says. "We tried to have meetings where it was 99% light and 1% heat." Ten-baggers like Chrysler do not come along often, Lynch notes, and it's important to wait for them. "All you need is one good stock every five or six years, not every five or six days. If, during the day, I can't find any good ideas, I don't buy anything."

In the nearly 13 years Lynch ran Magellan, he tallied annual gains averaging about 29%, approximately double the returns on the Standard & Poor's 500. Magellan's assets grew from $20 million to more than $14 billion, making it the most successful fund of its time. "The person who turns over the most rocks will win the game," Lynch says. "I just stayed on the offensive all the time…I'm a Red Sox fan, and if you're a Red Sox fan and grow up here, you have to be optimistic. You have to think things are going to turn out okay."

1983: Magellan becomes the largest fund in the world, with assets of $1.6 billion on December 31. The fund returns 38.6%, the S&P 500 22.4%. Some critics worry that with more than $1 billion in assets to manage, it will be impossible for Lynch to find enough bargain stocks. They warn Magellan's era of market-beating returns will end.

1984: Magellan returns 2.0%, the S&P 500 6.1%. Assets: $2 billion.

1985: Magellan returns 43.1%, the S&P 500 31.6%. Assets: $4.1 billion.

1986: Magellan returns 23.7%, the S&P 500 18.6%. Assets: $7.4 billion.

1987: Magellan returns 1.0%, the S&P 500 5.1%. Assets: $7.8 billion. During the October market crash, less than three percent of Magellan investors take money out of the fund, apparently heeding Lynch's longstanding advice to stick with the fund for the long term and ignore the market's short-term moves.

1988: Named trustee of Boston College. Magellan returns 22.8%, the S&P 500 16.6%. Assets: $9.0 billion.

1989: Magellan returns 34.6%, the S&P 500 31.7%. Assets: $12.7 billion. Lynch publishes his bestseller, *One Up on Wall Street.*

Leadership Lesson

Navigating Through the Unknown

Between 1519 and 1521, Ferdinand Magellan, a Portuguese explorer who sailed under the Spanish flag, commanded a fleet of five ships that crossed uncharted seas and faced untold hazards (including storms and mutinies) to accomplish a breakthrough: His crew became the first sailors in history to circumnavigate the globe. At Fidelity's Magellan Fund, Peter Lynch also navigated through financial turbulence and economic uncertainty to great success. Between 1977 and 1990, with Lynch at the helm, Magellan was the best performing mutual fund, its value increasing by more than 2,700%.

Achieving that kind of leadership in mutual fund performance requires a sure hand at managing risk. Lynch cultivated that ability by following a set of principles he distilled from years of investment experience.

Lynch has often said that in deciding whether or not a stock is worth buying or holding, it is useful to apply a simple test: Can you explain your reasons to a child in less than two minutes? Companies looking for capital often justify their needs and prospects with complicated explanations based on optimistic assumptions. Unless the value of an investment is so clear that even a child could understand it, however, it is likely that muddle-headed thinking (at best) or obfuscation (at worst) are at work. Lynch's criterion for investment resembles Buffett's view that investors should put their money only into businesses they understand.

Lynch also shares another trait with Buffett and Greenspan: His fondness for using unconventional signals to read the truth about the market. Just as Greenspan sometimes used the demand for paperboard, as noted earlier, to see if the economy was picking up, and Buffett wandered around steakhouses to see if American Express cards were still popular among diners, Lynch looked at products people were buying in their everyday lives. A well-known case in point: He urged Fidelity fund managers to buy Hanes, a stocking maker that had just come out with the L'eggs brand, sold in colorful egg-shaped containers at grocery stores and other retail outlets. Lynch learned of the product through his wife, who had raved about it. Hanes rose sixfold before the company was bought out.

In Lynch's view, small, aggressive companies are most likely to be profitable for investors. His goal as a mutual fund manager was to find such high-growth companies. The best of this lot, he believed, could rise ten-fold in value in a few years. Lynch called such firms "ten-baggers." "The very best way to make money in a market is in a small growth company that has been profitable for a couple of years and simply goes on growing," Lynch told *Money* magazine in an interview.

The search for high-growth companies is a key component of Lynch's investment philosophy. Even more importantly, however, it is an essential part of his strategy to manage risk in a mutual fund's portfolio. The main advantage of having a handful of

2000: The School of Education at Boston College is renamed The Lynch School of Education in honor of a $10 million gift received in 1999 from Peter and Carolyn Lynch. In the introduction to the 2000 edition of *One Up on Wall Street*, warns of the risk of the day's hot Internet stocks, arguing that investors should stick with companies they can understand. Argues it does not make sense to buy a stock at an escalated price that can only be justified if the company enjoys many years of rapid earnings growth that may not materialize. In his own investing, he says, he still relies on old-fashioned fundamentals. The dot-com crash of 2000 proves Lynch right.

2004: Inner-City Scholarship Fund provides more than $5 million to 5,000 students for the 2003–2004 school year. Under Lynch, the fund has raised more than $55 million for 45,000 students.

ten-baggers in a mutual fund portfolio is that they can offset bad or lackluster performance by other firms. As *Money* magazine wrote, "The occasional huge winner will offset a number of small losses. For example, if you had invested equal sums each in five stocks, and three of them plunged by 75%, and one rose by 20% and another by 900%, your entire portfolio would still be up by some 140%."Another aspect of Lynch's approach to managing risk is a variant of the old saw that wisdom means not just making good decisions but avoiding bad ones. He believes that one of the most risky moves investors can make is being seduced by companies that are high on sizzle and short on substance. "The stock [Lynch] would most want to avoid is the hottest stock in the hottest industry," writes *Money* magazine. "[This is] the one that generates the most favorable publicity, that every investor is told about by other investors. Usually, the high growth is a honey pot for the competition, which strikes the hot company just when it has spent huge sums to expand in order to hold on to market share."

10

Conclusion
Making It Work:
Lessons of Lasting
Leadership

What conclusions can be drawn from the experiences of the 25 leaders profiled in these pages? Are some leadership attributes "better" than others? Is there one definition of leadership that is a template for those seeking to become leaders themselves? The individuals in this book would most likely say that the secret of their success is as old and obvious as the ancient Greek injunction to "Know Thyself" (and thy company). In the same way that good negotiators adapt the principles of successful negotiation to their own personalities and goals, good leaders pay close attention to what their own experiences and instincts tell them is the right thing to do and the right time to do it. Andy Grove used his technical knowledge, courage and resolution to build Intel into a formidable IT powerhouse. Herb Kelleher believed in building a

motivated workforce knowing that, in return, his employees
would do whatever it took to sell the company, and its discounted
airfares, to the public. Michael Dell started a company based in
part on his experience as a frustrated consumer trying to buy a
computer. John Bogle created The Vanguard Group with the
knowledge that average investors were being exploited by money
managers.

In some cases, these leaders have become household names. Bill
Gates, long before he earned notoriety as the world's richest man,
was the first geek celebrity. Lee Iacocca wrote a best-seller about
his careers at Ford and Chrysler. Ted Turner, with his flair for outrageous overstatement and wacky antics, drew attention to his
fledgling cable business and turned it into a media empire. Oprah
Winfrey and Richard Branson, both of whom capitalized on an
extraordinary ability to connect with their markets, are probably
better known in their respective countries than most politicians.
But others are stars mainly because of their steady performance
within the boundaries of their profession: Peter Lynch and Warren
Buffett earned reputations as the best stock-pickers in the country; George Soros made billions of dollars in risky currency bets;
Alan Greenspan became the person who calmed markets and guided the U.S. economy through recessions as well as "irrational exuberance"; William George expanded Medtronic from a pacemaker
manufacturer into a leading maker of implantable biomedical
devices despite stiff opposition within the company.

Extraordinary achievement and, in some cases, fame have not
distorted these individuals' ability to see that success in corporate
life is a team effort. Jack Welch applauded foremen in GE factories who spoke up about what they saw as inefficient processes;
Kelleher likes to say that a baggage handler at Southwest is more
important than an executive. The all-important customer is
another focal point for these leaders. James Burke pointed to
Johnson & Johnson's credo—with its primary emphasis on responsibility to the customer—to win support for his controversial
decision to recall 31 million bottles of Tylenol. Jeff Bezos
relentlessly stressed service by continually soliciting, and responding to, customer feedback. Sam Walton's stores were more than
shopping destinations; they often served as outlets for the social
lives of their rural clientele.

These leaders have avoided the creative accounting and docu-
ment shredding that afflicted firms such as Enron, WorldCom,
Tyco, Adelphia, HealthSouth, Rite Aid and Parmalat. They did
this by folding their own healthy egos into the stronger ego of the
organization, thereby laying out a vision for the company that
transcended—and outlasted—themselves. Mary Kay Ash set up a
system of rewards and recognition for thousands of sales representatives that encouraged them to mentor each other up the "ladder
of success." Louis Gerstner repositioned a hidebound and stagnant
IBM into an integrator that would offer customers technology
solutions, not just hardware and software. Steve Jobs, who was
ousted from Apple after a bruising boardroom battle, returned to
lead the company to new heights and into new directions.

The ability to admit mistakes, and correct them, also stands out
among these individuals. Dell Inc. nearly crashed in the early
1990s after sales shot up so high that the company was unable to
meet demand. Founder Michael Dell brought in outside managers
to introduce stricter financial measures and ensure that future
growth spurts benefited the company. In 1999, Warren Buffett
wrote a letter to his shareholders apologizing for a stock loss at
Berkshire Hathaway of nearly 20% compared to an increase of
nearly 21% for the S&P 500. He stayed the course, however, and
one year later his refusal to jump on the high-tech bandwagon paid
off when the company's shares rose 26.6% compared to a loss of
9% for the S&P. Sam Walton said the biggest error he ever made
was limiting a company profit-sharing program to management
only, rather than opening it to rank and file employees. A year
later, he reorganized the program to include them. Jack Welch
admitted that the superstar environment he allowed to exist at
Kidder Peabody enabled a rogue trader to commit massive fraud.

Probably the single most common skill these leaders have
displayed is a knack for seeing into the future. Few could have imagined the impact that computers would have on businesses and
consumers once a user-friendly interface became possible. Steve Jobs
did, and that realization led to the Lisa and then the Macintosh.
Thirty years ago, Charles Schwab understood the need to get out
from under the SEC's requirement that all stock transactions be
recorded on paper forms. He "bet the company" on a plan to computerize the transaction order process, a move that gave him a huge
head start building the country's largest discount brokerage.

Jeff Bezos recognized a decade ago the potential of the Internet to revolutionize retailing. He imagined a bookstore with more than 10 times the inventory of the biggest brick–and-mortar stores, and then he created it, with the backing of initially reluctant (except for his parents) investors. Fred Smith rejuvenated Federal Express in the 1990s by starting up a system that could trace and track millions of packages as they were in transit. Lee Iacocca predicted the growth of the minivan, reasoning that Mustang buyers from the 1960s would morph into soccer parents, thereby setting up a whole new generation of loyal Chrysler customers.

Not all individuals in this book run companies, but all have demonstrated leadership in the sheer intellect they bring to their fields. Peter Drucker transformed the anecdotal study of management into an academic discipline by looking at corporations as both social systems and economic organizations. He spent his career consulting and teaching rather than tying himself to a single corporate employer. George Soros, who wants to be remembered as a philosopher as well as a philanthropist and financier, has given away billions trying to encourage his vision of more open societies in formerly repressive countries. Alan Greenspan's near-legendary ability to gather and interpret huge amounts of data has helped him retain his leadership in the global economy for decades.

Finally, an important characteristic of these leaders has been a willingness to speak out against unfair or misguided business practices. Muhammad Yunus openly criticizes traditional bankers, economists, and such agencies as the World Bank for attitudes that he says perpetuate the cycle of poverty. William George, in his book *Authentic Leadership*, censures today's executives for focusing on short-term numbers rather than the company's customers, employees, and shareholders. Warren Buffett has slammed companies for refusing to treat stock options as expenses on an income statement, arguing that by doing so these companies present a distorted picture of their finances to potential investors.

What's in It for Us?

The lives of the 25 leaders covered in these pages are instructive because of the choices they made—often in the face of adversity—on their way to defining success in their respective fields. Their experiences suggest questions worth considering when assessing the leadership potential of ourselves or others:

- Do we seek the positive seam when confronted with negative circumstances?
- How do we cultivate a corporate culture that inspires and empowers those around us?
- How do we emphasize the importance of honesty, especially at times when honesty is not the easiest course to pursue?
- Have we sought to identify and cultivate underserved markets?
- Can we see the invisible? Are we able to dig deeper and understand the connections between seemingly unrelated phenomena?
- Do we understand the role of price as a potential competitive advantage in our particular industry?
- Do we cultivate and maximize brand identity?
- Are we fast learners, able to make decisions quickly and reverse position when necessary?
- How well do we manage risk?

In the end, leadership boils down to a personal approach to the business of managing. Leaders are able to communicate their ideas, values and beliefs to employees and the business community at large. They encourage innovation at times when none seems necessary. They work in chaotic environments and bring discipline and a vision of the future to their stakeholders.

It is, after all, the future that drives many leaders forward. Muhammad Yunus, whose bank has so far loaned more than $4 billion to poor people around the globe, envisions a world that will be free of poverty, where the market for his bank will no longer exist. This would be a world, he says, "we could all be proud to live in."

References

INTRODUCTION

"People are leaders because they choose to lead." From a speech by John Bogle at the Wharton School, June, 2000

CHAPTER 1:
BEST OF THE BEST: INSIDE ANDY GROVE'S
LEADERSHIP AT INTEL

Challenge essay:

"...only once every 27,000 years of spreadsheet use." *Only the Paranoid Survive.* Andrew S. Grove, Doubleday, 1996, p. 12

"Your current computer is too accurate." "Intel to Users: 'Humbug!'" *Information Week,* December 19, 1994

"...back on the defensive again in a major way." *Only the Paranoid Survive.* Andrew S. Grove, Doubleday, 1996, p. 14

"...of how not to handle a delicate situation?" "Intel to Users: 'Humbug!'" *Information Week,* December 19, 1994

"…we had to made a major change," according to Grove. *Only the Paranoid Survive.* Andrew S. Grove, Doubleday, 1996, p. 15

"…five years' worth of the Pentium processor's advertising spending," says Grove. Ibid., p. 16

"…conference rooms with blackboards, based on data analyses," Ibid., p. 17

Timeline:

"…easily colored by political considerations, could decide the merits of my work." *One-on-One with Andy Grove: How to Manage Your Boss, Yourself and Your Co-Workers,* Putnam, 1987, p. 15

Chapter text:

"…and supported myself through my remaining years of college that way." *One-on-One with Andy Grove: How to Manage Your Boss, Yourself and Your Co-Workers,* Putnam, 1987, p. 16

"…that can be ethically wrong and will backfire every time." Ibid., p. 235

"…experience was unique to Intel, the lessons it teaches are universal." *Only the Paranoid Survive.* Andrew S. Grove, Doubleday, 1996, p. 82

"If you don't recognize the names, it's because these companies are long gone," notes Grove. Ibid., p. 84

"…was the availability of high-quality product priced astonishingly low," Grove wrote. Ibid., p. 87

"'Why shouldn't you and I walk out the door, come back and do it ourselves?'" Ibid., p. 89

"…that the microprocessor that's inside his or her computer *is* the computer." Ibid., p. 18

"…logos in consumer merchandising, up there with names like Coca-Cola or Nike." Ibid., pp. 18, 19

CHAPTER TWO:
LEADERSHIP AND CORPORATE CULTURE
HERB KELLEHER

Chapter text:

"It's going to be a battle for our lives." *The New York Times*, March 25, 2004

MARY KAY ASH

Challenge essay:

"...will often work for recognition when she won't work for money." *Mary Kay: You Can Have It All*, Prima Publishing, 1995, p. 121

"...the first thing you know, [these salespeople] actually become successful." *Mary Kay*, Harper Row, 1981, p. 160

"Wearing an invisible sign that says, 'Make me feel important.'" *Mary Kay: You Can Have It All*, p. 9

"Their applause ranks among the most meaningful praise anyone can receive." Ibid., p. 122

Timeline:

She replies, "I like to think God is using me." Interview with Morley Safer on CBS's *60 Minutes*, 1979

Chapter text:

"...takes [the newcomer] under her wing and treats [her] as one of her own." *Mary Kay: You Can Have It All*, Prima Publishing, 1995, p. 161

"And neither would our directors with their adoptees." Ibid., pp. 161-162

"These vows are not idle words: At Mary Kay, they are how we live." Ibid., p. 17

...offered women "the ultimate opportunity, with no ceilings, no boss." *Orange County Register*, Nov. 2, 2001

"Now, it allows women to stay home." Fairchild Publications, April 6, 2001

"Truths about beauty, equality, success and the color pink." *The Washington Post*, Nov. 24, 2001

"Home life, a family and be involved in [their] community." *National Post,* Nov. 24, 2001

"Use their God-given talents and abilities." *Mary Kay,* Harper & Row, 1981, dedication

"...to create better lives and to realize their dreams." *Mary Kay: You Can Have It All,*
Prima Publishing, 1995, p. 4

JAMES BURKE

Timeline:

...campaign's theme is "Stop. Think. Tylenol." *The New York Times,* March 17, 2004

Chapter text:

"He continually energized the system." "At Johnson & Johnson, a Mistake Can Be a
Badge of Honor," by C. Power. *Businessweek,* Sept. 26, 1988

"Until they prove themselves unworthy of that trust, a lot more happens." American
Management Association's Management Review, Oct. 1, 1996, Vol. 85, No. 10

"...hiring boards of directors that feel beholden to the CEO." Harvard Business School
Alumni Achievement Awards: 2004

CHAPTER 3: TRUTH TELLERS

Introduction:

"...no force in the world that is so direct or so swift in working." Young India,
Mohandas Gandhi. Feb. 27, 1930

JACK WELCH

Chapter text:

"...it brought relief, and eventually McCann made up with his friend." "The Truth Is, the
Truth Hurts," *Fast Company,* April 14, 1998

"...as we were in Louisville and Schenectady," Welch writes in his autobiography.
Straight from the Gut. Jack Welch and John A. Byrne. Warner Books, 2003. p. 186

"The two cultures and their differences never stood out so clearly in my mind."
Ibid., p. 226

PETER DRUCKER

Challenge essay:

"An observer, not a participant—making him, for his refusal to participate, all the keener as an observer," *Forbes* magazine said of him. "Seeing Things As They Really Are," Robert Kenzner and Stephen S. Johnson, *Forbes*, March 10, 1997

...moving the majority of the world's largest companies to "radical decentralization," wrote John Micklethwait and Adrian Wooldridge. *The Witch Doctors*, Crown Business, 1996

"...a mob into an organization, and human effort into performance." *Managing Turbulent Times*. Peter Drucker, HarperBusiness, 1980, p. 104

Chapter text:

"...the most prescient business-trend spotter of our time." *Fortune*, Sept. 28, 1998

...such terms as "privatization," "knowledge workers," and "management by objective," *Fortune*, January 12, 2004

...that Drucker "has remained consistently fresh and ahead of the times." *The Wall Street Journal*, Dec. 31, 1999

"Such relationships are the way the world economy is going." Training & Development, Sept. 1, 1998

"...totally absent today for executives—information about the world outside the company." Ibid.

"These are all areas on which our modern technology gives absolutely no information." Ibid.

"I am teaching, above all, how to manage oneself." Ibid.

"...think through what results are wanted in the organization—and have then to define objectives." "Age of Social Transformation," *The Atlantic Monthly*, November 1994

...develop "meaningful objectives based on a thorough understanding of the work." *Christianity Today*, Nov. 15, 1999

...do not exist to "make and sell things" but rather to "meet human needs." Ibid.

WILLIAM GEORGE

Timeline:

"...employees, and—ironically, since the Game is supposed to be all about them—shareholders." *Fortune*, Sept. 29, 2003

Chapter text:

"That superstar CEO has now been indicted for fraud." Authentic Leaders.org website

"No wonder many CEOs went to extreme measures to satisfy shareholders!" *Authentic Leadership: Recreating the Secrets to Discovering Lasting Value.* Bill George, Jossey-Bass, 2003

CHAPTER 4:
IDENTIFYING AN UNDERSERVED MARKET

CHARLES SCHWAB

Challenge essay:

Schwab employees used something akin to a plunger to unplug the jam. *Charles Schwab: How One Company Beat Wall Street and Reinvented the Brokerage Industry.* John Kador, John Wiley and Sons, 2002, p. 53

"...calculating margin trades, and moving cash from trading accounts to money market funds." Ibid., p. 54

"...no paper tickets generated by BETA, the NYSE refused to certify Schwab's system." Ibid., p.54

"...only *save* paper tickets but did not require them to *write* paper tickets." Ibid., p.55

Timeline:

"...which he later describes as his 'first fully integrated venture.'" *Fortune Small Business*, September 2003

Chapter text:

"...individual investors were sold stocks; they didn't buy them," recalls Schwab. *Fortune Small Business*, September 2003

MUHAMMAD YUNUS

Challenge essay:

"…people earning less than $1 a day." "Debate Stirs Over Tiny Loans for World's Poorest," *The New York Times*, April 29, 2004

"…we could all be proud to live in." *Banker to the Poor*, PublicAffairs 2003, p. 262

Timeline:

…"'Oh, I don't need money.' When you hear that, you have found your person." "World Bank for the Little People," by Jessica Mathews. *The Toronto Star*, Dec. 23, 1993

Chapter text:

"You never find out. That's poverty." *Financial Times*, April 14, 1998

"Such conceptual vagueness greatly damaged our efforts to alleviate poverty." *Banker to the Poor.* Muhammad Yunus, PublicAffairs, Perseus Books Group, 2003, pp. 40-41

"…had absolutely no chance of improving their economic base. Each one was stuck in poverty." Ibid., p. 41

"In all these families, all for the lack of $27." Ibid., pp. 46-50

"Any credit because it very quickly gets politicized." Interview with Yunus in *The Hindu Business Line*, Jan. 11, 1999

"Put into practice the skills they already know." *Banker to the Poor*, p. 140

"If they screw up, they won't have access to lending." From article in *US Banker*, Aug. 1, 2003, entitled "Doing Good by Doing Well: As Third-World NGOs Morph into Full-Fledged Banks, Profits Are Swelling — and Global Bankers Are Taking Notice."

CHAPTER 5: SEEING THE INVISIBLE

Introduction:

"It had a crude menu system. It had crude panels and stuff. It didn't work right, but it basically was all there." The Smithsonian Institution's oral history archive.

STEVE JOBS

Challenge essay:

"...we felt we were fashioning collective works of art." The Smithsonian Institution's oral history archive.

"It was the combination of those two things that I'm the most proud of." Ibid.

Chapter text:

"Customers pay 99 cents to download each song. After that, it's almost like buying music on a CD, LP, or tape. The user can play it on the computer, burn it to a CD that can be played on any device, or transfer it to an MP3 player." "Online Music Wings Its Way to the Celestial Jukebox." *Knowledge@Wharton*, July 2, 2003

"The success of Apple's iTunes service isn't the downloading per se; it's the interface— the fun of use." "Which Online Music Service Will Have the Longest Playing Time?" *Knowledge@Wharton*, January 14, 2004

"...music lovers bought 7.7 million songs online, but only 4 million single-song CDs at stores." "Online Music Wings Its Way to the Celestial Jukebox." *Knowledge@Wharton*, July 2, 2003

"...unmatched by even his most powerful computer industry rivals." *The New York Times*. April 25, 2004

TED TURNER

Challenge essay:
Turner won and CNN launched on schedule. *Ted Turner: It Ain't As Easy As It Looks.* Porter Bibb, Johnson Books, 1993. pp. 171-172

Chapter text:
"...that of an oil refiner short of crude during OPEC's heyday." *Forbes* magazine, Nov. 4, 1985

GEORGE SOROS

Challenge essay:

...with Soros himself "maintaining a low profile and keeping his ego out of it." "The World According to Soros," *The New Yorker*, 1995, pp. 62, 64

"...and I made some wrong steps: *Soros: The Life and Times of a Messianic Billionaire.* Michael T. Kaufman, Knopf, 2002, p. 178

"...whatever I did made me an accomplice of the system." *Soros On Soros*, John Wiley & Sons, Inc. 1995, pp. 114-115

"In effect, the foundation was run by the secret police: Ibid., pp. 126-127

"...signified citizen involvement in finding data and passing it on: *Soros: The Life and Times of a Messianic Billionaire*. Michael T. Kaufman, Knopf, 2002, p. 197

"...difficult to run a foundation in a revolutionary environment." *Soros On Soros*, John Wiley & Sons, Inc. 1995, pp. 128 and 129

"...emerging societies not from the bottom but from the top." *The New Yorker*, p. 65

"...and not profit whenever this possibility arises." *Soros on Soros*, p. 142

"If I did, I would not be alive today." Ibid., p. 145

"In philanthropy as in business, Soros was pulling the trigger." *Soros: The Life and Times*, p. 256

"Giving him Leverage if performance falters." "Soros Has a Hunch Bush Can Be Beat," Jeanne Cummings, *Wall Street Journal*, Feb. 5 2004, p. A4

"It is a unique combination." *Soros on Soros*: p. 111

Chapter text:

"A clear sign that sterling was also vulnerable." *Soros on Soros: Staying Ahead of the Curve*. George Soros. John Wiley & Sons, 1995, p. 81

"Very often those signs come from politics." *Fortune*, Oct. 27, 2003

"...than Kohl was predicting, than anyone was predicting." *The Observer Magazine*, Jan. 16, 1994

"Where perception lagged behind reality, leaving room for exploitation." "The World According to Soros," Connie Bruck. *The New Yorker*, January 1995, p. 61

"...And learning that before others did." Ibid., p. 61

"Disengage from the herd and look for a different investment thesis." *Soros on Soros: Staying Ahead of the Curve*. George Soros. John Wiley & Sons, 1995. p. 12

"...paid off handsomely. It would not be the last time." *Soros: The Life and Times of a Messianic Billionaire*. Michael Kaufman, Alfred A. Knopf, 2002. pp. 124-125

"Fixed exchange rates gave way to floating parities a year later." Ibid., pp. 138-139

"When he thinks he's right, he'll bet the ranch." *The Observer Magazine*, Jan. 16, 1994

"Not something that can be learned. It is totally intuitive." Kaufman, p. 142

"That's when you have lost your ability to get out of trouble." *Soros on Soros*, pp. 56, 57

CHAPTER 6:
USING PRICE TO GAIN COMPETITIVE ADVANTAGE

Introduction:

"They just didn't spend it," Walton writes in his autobiography, *Sam Walton: Made in America*. Bantam, republished 1993. p. 5

"…the overall profit was much greater. Simple enough." Ibid., p. 25

SAM WALTON

Challenge essay:

"…when you went inside the store, the mess just continued." *Fortune*, Jan. 30, 1989

"I've probably been in more Kmarts than anybody in the country." *Sam Walton, Made in America*, p. 190

"We got so much better so quickly you couldn't believe it." Ibid., p. 190

"…adopted the attitude that competition was healthy," Brand notes." *Masters of Enterprise: Giants of American Business from John Jacob Astor and J.P. Morgan to Bill Gates and Oprah Winfrey*. H.W. Brands, Free Press, 1999. pp. 229-230

"…attractive prices and store the merchandise." *Forbes*, Aug. 16, 1982

"…new confidence that we could conquer anything." *Sam Walton: Made in America*, p. 198

"We'll never know because we chose the other route." Ibid., p. 189

"It's truly amazing what they can accomplish." *Fortune*, January 30, 1989

Chapter text:

"And just blow that stuff out the store." *Sam Walton: Made in America*, p. 24

"Everybody in town had a pair." *Masters of Enterprise*, H.W. Brands, Free Press, 1999. p. 227

"…could beat going to the Wal-Mart." *Sam Walton: Made in America,* p. 160

"…sponsored local scholarships to help local kids attend college: *Masters of Enterprise*: p. 232

"To break the mold and fight monotony." *Sam Walton: Made in America,* p. 159

"How much better off they would be as the company did better." Ibid., p. 129

"…higher degree than most any other retail company." *USA Today,* March 28, 1991

"Which is where we always plan to be." *Sam Walton: Made in America,* p. 10

"…averaged less than one dollar per square foot." *Masters of Enterprise,* p. 228

"And profits totaled $1 billion." Ibid., pp. 229, 233

"Faced a real decline in its purchasing powers." *Value Migration: How to Think Several Moves Ahead of the Competition.* Adrian Slywotsky. Harvard Business School Press, 1996. pp. 210-211

"Two hours a week off their shopping time." Ibid., pp. 211-212

"The enemy of small-town America." *Sam Walton: Made in America,* p. 177

"Doing business the old-fashioned way." *Sam Walton: Made in America,* p. 178

MICHAEL DELL

Challenge essay:
"…was now unable to support our business." *Direct from Dell: Strategies that Revolutionized an Industry,* Harper Collins, pp. 44-45

Chapter text:

"…mastery of the computer industry's central dynamic: falling prices." "Picking a Big Fight with Dell, H-P Cuts PC Profits Razor-Thin. "*The Wall Street Journal,* May 12, 2004.

"…and deliver a lot of value," said Dell in a magazine interview, referring to the printer market. *PC Magazine,* February 2004

"It's music, it's videos and it's television." CNET news. September 2003

"We will keep pushing those as well." *PC Magazine,* February 2004

JEFF BEZOS

Chapter text:

"Spend money on things that matter to customers." *The New York Times*, March 31, 1999

"...guaranteeing that almost no one would make any money." CNET News.com, May 17, 1999

"Provide an even better customer experience." CNET News.com, April 11, 2001

"Less than a week later, Barnesandnoble.com followed suit." CNET News.com, July 2, 2001

"One area of the country to geographic hubs." CNET News.com, August 26, 2002

"He had the packaging redesigned." *The New York Times*, March 31, 1999

"Also tell 5,000 people how horrible we are." *The New York Times*, March 31, 1999

CHAPTER 7: MANAGING THE BRAND

OPRAH WINFREY

Challenge essay:

"How do you not cry about that?" *Oprah Winfrey: The Real Story*. George Mair, Birch Lane Press, 1994, pp. 44-45

"...short man can make love to all the very tall girlfriends Moore has had." Ibid. p.52

"You are responsible for your own life," she told *Fortune*. *Fortune*, April 1, 2002

"She also signaled that it was all right to fail," *Newsweek* said. *Newsweek*, Jan. 8, 2001

"And then people would fall out of their chairs laughing." *Fortune*, April 1, 2002

"And she guards her off-air ventures as fiercely." *Newsweek*, Jan. 8, 2001

"Owning myself is a way to be myself." *Fortune*, April 1, 2002

Chapter text:

"...teadfastly resisted these entreaties." *Fortune*, April 1, 2002

"It's easy to be a true believer." *Essence*, October 2003

"...just sitting up talking to you about service?" *Newsweek*, January 2001

"I feel I can learn something." *Investor Business Daily*, Sept. 1, 1999

"What is happening in pop culture." *Broadcasting and Cable*, Dec. 8 2003

"Recalls Hearst's [magazine president] Cathleen Black." *Fortune*, April 1, 2002

"Encouraging readers to revamp their souls." *Newsweek*, Jan. 8, 2001

"Oppressed women in Afghanistan." *Fortune*, April 1, 2002

"But it's oh-so-Oprah." *Fortune*, April 1, 2002

"My constant focus is on being better." *Fortune*, April 1, 2002

LEE IACOCCA

Challenge essay:

"...And laid off more than 15,000 salaried workers." *Iacocca: An Autobiography*. Lee Iacocca with William Novak. Bantam Books, 1984. p. 189

Chapter text:

"...cause the entire enterprise to backfire." Ibid., pp. 268-269

"And when they don't, I'll buzz you:'" *Talking Straight*. Lee Iacocca with Sonny Kleinfeld, Bantam Books, 1988. p. 115

RICHARD BRANSON

Challenge essay:

All quotes in this section are from Richard Branson's autobiography, *Losing My Virginity: How I've Survived, Had Fun, and Made a Fortune Doing Business My Way*, Three Rivers Press, 1999, and Virgin Books Ltd., © Richard Branson, 1998

Timeline:

"Declines offer of knighthood in 1999." *Forbes*, July 13, 2000

Chapter text:

"…would recognize as having certain key values." *Losing My Virginity: How I've Survived, Had Fun, and Made a Fortune Doing Business My Way.* Richard Branson. Three Rivers Press, 1999. p. 47, and Virgin Books Ltd., © Richard Branson, 1998

"…bought Mantovani or Perry Como." Ibid., p. 59

"…framework of what Virgin later became." Ibid., p. 59

"…That there was room for new competition." Ibid., p. 153

"…had been filmed earlier in a flight simulator." Ibid., pp. 163-64

"Probably gone as far as we can in the UK." *The Observer Guardian*, March 2002

"…too informal, too restless, and I like to move on." *Losing My Virginity*: p. 351

CHAPTER 8: FAST LEARNERS

WILLIAM H. GATES

Challenge essay:

"A neglected orphan of AOL Time Warner to a candidate for euthanasia." CNET News.com May 29, 2003

"…but it no longer poses a threat to the company's survival." "Sir Bill and his Dragons – Past, Present and future," *The Economist*, Jan. 29, 2004

"…technology that allows people to play music and videos on their PCs, regulators said." "Microsoft and the EU: Who's Right and Does It Really Matter?" *Knowledge@Wharton*, June 2, 2004

"…under traditional antitrust law, [makes] it clear that it is overcharging for the operating system." Ibid.

"…another separate market—search engines this time—at the expense of competitors." Sir Bill and his Dragons – Past, Present and future," *The Economist*, Jan. 29, 2004

"…agreement with Siemens that allowed both companies access to one another's patents." "Microsoft: Kinder, Gentler." *The Economist*, May 13, 2004

Timeline:

..."this is the biggest, splashiest software rollout yet concocted." *Gates: How Microsoft's Mogul Reinvented an Industry – and Made Himself the Richest Man in America.* Stephen Manes and Paul Andrews, Doubleday, 1993. p. 1

Chapter text:

"...and a modem that could connect the unit via telephone to the outside world." *Gates: How Microsoft's Mogul Reinvented an Industry – and Made Himself the Richest Man in America.* Stephen Manes and Paul Andrews, Doubleday, 1993. pp. 25, 27

"It wasn't just a fair deal for Microsoft. It was the deal of the century." Ibid., p. 175

"...most fantastic thing to happen in the world of computing since the original PC." *Internet World,* 1996, remarks by Bill Gates, April 30, 1996

"...critical mass of people who might want to use the PC to communicate with one another. Harvard Conference on Internet society, Bill Gates keynote address, 1996

"...more powerful in many ways than any of these other communications devices." Ibid.

"...value of those systems is really hard to exaggerate." *Internet World,* 1996

FREDERICK WALLACE SMITH

Chapter text:

"...and electronic connections—be erected alongside the air and vehicle networks," "Why FedEx Is Flying High," by Linda Grant. *Fortune,* Nov. 10, 1997, p.158

"...and you're determined to get there, that's worth a lot." *Investor's Business Daily,* 1998

"I wanted to do something productive after blowing so many things up," he told *Fortune* magazine in 1997. "Why FedEx Is Flying High," by Linda Grant. *Fortune,* Nov. 10, 1997

LOUIS V. GERSTNER, JR.

Challenge essay:

"…can do is create the conditions for transformation, provide incentives." *Who Says Elephants Can't Dance? Inside IBM's Historic Turnaround.* Louis V. Gerstner, Jr., HarperBusiness, 2002, p. 187

Chapter text:

"…before they can succeed as leaders, they must first become effective workers and managers." Louis Gerstner's interview with *Knowledge@Wharton,* April 2004.

CHAPTER 9: MANAGING RISK

Introduction:

"The thing about Greenspan is that he doesn't stay wrong." From *The Man Behind the Money,* by Justin Martin, quoted in *Knowledge@Wharton,* "Alan Greenspan: Woody Allen with Math Skills," Feb. 2, 2001

WARREN BUFFETT

Challenge essay:
"…compared to the S&P, the worst relative performance as well," 1999 Letter to Shareholders, published March 1, 2000

"What really gets our attention, however, is a comfortable business at a comfortable price." Ibid.

"Companies that operate in fast-changing industries is simply far beyond our perimeter." Ibid.

"…the stock might never again provide big returns," Bianco wrote. *Businessweek,* March 20, 2000

"It's no sure thing that they will quickly regain their stride." 1999 Letter to Shareholders, published March 1, 2000

"…industries as brick, carpet, insulation, and paint. Try to control your excitement." 2000 Letter to Shareholders, published Feb. 28, 2001

Chapter Text:

"As the negative publicity went on, the stock price plunged further." Buffett: *The Making of an American Capitalist.* Roger Lowenstein. Main Street Books, 1995, p. 80

"Though our corporate performance last year was satisfactory, my performance was anything but," Buffett wrote. Annual Letter to Shareholders regarding 2001 results. Written in 2002.

ALAN GREENSPAN

"...has come to involve at its core crucial elements of risk management." Risk and Uncertainty in Monetary Policy, speech to American Economic Association, Jan. 3, 2004

"...with outsized adverse feedback to the performance of the US economy." Risk and Uncertainty in Monetary Policy, speech to American Economic Association, Jan. 3, 2004

"Where it doesn't, I recognize that it doesn't." *Greenspan: The Man Behind the Money.* Justin Martin. Perseus Publishing 2000, p. 110

"Greenspan was forever adding to his toolbox of indicators." Ibid. p. 56

"In fact, uncertainty characterized virtually every meeting." Risk and Uncertainty in Monetary Policy, speech to American Economic Association, Jan. 3, 2004

Timeline:

Biographic material mainly from *Greenspan: The Man Behind the Money.* Justin Martin. Perseus Publishing, 2000

Chapter text:

"Greenspan began to see mounting signs that the economy was overheating," *Greenspan: The Man Behind the Money* by Justin Martin. Perseus Publishing, 2000, p. 171

"Greenspan knew the value of appearing blasé in the face of a mounting financial crisis," says Martin. Ibid., p. 173

"...in this instance by his age, his experience, and his knowledge of economic history," Martin notes. Ibid., p. 175

"...did a bit of canny arm twisting, made sure they actually made the loans available," writes Martin. Ibid., p. 177

"...bubble's consequences rather than the bubble itself has been successful," he said. Risk and Uncertainty in Monetary Policy, speech to American Economic Association, Jan. 3, 2004

PETER LYNCH

Chapter text:

"...has been profitable for a couple of years and simply goes on growing," Lynch told *Money* magazine in an interview. *Money.* Feb 1, 2003

"...and one rose by 20% and another by 900%, your entire portfolio would still be up by some 140%." Ibid.

"...just when it has spent huge sums to expand in order to hold on to market share." Ibid.

INDEX

A

addiction, work in (James Burke), 44-46
Adelphia, 239
Akers, John, 108
Akhter, Firuza, 93
Allen, Paul, 184, 191
Amazon.com, xv, 132. *See also* Bezos, Jeff
    capital investment in, 151-154
    pricing strategy, 155-157
American Association of Advertising Agencies, 44
American Bankers Association, 225
American Economic Assocation, 228
American Express, 206-207, 212, 215, 217, 235
American Motors, 173
Amit, Raffi, xv
antitrust regulation, 16-17, 185-189
AOL Time-Warner, 187
Apollo Investment Fund, 119
Apple Computer, xv, xix, 103, 150, 191, 239.
    See also Jobs, Steve
    competition from industry leaders, 106-111
    online music business, 112-113
Apple Confidential: The Real Story of Apple Computer
    (Linzmeyer), 108
Aresty Institute of Executive Education, xv
Arterial Vascular Engineering, 67
Ash, Mary Kay, xv, xix, 22, 239
    biographical timeline, 30-33
    challenges for, xix, 30-33
    corporate culture, 34-37

AT&T, 16, 163
attributes of leadership. *See* character traits of
    leaders
authentic leadership, 68-71
Authentic Leadership (George), 69, 240
AVECOR Cardiovascular, 67

B

Banker to the Poor (Yunus), 96, 99
Barnesandnoble.com, 132, 155
Barrett, Craig, 12-13, 18
Barry, Nancy, 101
Beatty, Jack, 57
Bell Labs, xvi
Berkshire Hathaway, xiv-xv, xvii, 217-218, 239
    See also Buffett, Warren
    long-term investment challenge, 211-214
Bezos, Jeff, xv, xix-xx, 132, 238, 240
    biographical timeline, 151-154
    challenges for, 151-154
    price, using for competitive advantage, 155-157
Bianco, Anthony, 213
"Big Brother" commerical, 109
Black, Cathleen, 167
Black, Leon, 119
"Black Monday," 225-227
Bogle, John, xiii-xv, xix, 73, 238
    biographical timeline, 75-79
    challenges for, 75-79
    character traits of leaders, xvii
    targeting underserved markets, 80-83

Borders.com, 132, 155
Bower, Marvin, 62
brand recognition, 159-160
  Richard Branson, 179-181
  Andrew Grove, 15-16
  Lee Iacocca, 172-174
  Oprah Winfrey, 165-167
Brands, H.W., 135
Braniff, 28
Branson, Richard, xv, xix, 159-160, 238
  biographical timeline, 175-177
  brand recognition, 179-181
  challenges for, 175-178
British Airways, 175-176, 178
Buffett, Warren, xiv-xv, xix, 48, 121, 206, 235,
      238-240
  biographical timeline, 211-216
  challenges for, 211-214
  character traits of leaders, xvii
  risk management, 215, 217-219
Buffett: The Making of an American Capitalist
      (Lowenstein), 215
Burke, James, xv, xix, 22, 238
  addiction, work in, 44-46
  biographical timeline, 38-42
  challenges for, 38, 40-41
  character traits of leaders, xviii
  corporate culture, 42-44
Bush, George W., 125
Business @ The Speed of Thought (Gates), 190

C

Cable News Network. *See* CNN
cable television. *See* satellite broadcasting
      challenge (Ted Turner)
Canon, 148
capital investment in Amazon.com (Jeff Bezos),
      151-154
Cappelli, Peter, xv, xvii, 22, 56, 82
Carrey, Jim, 167
Carter, Dennis, 9
Cartoon Network, 117, 120
Carville, James, 174
Center for Human Resources, xv
Center for Leadership and Change Management, xv
challenges for leaders, xix
  antitrust regulation (Bill Gates), 185-189
  capital investment in Amazon.com (Jeff
      Bezos), 151-154
  Chrysler management (Lee Iacocca), 168-171
  competition between Wal-Mart and Kmart
      (Sam Walton), 133-136
  competition from industry leaders (Steve
      Jobs), 106-111
  growth of Dell Inc. (Michael Dell), 142-145
  growth of Medtronic (William George), 64-68
  IBM turnaround (Louis Gerstner), 202-205
  information systems (Fred Smith), 195-198
  investment in Chrysler (Peter Lynch), 230-233
  long-term investments (Warren Buffett),
      211-214
  management studies (Peter Drucker), 57-61
  microcredit (Muhammad Yunus), 93-96
  mutual fund company management (John
      Bogle), 75-79

Pentium flaw (Andrew Grove), 4-9
personal business control (Oprah Winfrey),
      161-164
philanthropy (George Soros), 121-126
restructuring of General Electric (Jack
      Welch), 50-53
sales force motivation (Mary Kay Ash), 30-33
satellite broadcasting (Ted Turner), 114-117
Southwest Airlines startup (Herb Kelleher),
      23-26
technology integration (Charles Schwab),
      84-89
Tylenol crisis (James Burke), 38-41
uncertainty, dealing with (Alan Greenspan),
      220-224
Virgin Music versus Virgin Atlantic (Richard
      Branson), 175-178
character traits of leaders, xvii-xxi, 237-241
  brand recognition, 15-16, 159-181
  corporate culture, 17-44
  fast learning, 183-208
  price, using for competitive advantage, 131-157
  risk management, 16-17, 209-236
  tartgeting underserved markets, 13-15, 73-101
  teamwork, 11-13
  thrift, 27-29
  truth-telling, 10, 47-71
  vision of future, 103-129, 200
Charles Schwab & Co., xv, 90, 92. *See also*
      Schwab, Charles
  technology integration, 84-89
Chrysler, xv, 160, 238, 240. *See also* Iacocca, Lee
  brand recognition, 172-174
  investment in (Peter Lynch), 230-233
  management of, 168-171
Clark, Howard, 215, 217
Clemons, Eric, 188
CNN (Cable News Network), xv, 105,
      114-117. *See also* Turner, Ted
Coca-Cola, 16, 38, 160, 181, 212-213, 217
Cody, William, 141
Commodore, 191
Communist Youth League, 123
Compaq Computer, 15, 149, 203
competition. *See also* global competition
  from industry leaders (Steve Jobs), 106-111
  Wal-Mart and Kmart, 133-136
competitive advantage, using price for, 131-132
  Jeff Bezos, 155-157
  Michael Dell, 146-150
  Sam Walton, 137-141
ComputerLand, 108
Concept of a Corporation (Drucker), 59-60, 63
consumer trends. *See* vision of future
corporate culture
  Mary Kay Ash, 34-37
  James Burke, 42-44
  Andrew Grove, 17-19
  IBM, 204-208
  Herb Kelleher, 21-22, 27-29
Corrigan, Gerald, 227
criticism of unfair business practices, 240
Croson, David, 148-149
Cultural Initiative Foundation, 123

culture. *See* corporate culture
customers, importance of, 238

D

Dayton's, 133
Dell Inc., xv, 132, 203, 239. *See also* Dell, Michael
 growth of company, 142-145
Dell, Michael, xv, xix-xx, 132, 238-239
 biographical timeline, 142-144
 challenges for, 142-145
 price, using for competitive advantage, 146-150
Della Femina, Jerry, 38
Digital Research, 191
*Direct from Dell: Strategies that Revolutionzed an
 Industry* (Dell), 143
Donahue, Phil, 162
Dougall, William, 190
Dow Chemical, 232
Drexel Burnham Lambert, 119
Druckenmiller, Stanley, 124
Drucker, Peter, xv, xix, 12, 48, 240
 biographical timeline, 57-61
 challenges for, 57-61
 truth-telling, 62-63

E-F

education. *See* fast learning
Enron, 46, 48, 68, 239
Exxon, 136

F.W. Woolworth, 133
Fader, Peter, 113
Fairchild Semiconductor, xvi, 11
Fannie Mae, 232
fast learning, 183-184
 Bill Gates, 190-194
 Louis Gerstner, 206-208
 Fred Smith, 199-201
Federal Express, xv, 184, 199-201, 240. *See also*
 Smith, Fred
 information systems, 195-198
Federal Open Market Committee (FOMC),
 221-222, 224
Federal Reserve System, xv, 196
 dealing with uncertainty, 220-224
FedEx. *See* Federal Express
Fidelity, 92
Fidelity Magellan Fund, xv. *See also* Lynch, Peter
 investment in Chrysler, 230-233
 risk management, 234-236
Firestone, 38
Flying Tigers, 197
FOMC (Federal Open Market Committee),
 221-222, 224
Ford Motor Company, 60, 168, 170, 172-173, 238
Ford, Henry, II, 60, 168, 170, 172
Freddie Mac, 212
Fund for the Reform and Opening of China, 123
future, vision of, 103-105, 239
 Steve Jobs, 112-113
 Fred Smith, 200
 George Soros, 126-127, 129
 Ted Turner, 118-120
The Future of Industrial Man (Drucker), 58

G

Gates, Bill, xiv-xv, xix, 184, 238
 biographical timeline, 185-190
 challenges for, xix, 185-189
 character traits of leaders, xviii
 fast learning, 190-194
*Gates: How Microsoft's Mogul Reinvented an Industry—
 and Made Himself the Richest Man in
 America* (Manes and Andrews), 190
GE Captial, 52
General Electric, xv, xviii, 48, 238. *See also*
 Welch, Jack
 restructuring of, 50-53
General Motors, 58-60
General Reinsurance, 213, 218-219
George, William, xv, xix, 49, 238, 240
 biographical timeline, 64-66
 challenges for, 64-68
 character traits of leaders, xviii
 truth-telling, 68-71
Gerstner, Louis, xv, xix, 184, 239
 biographical timeline, 202-204
 challenges for, 202-205
 fast learning, 206-208
Gharib, Susie, xvi
Gillette, 212
Glass, David, 133
global competition, restructuring of General
 Electric, 50-53. *See also* competition
GM (General Motors), 58-60
Goergen Entrepreneurial Research Program, xv
Goodyear Tire, 170
Google, 188
Grameen Bank, xv, xviii, 73, 97, 99-100. *See also*
 Yunus, Muhammad
 microcredit, 93-96
Greenspan, Alan, xv, xix, 235, 238, 240
 biographical timeline, 220-228
 challenges for, 220-224
 risk management, 225-229
Grokster, 112
Grove, Andrew, xiv-xv, xix, 1-3, 237
 background of, xvi
 biographical timeline, 4-9
 challenges for, xix, 4-9
 character traits of leaders, xvii
  brand recognition, 15-16
  corporate culture, 17-19
  risk management, 16-17
  targeting underserved markets, 13-15
  teamwork, 11-13
  tenacity, xxi
  truth-telling, 10
growth of company
 Michael Dell, 142-145
 William George, 64-68
Gutfreund, John, 48

H

Hanes, 235
Hanna-Barbera animation studio, 117, 119
Harpo Inc., xv, 159, 164, 167. *See also*
 Winfrey, Oprah
 personal business control, 161-164

HBO, 116
HealthSouth, 239
Hearst, 167
Heinz, John, 174
Hewlett-Packard, 148-149
Hitachi, 203
Homebrew Computer Club, 107
honesty. See truth-telling
Hotmail, 194
hubris, 68
The Human League, 177

I-J
Iacocca, Lee, xv, xix, 160, 231, 238, 240
  biographical timeline, 168-170
  brand recognition, 172-174
  challenges for, 168-171
Iacocca: An Autobiography (Iacocca), 173
IBM, xv-xvi, xix, 15-16, 52, 85-86, 107-110, 148,
        160, 184, 190, 239. See also Gerstner,
        Louis
  corporate culture, 204-208
  deal with Microsoft, 191-192
  turnaround of, 202-205
index funds, 77-78
information systems (Fred Smith), 195-198
insurance, risk management, 218-219
integrity. See truth-telling
Intel, xv-xvi, xix, xxi, 2-3, 38, 107, 148, 163, 237.
        See also Grove, Andrew
  brand recognition, 15-16
  corporate culture, 17-19
  Pentium flaw challenge, 4-9
  risk management, 16-17
intellect and leadership ability, 240
Internet revolution and Microsoft, 192-194
Internet World Conference, 192
Intuit, 186
investment in Chrysler (Peter Lynch), 230-233
investment principles (Warren Buffett), 217

J.C. Penney, 139
Jack: Straight from the Gut (Welch), 48
Jackson, Thomas Penfield, 187
Jain, Ajit, 218
Jefferson Airplane, 179
Jett, Joseph, 56
Jobs, Steve, xv, xix, 239
  biographical timeline, 106-111
  challenges for, xix, 106-111
  vision of future, 103-104, 112-113
Johnson & Johnson, xv, xviii, 22, 238. See also
        Burke, James
  challenges for, 38-41
  corporate culture, 42-44
Johnson, General Robert Wood, 43
Jones, Lewis, 58

K-L
Kahn, Barbara, xv, 167
Kaufman, George (*Soros: The Life and Times of a
        Messianic Billionaire*), 127
Kaufman, Michael T., 122
Kazaa, 112

Kelleher, Herb, xv, xix, 23-29, 237
  biographical timeline, 23-26
  challenges for, xix, 23-26
  character traits of leaders
    corporate culture, 21-22, 27-29
    thrift, 27-29
Kenyon & Eckhardt, 173
Kidder Peabody scandal, 56, 239
King, Coretta Scott, 166
Kinko's, 198
Kleiner Perkins Caufield & Byers, 154
Kmart, xix, 137, 139
  competition with Wal-Mart, 133-136
knowledge workers, 62
Kohl, Helmut, 127
Kozlowski, Dennis, 69
Kuhn's Big K, 136

La Quinta, 232
leaders
  challenges for. See challenges for leaders
  character traits. See character traits of leaders
  reasons for studying, xiv
leadership, heart of, xiv
The Leadership Moment (Useem), 48
learning quickly. See fast learning
Long-Term Capital Management (LTCM), 220, 222
long-term investment challenge (Warren
        Buffett), 211-214
long-term vision. See tenacity; vision of future
Losing My Virginity (Branson), 175
LTCM (Long-Term Capital Management), 220, 222
Lynch, Peter, xv, xix-xx, 238
  biographical timeline, 230-235
  challenges for, 230-233
  risk management, 234-236

M
M&T Bank, 212
Magellan Fund. See Fidelity Magellan Fund
Mair, George, 162
The Man Behind the Money (Martin), 223, 225, 227
management by objective, 63
management studies, invention of (Peter
        Drucker), 57-61
Markkula, Mike, 107
Marks & Spencer, 57
Mary Kay Inc., xv. See also Ash, Mary Kay
  challenges for, 30-33
  corporate culture, 34-37
Mary Kay: You Can Have It All (Ash), 31-32, 35, 37
Matsushita, 119
MCA, 119
McCann, Jim, 54
McDonald's, 232
McGraw, Phil, 167
McKinsey & Co., 62
McNeil Consumer Products Co., 38, 42
Medtronic, xv, xviii, 49, 238. See also George,
        William
  challenges for, 64-68
MGM movie studio, 116, 118
Micro Interventional Systems (MIS), 64
microcredit, xviii, 93-96

Microsoft, xv-xvi, xviii-xix, 16, 104, 110, 113,
        148, 184, 190. *See also* Gates, Bill
    antitrust regulation, 185-189
    deal with IBM, 191-192
    Internet revolution, 192-194
Midas Rex, 67
MIS (Micro Interventional Systems), 64
mistakes, importance of admitting, 239
Mittelstaedt, Robert E., Jr., xv, xvii-xviii
Moore's Law, 11
Moore, Dudley, 162
Moore, Gordon, xvi, 11-14
Morpheus, 112
Mostek, 13, 15
motivation of sales force (Mary Kay Ash), 30-33
mutual fund company management (John
        Bogle), 75-79

N
Napster, 112
National Steel, 170
NBC, xviii, 51, 116
NBR (Nightly Business Report), 25th
        anniversary, xiv
Netscape, 153, 186-187, 190, 193
New York Stock Exchange (NYSE), 84
Nightly Business Report (NBR), 25th
        anniversary, xiv
Nike, 16, 181
no-load mutual funds, 78
"Noah rule," 219
Norris, James, xiii
Noyce, Robert, 11-12
NYSE (New York Stock Exchange), 84

O-P
O'Neill, Thomas "Tip," 174
O, The Oprah Magazine, 162, 167
online music business, 112-113
Only the Paranoid Survive (Grove), 7, 13-14
Open Society Foundation, xv, 105
    philanthropy, 121-126

Palmisano, Sam, 205
Palo Alto Research Center, 103-104, 108
Pandya, Mukul, xv
paper trail challenge (Charles Schwab), 84-89
Parmalat, 48, 239
Partnership for a Drug-Free America, 44-46
Paychecks of the Heart (Mary Kay Inc.), 35
Pearson, Bill, 84-85
Pendleton, Yvonne, 35
Pentium flaw challenge (Andrew Grove), 4-9
People Express, 180
Perkins, Brian, 42-43
personal business control (Oprah Winfrey),
        161-164
philanthropy (George Soros), 121-126
Physio-Control International, 67
Pixar, 103, 106
Pottruck, David, 92
poverty
    microcredit, 93-96
    targeting underserved markets, 97-101
The Practice of Management (Drucker), 12

price, using for competitive advantage, 131-132
    Jeff Bezos, 155-157
    Michael Dell, 146-150
    Sam Walton, 137-141
Procter & Gamble, 43

Q-R
qualities of leadership. *See* character traits of
        leaders
Quantum Hedge Fund, 121, 124, 127
Quarterman, John S., 154
quick learning. *See* fast learning

Radio Shack, 191
Ralph Lauren, 163
Rand, Ayn, 226
RCA, 51, 116
Reagan, Ronald, 227
Real Networks, 187
Recording Industry Association of America, 112
The Republic (Plato), 183
restructuring of General Electric (Jack Welch),
        50-53
risk management, 209-210
    Warren Buffett, 215, 217-219
    James Burke, 43-44
    Alan Greenspan, 225-229
    Andrew Grove, 16-17
    Peter Lynch, 234-236
Rite Aid, 239
RJR Nabisco, 206-207
Rogers, Richard, xix, 30, 35-37
Rollins, Kevin, 145

S
S.S. Kresge, 133
sales force motivation (Mary Kay Ash), 30-33
Salomon Inc., xvii, 48
Sam Walton: Made in America (Walton), 131, 134
Sam's Club, 140
satellite broadcasting (Ted Turner), 114-117
Satyagraha, 47
Schmidt, Al Xavier, 1-2, 7, 10
Schwab, Charles, xv, xix, 73, 239
    biographical timeline, 84-89
    challenges for, 84, 86-87, 89
    targeting underserved markets, 90-92
Scott, Ridley, 109
Sears Roebuck, 57, 108
Seattle Computer, 192
SEC (Securities and Exchange Commission), 84,
        90
Siegel, David, 29
Siemens, 189
Six Sigma, 53
Sloan, Alfred P., 58-59
Smith, Fred, xv, xix, 184, 240
    biographical timeline, 195-198
    challenges for, 195-198
    fast learning, 199-201
Sofamor Danek Group, 67
Sony, 113, 149
Soros Fund Management, 105, 127-128
Soros on Soros (Soros), 122, 126-128

Soros, George, xv, xix, 105, 238, 240
    biographical timeline, 121-125
    challenges for, 121-126
    vision of future, 126-129
Soros: The Life and Times of a Messianic Billionaire
        (Kaufman), 127
Southwest Airlines, xv, xix, 238. See also
        Kelleher, Herb
    challenge in starting up, 23-26
    corporate culture, 21-22, 27-29
    thrift, 27-29
stock market, "Black Monday," 225-227
Stoker, Angela, 37
Sun Microsystems, 189

T
Taco Bell, 232
Talking Straight (Iacocca), 173
Target, 133, 137
TBS (Turner Broadcasting System), 115-116, 119
teamwork, 11-13, 238
technology integration (Charles Schwab), 84-89
telegraph versus telephone analogy, 108
television. See satellite broadcasting (Ted Turner)
tenacity, xxi. See also vision of future
Thorn EMI, 177-178
Thorndike, Doran, Paine and Lewis Inc., 75
thrift, 27-29
TNT (Turner Network Television), 105, 114
traits. See character traits of leaders
trend-spotting. See vision of future
trust, 45
truth-telling, 47-49
    Peter Drucker, 62-63
    William George, 68-71
    Andrew Grove, 10
    Jack Welch, 54-56
Turner Broadcasting System (TBS), 115-116, 119
Turner Classic Movies, 117, 120
Turner Network Television (TNT), 105, 114
Turner, Ted, xv, xix, 105, 238
    biographical timeline, 114-119
    challenges for, 114-117
    vision of future, 118-120
Tyco, 68-69, 239
Tylenol crisis (James Burke), xviii, 38-41

U-V
uncertainty, dealing with (Alan Greenspan),
        220-224
underserved markets, targeting, 73-74
    John Bogle, 80-83
    Andrew Grove, 13, 15
    Charles Schwab, 90-92
    Muhammad Yunus, 97-101
unfair business practices, speaking out against, 240
Unisem, 13, 15
UPS, 197
US Airways, 29
Useem, Michael, xv, xvii-xviii, 48, 59, 61
Utah International, 51

Value Migration (Slywotsky), 140
Vanguard Group, xiii-xv, xvii, 73, 80-82, 92, 238.
        See also Bogle, John
    mutual fund company management, 75-79
Virgin Atlantic, 175-178, 180
Virgin Group, xv. See also Branson, Richard
    brand recognition, 179-181
    challenges for, 175-178
Virgin Mobile, 181
Virgin Records, 159-160, 175-178
vision of future, 103-105, 239
    Steve Jobs, 112-113
    Fred Smith, 200
    George Soros, 126-129
    Ted Turner, 118-120

W
Wagner, Mary Kathlyn. See Ash, Mary Kay
Wal-Mart, xv, xvii, 131-132, 137-141. See also
        Walton, Sam
    competition with Kmart, 133-136
Walton, Sam, xv, xix, 131-132, 146, 238-239
    biographical timeline, 133-136
    challenges for, xix, 133-136
    character traits of leaders, xvii
    price, using for competitive advantage, 137-141
The Washington Post Co., 212, 217
Welch, Jack, xv, xix, 48, 238-239
    biographical timeline, 50-53
    challenges for, 50-53
    character traits of leaders, xviii
    truth-telling, 54-56
Wellington Management Company, 75, 77-78
Wells Fargo, 212
Wharton School Publishing, xiv-xv
Whatley, Tom, 36
Who Says Elephants Can't Dance? Inside IBM's
        Historic Turnaround (Gerstner), 205
Winfrey, Oprah, xv, xix-xx, 159, 238
    biographical timeline, 161-165
    brand recognition, 165-167
    challenges for, 161-164
Women's World Banking, 101
Woolco, 133
work-out sessions (General Electric), 55
World Bank, 240
WorldCom, 48, 68, 239
Wozniak, Steve, 106-107

X-Z
Xerox, 103-104, 108
Xomed Surgical Products, 67

Yahoo, 153
Yunus, Muhammad, xv, xix, 73, 240-241
    biographical timeline, 93-99
    challenges for, 93-96
    character traits of leaders, xviii
    targeting underserved markets, 97-101

Zapmail, 196